Exuberant praise for Tad Friend's

CHEERFUL MONEY

*Me, My Family, and
the Last Days of Wasp Splendor*

"American Wasps are now as rare as black truffles, and rarely has their story been told so candidly or entertainingly as it is in Tad Friend's wonderful new memoir, *Cheerful Money*.... Friend's book is such a winning family chronicle that the decline he describes is less a fall than an exhilarating ride, less sad than heartwarmingly comic....Friend's book is a fascinating mix of cultural, family, and personal history....*Cheerful Money* absolutely sings....This is a memorable hymn to a vanishing America. Exceptionally warmhearted, full of good cheer, and ruthlessly funny, it may even have you singing along."
— Marie Arana, *Washington Post*, "Best Books of 2009"

"In Tad Friend's stunning memoir about the lost world of the Wasp elite, the Hamptons' Georgica Pond comes to seem as Edenic as Thoreau's Walden. Friend animates a deeply private, aristocratic way of life with detailed, moving intimacy."   — Susan Cheever

"Be reassured: Tad Friend does fall far enough from the tree to give us not only a delightfully rendered account of his self-discovery but an examination of 'the last days of Wasp splendor.' It is gorgeously written....Nowhere in this book does Friend allow self-pity or longing for times past or accusations

against self or others to creep in. His account of losing his armor is straightforward, funny, and often moving.... *Cheerful Money*, in a way, is Friend's own letter to his father from a son who sees his flaws as his own, his strengths issuing from his father, deepened and enriched by his own efforts. In Tad's case, the sweetness flows and we the readers are richer for it."
—Jane Juska, *San Francisco Chronicle*, "Best Books of 2009"

"*Cheerful Money* is side-splittingly funny and touching, without being the least predictable. It has the verve of Nick and Nora Charles, with their silver martini shakers, and some insights mournful as Kafka's. This will become a classic."
—Mary Karr, author of *Lit* and *The Liars' Club*

"Using cash as a 'behavioral-management tool' is just one Wasp peccadillo that Friend nails in *Cheerful Money*, a suave, sharp-witted, generally intoxicating but occasionally sobering exposé of his native culture....Friend is not the first to write about emotionally constipated ancestors, the waning of Wasp power, or the painful erosion of beloved family holdings. But drawn to 'the ruinous romance of loss,' Friend is one of the least whiny and most incisive insiders to chronicle this privileged world, and he does so with style and soul."
—Heller McAlpin, National Public Radio,
"Best Memoirs of 2009"

"*Cheerful Money*, by a self-stinging Wasp, is sharp as well as blunt about this problematic caste, but also rather proud of its salty aspects. An insightful, highly humorous memoir, exceptionally well written."
—Peter Matthiessen, author of *Shadow Country*

"There is so much grace here.... *Cheerful Money* is taxonomy-as-memoir, an absolutely brilliant gift to the reader, wherein Friend essentially holds open the door to the exclusive club.... Friend is very funny, as when he notes that one of his talents, as befitting a good Wasp male, is 'the rarely called-for ability to carve a watermelon into the shape of a whale.' But he also is sad, sometimes angry, and in an effort to understand why his family withheld and bequeathed affection, hauls us with him over the emotional shoals."
— Nancy Rommelmann, *Portland Oregonian*

"With its Waspish brew of aunts, alcoholics, and dashed promise (not to mention an assortment of Inkys, Wassas, Lettys, Goggys, and Hannys), *Cheerful Money* goes down like a bittersweet late-summer cocktail made with a jigger of Cheever and a splash of Wodehouse."   — Graydon Carter

"A rare memoir, both bittersweet and psychologically insightful as it mines the family's grievances.... *Cheerful Money* rings with the sounds of tinkling ice cubes, robust laughter, and cruel madness.... Tad Friend has written the memoir of the season—and one for all time."
— Kirk Davis Swinehart, *Chicago Tribune*,
"Best Books of 2009"

"The world laid bare here in Tad Friend's winning voice emerges from struggles he's waged in his heart. *Cheerful Money* is a terrific memoir about the nuances of loss, wrenching revelations from a golden boy who has chosen to face the cost of a legacy of denial."
— Adrian Nicole LeBlanc, author of *Random Family*

"In *Cheerful Money*, Tad Friend is able to paint a picture of the now-faded cultural elite of America with the delight and disgust that only an insider can. [In a book] part memoir and part analysis, Friend shares the funny and occasionally heartbreaking stories of his life, family, and friends just as the money is running out and prestige is waning....He catalogs servants, summer homes, and Shetland sweaters that define the culture. But more intriguing, he deftly captures the delightful torture of being raised in a culture of restraint....Ultimately the book reflects on more than birthright, with Friend's take on the influence of family, tradition, and loss that shapes one's life."

—Sarah Skidmore, Associated Press

"A lively, heartbreaking, insider look at what it means to be a Wasp....Friend writes brilliantly, sometimes scathingly, always lovingly about his people."

—Laura Wells, *East Hampton Star*

"Friend is a ruthlessly brilliant social taxidermist and a joyous chronicler of life's telling bric-a-brac. With compassion, humility, and wit, he transforms his exotically accomplished and eccentrically intelligent Wasp relatives into a winsomely flawed American Everyfamily."

—Heidi Julavits, author of *The Effect of Living Backwards*

"Wasps' legendary courtesy is at the heart of Tad Friend's winsome memoir, which recounts, with amiable nostalgia, the foibles and predilections of a declining caste....But Friend's book derives a good part of its fun from the more eccentric relatives who broke from traditional Wasp patterns....Friend, a staff writer at *The New Yorker*, is very

good at cataloging the more salient Wasp idiosyncrasies: the Wasp 'sprezzatura,' as he calls it, which avoids any evidence of striving or seriousness because it would suggest 'that you aren't yet at—haven't always been at—the top.'"
— Francine du Plessix Gray, *New York Times Book Review*

"A brilliantly braided book: a hilarious coming-of-age memoir, a sharp stake through the zombie heart of the Wasp ascendency, and the bravest work of filial love I've ever read."
— Nelson W. Aldrich Jr., author of *Old Money: The Mythology of Wealth in America*

"Friend's memoir is a droll, psychologically astute, and sometimes nostalgic look backward at the Wasp world that was. Friend does much more here than just crack exquisite, Bertie Wooster–ish jokes at the expense of his bloodlines. He takes readers on an anthropological journey deep into the consciousness of a class. And in so doing, [he] mulls over the question of whether all those motley ancestral genes have mattered more than he would like to think in shaping his life and identity.... As befits a Wasp to the manner born, Friend tells his personal and familial tale without self-pity. Recognizing that it's his inherited duty to entertain and amuse his audience, even as he's occasionally serving up grisly confessions and nut-hard kernels of emotional truth."
— Maureen Corrigan, National Public Radio

"Friend's recollections of Wasp America in the throes of decline are frequently amusing, carefully modulated.... Friend is one of those journalists with an admirable eye for the telling detail."   — Tim Rutten, *Los Angeles Times*

"In *Cheerful Money*, Tad Friend writes a multigenerational portrait of his family, an impressive set of Wasps whose ancestors include a signer of the Declaration of Independence. Clearly an expert on the breed, Friend sprinkles hilarious aphorisms throughout the text: 'Wasps name their dogs after liquor and their cars after dogs and their children after their ancestors'; 'Wasps emerge from the womb wrinkly and cautious, already vice presidents, already fifty-two.'...The scenes with Friend's parents are touching and poignant. At the beginning of the book, Friend writes, 'I am a Wasp because I harbored a feeling of disconnection from my parents, as they had from their parents, and their parents had from *their* parents.' *Cheerful Money* is Friend's funny and enlightening way of piecing together that disconnect." —Eliza Borné, *BookPage*

"Abundantly rich in character, setting, and incident....Friend writes with irresistible humor and unsparing candor....This is a book crowded with ghosts, clinking phantom glasses at a party none have been told is over." — Geoff Pevere, *Toronto Star*

"In the hands of a lesser writer, a book like this could read like the empty lament of a poor little rich boy, a tale likely to elicit little sympathy from readers without Friend's resources or options. But Friend's talents are well suited to his material. He broadens his tale into the chronicle of an entire slice of society and not just that of one cluster of families....The tone he strikes is elegiac, even tender (at times) as he chronicles the futile pursuit of gracious living, now sinking into the 'ruinous romance of loss.'" —Marjorie Kehe, *Christian Science Monitor*

CHEERFUL MONEY

*Me, My Family, and
the Last Days of Wasp Splendor*

TAD FRIEND

BACK BAY BOOKS
LITTLE, BROWN AND COMPANY
NEW YORK   BOSTON   LONDON

Back Bay Books / Little, Brown and Company
Hachette Book Group
237 Park Avenue, New York, NY 10017
www.hachettebookgroup.com

Originally published in hardcover by Little, Brown and
Company, September 2009
First Back Bay paperback edition, July 2010

Back Bay Books is an imprint of Little, Brown and Company.
The Back Bay Books name and logo are trademarks of
Hachette Book Group, Inc.

AUTHOR'S NOTE

I have changed the names of a few people: the Viscontis and
Giovanna Visconti's boyfriends; Sally Cottone and her family;
Melanie Grayboden and her family; Francesca; and
Christine Wells.

Portions of this book were previously published,
in different form, in *The New Yorker* and *The Paris Review*.

Copyright acknowledgments appear on page 351.

Library of Congress Cataloging-in-Publication Data
Friend, Tad.
Cheerful money : me, my family, and the last days of Wasp
splendor / Tad Friend. — 1st ed.
    p.   cm.
ISBN 978-0-316-00317-9 (hc) / 978-0-316-00318-6 (pb)
1. Friend, Tad.   2. Friend, Tad—Family.   3. Wasps
(Persons)—Biography.   4. Journalists—United States—
Biography.   5. Upper class—United States—Biography.
6. Social classes—United States—Psychological aspects.
7. Social status—United States—Psychological aspects.   I. Title.
CT275.F715A3 2009
305.5'20973092—dc22
[B]   2009006622

10   9   8   7   6   5   4   3   2   1

RRD-IN

Printed in the United States of America

For my family

We said good-bye with a highball
Then I got "high" as a steeple.
But we were intelligent people
No tears, no fuss,
Hurray for us.
So thanks for the memory,
And strictly entre nous,
Darling, how are you?
And how are all the little dreams
That never did come true?

— RALPH RAINGER AND LEO ROBIN,
"Thanks for the Memory"

CONTENTS

Tad Friend's Family Tree*

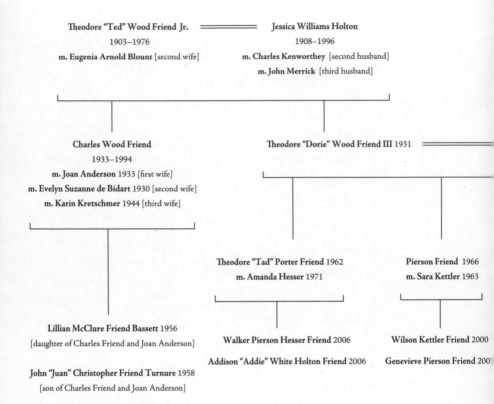

Theodore "Ted" Wood Friend Jr. ══════ Jessica Williams Holton
1903–1976   1908–1996
m. Eugenia Arnold Blount [second wife]   m. Charles Kenworthey [second husband]
                                          m. John Merrick [third husband]

Charles Wood Friend
1933–1994
m. Joan Anderson 1933 [first wife]
m. Evelyn Suzanne de Bidart 1930 [second wife]
m. Karin Kretschmer 1944 [third wife]

Theodore "Dorie" Wood Friend III 1931 ══════

Theodore "Tad" Porter Friend 1962   Pierson Friend 1966
m. Amanda Hesser 1971   m. Sara Kettler 1963

Lillian McClure Friend Bassett 1956
[daughter of Charles Friend and Joan Anderson]

Walker Pierson Hesser Friend 2006   Wilson Kettler Friend 2000

Addison "Addie" White Holton Friend 2006 Genevieve Pierson Friend 200?

John "Juan" Christopher Friend Turnure 1958
[son of Charles Friend and Joan Anderson]

Andrea "Daisy" Victoria Friend 1966
[daughter of Charles Friend and Suzanne de Bidart]

*somewhat simplified

John Herman Groesbeck Pierson ═══════════ Gertrude "Timmy" Trumbull Robinson
1906–2001   1908–1992
m. Sherleigh Glad [second wife]   m. Henry "Tom" Thomson Bourne
m. Harriet-Anne "Hanny" Duell Kelso [third wife]   1900–1998 [her second husband]
                                                                       m. Gertrude Williams [his first wife]

Pierson Stepsiblings:

Elizabeth Groesbeck Pierson   John "Paddy" Trumbull Robinson Pierson 1937   Henry "Tom" Thomson Bourne Jr. 1925
1933–2003   m. Karen Zamecnik 1940   m. Gladys "Jan" Janet Goldsmith

Joanne "Nan" Williams Bourne
1928–1999
m. Samuel Schwartz

Edith "Nicki" Nettleton Bourne 1935
Elizabeth "Timmie" Robinson   Eliza Trumbull Pierson 1971   m. William Cooley Greene Jr.
Friend Haskins 1968
m. Scott Haskins 1964   Katherine Conner Pierson 1974

                                             Isabella Zamecnik Pierson 1976
Lucia Elizabeth Webb Haskins 2007
                                                                                                       Gaylord Bourne 1954
                                                                                              [daughter of Tommy and Jan Bourne]

                                                                                                   Brett Williams Bourne 1956
                                                                                                [son of Tommy and Jan Bourne]

                                                                                                 Anne Williams Schwartz 1960
                                                                                         [daughter of Nan Bourne and Sam Schwartz]

                                                                                                   Jean Frances Schwartz 1961
                                                                                         [daughter of Nan Bourne and Sam Schwartz]

                                                                                             Anne Nettleton Greene Santos 1959
                                                                                              [daughter of Nicki and Bill Greene]

                                                                                            Elizabeth "Lizz" Barrett Greene 1961
                                                                                              [daughter of Nicki and Bill Greene]

CHEERFUL MONEY

Snow

F ROM AN UPSTAIRS window, I see my father walking away down his snowy lawn. He moves uncertainly, his hands cupped around his eyes like an Arctic explorer in a whiteout. It takes a moment to realize that he is peering through my mother's old Olympus camera, aiming it here and there. The set of his shoulders suggests dissatisfaction with what he sees this Christmas season: the bare apple trees, the frozen pond. Turning to face the house at last, he lowers himself onto one knee like a hopeful fiancé and pans across the stone exterior, slowly now. Watching him out there leaves me lonely.

My father, Dorie Friend, is a historian and a highly rational man; his Easter Island–size head is stuffed with knowledge. In our family, he was in charge of logic and money. He husbanded our declining fortunes, a decline that, as he recognized, mirrored the broader Wasp ebb: the outflow of maids and grandfather clocks and cocktail shakers brimming with gin.

My mother, who utterly ignored this decline, was in charge of everything else. She set the tone. Elizabeth Pierson Friend was Lib to her oldest friends, classmates at Smith who possessed all the graces. They were stylish and sparkling women, prepared by birth—and since birth—to charm the Burmese or Nigerian ambassador, but Mom was particularly conscientious. She took occasions so seriously. "After much ado," she e-mailed her friends about one party, "I had settled on a periwinkle blue dress: Fortuny-like silk pleats in a tea-length skirt, horizontal tucks in a long-sleeved tunic top. A necklace of eight strands, each a different size, of silver-gray freshwater pearls, twisted to almost choker length . . ." Slim and vivacious and determined, with a pouf of chestnut hair and snapping blue eyes, she drew you out at the table, exclaiming at just the right moment, and her own conversation built to jubilant punch lines.

There was the story about how she had received a terrific rush in her early twenties, with a date every night, including a series with a tremendously tall young man who later supervised the secret bombing of Cambodia. And then, suddenly, the phone didn't ring for two weeks: "And I thought, *So this is menopause.*" There was the story about a trip to India, during which it became necessary for her to hide a suitor's turban in an icebox. Before you could wonder, Why an icebox, exactly? she cried, "So there I was, dancing cheek to cheek with a Sikh!" When my father first heard that story— overheard it, actually, from an adjoining booth in a New Haven diner—he thought, *Who is that horrible woman?* When he heard it for the second time, years afterward, it was too late.

She pounced past your defenses. When I was in my twenties, a married woman I'd been idly flirting with at a gallery opening in New York introduced herself to my mother as we all took the elevator down and said, "I've been talking to your son all night. He's *fascinating.*" I reddened, embarrassed but pleased.

"You should see the rest of the family," Mom replied, instantly. You had to love her for that.

She spelled basic words as if she were Corsican (snug was "cosi"; gloves were "mittons"); trespassed wherever a stylish driveway beckoned; sobbed if she caught a bad cold. Her character was chatoyant, like a cat's eyes, candid and then suddenly bleached and desolate. But her darker recesses were usually masked by virtuosity: a gifted cook, painter, and designer, she had also shown early promise as a poet. As a sophomore at Smith, she came in second to Sylvia Plath in a poetry contest judged by W. H. Auden (who, when my mother was introduced to him a year later, delighted her by saying, "I believe I have read your verse"). She longed to best Plath, her nemesis. Later, though, she would toss her head and say, "Just as well I didn't win. Head in the oven, and so forth."

From time to time, I find myself studying a photograph of her taken in the summer of 1962, when she was pregnant with me, the first of her three children. She stands on the lawn in a blue maternity dress, looking pale and watchful. A soccer ball rests under her bare right foot. Soccer was my father's sport, and would be mine, but she liked to flash out into the yard and perform "the high trap." He would fling the ball into the air, and Mom would judge its fall perfectly and smother it with her right sole. And then, in triumph, she'd depart to rule her own realm, which consisted of tennis, tomato sandwiches, gossip, bread-and-butter letters, chore lists, conviviality, wit, and worrying. It all fell under the heading of keeping the house in order, wherever the house was. Her last campaign began in 1989, with this house in the Philadelphia suburb of Villanova: the one being photographed by my father.

After years without a home to make her own — in Buffalo, in the sixties, my parents had no income to speak of, and then for nearly twenty years they lived first in an imposing pile belonging to Swarthmore College, when my father was the college's president, and later in a rented bungalow — the Villanova house was her epic work. An anonymous fieldstone relic at first, the place soon grew thick with her, with the snares and honeypots she concealed in plain sight: the bottom kitchen drawer pull that rewarded you with a small collapsible stepladder; the closets stuffed with Christmas gifts, so that you couldn't approach a doorknob without having her call out, from three rooms away, "Ooh, ooh — don't go in there!" Walking through the Villanova house was like reading a series of Rorschach blots that inked out her emotional history (except that she hated blots of any sort). She had it all planned, having long considered how best to arrange a house and its contents, including us.

Since she died, suddenly, a few years ago, my father has taken to photographing what remains. From his vantage on the lawn, he can see three facets of her hexagonal dining room; the stone wall rebuilt to set off two new decks of weathered moleskin-colored ipe wood; and the glint from the nine windows on the south-facing "gallery," a sun-shot passageway lined with her own paintings. When the contractor installed bamboo blinds there, she exclaimed that the filtered light made the house look "so Japanesey!" From the next room, my father observed, "Elizabeth, there is no such word as 'Japanesey.' "

He can see the second-floor deck railing that she had rebuilt after she found her excitable Tibetan spaniel, Sam, poking his head between the palings—or, as she insisted, "poised to hurl himself to his death!" She took a tape measure to his five-inch-wide head and then had the pickets established a prudential three and a half inches apart. Sam lived a long life untroubled by further barks for help, and is now buried beneath the cutleaf maple in the back, alongside his toy bear. And my father can pick out the porthole window in his study in the former garage, a window placed low on the wall so that he could lie on his futon and look west at the very spot where he is now. The study appeared ten years into her campaign, a Trojan horse that surprised no one but him, for her clear intent had long been to surround his makeshift office in the entry hall with beauty until he surrendered the position. There was something inexorable about her, something of the Emperor Augustus, who said, "I found Rome brick, and left it marble."

My father, leaning now against Sam's maple, lowers the camera and closes his eyes.

ONE

Tomatoes

W HEN I GRADUATED from Shipley, a small prep
school in Bryn Mawr, my father's mother,
Grandma Jess, wrote to congratulate me on my
academic record: "A truly tremendous achievement—but
then I could expect nothing less due to your marvelous
background—Robinson, Pierson, Holton, Friend!" I remember scowling at her airy blue script, noting the point—after
the first dash—where the compliment turned into a eugenic
claim. As my grandparents happened to constitute a Wasp
compass, the way ahead was marked in all directions: I could
proceed as a Robinson like Grandma Tim's family (loquacious, madcap, sometimes unhinged); a Pierson like Grandpa
John's family (bristling with brains); a Holton like Grandma
Jess's family (restless, haughty show ponies); or a Friend like
Grandpa Ted's family (moneyed, clubbable, and timid).

I believed, then, that my family was not my fate. I believed
my character had been formed by charged moments and
impressions—the drift of snow, the peal of church bells, the

torrent of light cascading through the elms out front into our sunporch. Though my parents gave me love and learning and all the comforts, I believed I could go it alone. My grandparents were distant constellations, and as they wheeled across the sky I felt unshadowed by their marriages, their affairs, their remarriages, or their quarrels. On the question of how to pronounce "tomato," for instance, the family was split. On my father's side, the Friends and Holtons unselfconsciously said "tomayto." On my mother's, the Robinsons were staunchly in the Anglophile "tomahto" camp, while the Piersons, on the even more superior view that "tomahto" was pretentious, were ardently pro-"tomayto." At the family beach house on Long Island, my great-uncle Wilson Pierson would rebuke my mother, a Robinson in such matters, if she asked for a "tomahto." "Would you like some potahtoes with that?" he'd say.

It was unclear why such nuances should matter to me. The deeper history, the cultural history, filtered down only piecemeal: my father was embarrassed by some of his forebears, and my mother blithely assumed everyone knew all about hers. She might mention, in passing, the lace she'd worn at their wedding, lace handed down from mothers to their firstborn daughters for thirteen generations, beginning in England with Goodith Constantine in 1629 and continuing through such delightfully named ancestors as Lettice Beach and Damaris Atwater. A poem that accompanies the lace reads, in part:

> Guard it, dear child, as these have done,
> Good women, pure and true,
> Who hand it, with their own fair names
> Unblemished, down to you.

Keep ever in the one straight path
Of duty they have trod;
And guided by the same pure light
Of love, for man and God.

That sort of exacting heirloom, which my sister, Timmie, later wore at her wedding, contributed to a sense that we should hold ourselves apart, in readiness. But what for was never declared. The mission was a jigsaw puzzle of watchwords, affiliations, expectations, furniture, clothes, habits, rituals, empties, and stories that lacked one key detail: why?

Three years after my mother died, I published a piece about her in *The New Yorker.* In it, I tried to describe her aspirations and disappointments and her search for consolation; what she had taken from her parents, and handed on to us, and the gifts she herself brought to the party. I thought it was a loving portrait, but it was also unsparing, perhaps even more than I'd intended. Anger can impeach you. The piece rattled my family in ways that slowed the writing of this book yet clarified its true subject. Some of my relatives felt I was ungenerous, and some simply wondered, *Whose side are you on?*

Yet apostasy is in our blood too. Every so often in my family, someone writes a candid book or gets knocked up by the wrong guy. Now it was my turn.

THE ACRONYM "Wasp," from "White Anglo-Saxon Protestant," is one many Wasps dislike, as it's redundant — Anglo-Saxons are perforce white — and inexact. Elvis Presley was a white Anglo-Saxon Protestant, as is Bill Clinton, but they are not what anyone means by "Wasp." Waspiness is an overlay on human character, like the porcelain veneer that protects the biting surface of a damaged tooth. Worse, the adjective is pejorative: "Waspy" is reserved for horse-faced women, tight-assed men, penny-pinchers, and a cappella groups.

I'm too cheap to spring for a new acronym. But my family and their friends, as Wasps, were circumscribed less by skin tone and religion than by a set of traditions and expectations: a cast of mind. They lived in a floating Ruritania loosely bounded by L.L. Bean to the north, the shingle style to the east, Robert Falcon Scott's doomed polar expedition to the south, and the limits of Horace Greeley's optimism to the west.

That cast of mind is excessively attuned to such questions as how you say "tomato"—a word I now find myself pronouncing both ways, usually at random and always with misgiving. In this and more important respects I seem to have become, somehow, a motley product of my famously marvelous background. Oh, sure, I don't belong to any clannish or exclusive clubs, I prefer beer to hard liquor, I am neither affable nor peevish—the alternating currents of Wasp—and I love pop culture.

And yet. Until quite recently, I had the Wasp fridge: marmalade, wilted scallions, out-of-season grapes, seltzer, and vodka—nothing to really *eat*. (The Wasp fridge is like the bachelor fridge, but Wasps load up on dairy, including both 1 and 2 percent milk, moldy cheese, expired yogurt, and separated sour cream. And atop the Wasp fridge sit Pepperidge Farm Milanos, Fig Newtons, or Saltines—some chewy or salty or otherwise challenging snack.) I have a concise and predictable wardrobe, and friends even like to claim that I invariably wear the same oatmeal-colored Shetland sweater. I will never experience the pleasures of leather pants or a shark's tooth on a thong dangling in my chest hair. I will never experience the pleasures of chest hair. And, like the Tin Man, I don't articulate my upper body in sections; it moves en masse or not at all.

I politely stand aside: no, no, after *you*. I have a soft laugh, and I rarely raise my voice. Though I have an outsize grin, and friends take pleasure in trying to elicit it, I am reserved upon first meeting (it's Wasp women who are expected to charm). I used to like being told I was "intimidating," because it seemed to sanction my verbal jabbing to maintain a perimeter. Making everyone a little uneasy came naturally. When I characterized a college roommate's dancing style as "Jimmy Cracked Corn," he nursed the wound for decades, and a woman I fooled around with in my early twenties told me, years later, that she had to get a new mattress and headboard after I remarked on her "game-show bed." I am slow to depend on people because I hate being disappointed, hate having to withdraw my trust. All this has often led people to read me as aloof or smug.

I am fiercely but privately emotional—I was embarrassed, recently, when my wife, Amanda, found me having put *The Giving Tree* down while reading it to our twins, Walker and Addie, because I was in tears. I married Amanda, a strong-minded food writer, seven years ago: she revamped my fridge, and some of my other disaster areas. And I convinced her to have children, the best thing we have done together.

I walk into parties with a confident air but wait to speak until I have a point to make or self-deprecating joke to offer.

I can give a handsome wedding toast. I am slow to pitch in on manual labor and not particularly handy, though I pride myself on the rarely called-for ability to carve a watermelon into the shape of a whale (a sprig of parsley makes the spout). I am frugal to the point of cheapness—when out to dinner with friends, I used to contribute only for the dishes I had ordered. I dislike having to eat quail or crab, all that effort and mess for scant reward, an aversion Amanda calls "No sex in public!"

For a long time I didn't think of myself as particularly competitive, though my friends kept assuring me, as they pointed out where my helicoptered five-iron had landed, that I was. My belief that you shouldn't do something you care about in a half-assed way often provokes the charge that I don't want to take part in any activity I can't do well, that I fear public ineptitude, which is certainly true for karaoke. Despite my standoffishness, I am a good listener, and loyal, and friends often turn to me for advice. A Wasp friend remarks that I would have made an imposing country parson.

Most of all, I am a Wasp because I harbored a feeling of disconnection from my parents, as they had from their parents, and their parents had from *their* parents. And because, deep into my thirties, most of my relationships had the life span of a child's balloon. I felt that I was carrying around a brimming bucket of walnut stain and that if anyone got too close it would spill all over both of us. So I ended up spending my inheritance and then some on psychoanalysis. I was in trouble, but it was nearly impossible for anyone who didn't know me well to tell, and I made it nearly impossible for anyone to know me well.

WHEN I was twelve, my father, looking around the dinner table meaningfully, repeated a biblical quotation a Swarthmore student had reminded him of earlier in the day: "For unto whomsoever much is given, of him shall be much required." "That lets *me* out," I said, and my parents laughed. In Swarthmore, the dinner table was where we performed, auditioning for attention. We'd sit at the round butcher-block table Mom had commissioned in Buffalo, eating her quiche lorraine and waiting for my parents to stop discussing college business—and at last Mom would turn to us for brief accounts of our days. My younger brother, Pier, who in memory always wore a striped rugby shirt, would remark that his team had won its Little League game—he was the star pitcher—and beam at the resulting praise. Our sister, Timmie, the youngest, would excitedly announce that she'd had six hot dog halves at Oonie Ryan's half-birthday party. "I can see that you did," Mom would remark, smiling; in those days Timmie was a little chubby. Timmie would blink and crimson, then bolt from the table. Mom would exchange a chagrined glance with my father—she always hoped for a blithe, Noel Cowardish return of serve—and then stand in exasperated remorse and fold her napkin and go find Timmie.

We were expected to appreciate what we'd been given and make conspicuous use of it. (Wasps are credentialists, but my father particularly so: he thumbnailed people by their résumés: "A very able guy with a PhD in microeconomics from Stanford . . . head of the Asia Society . . . served on the

National Security Council.") Yet my parents had also sought, in different ways, to escape the way of life that had sustained their own achievements. So we received a tricky set of imperatives: meet the unspoken standard without thinking about it too much. Brooding on ancestral benchmarks could suck you into a life on the couch, the long parenthesis; Wasps don't rebel so much as drink, sink, and drop away.

My parents would mention our parenthetical relatives (John Anthony Walker, Tisha Pierson, various Robinsons) in tones of sorrow and then change the subject. Only much later would I learn that John Anthony Walker, my father's cousin, never held a job before dying in India of a kidney infection he'd treated with Ayurvedic medicine. And that Mom's cousin Tisha Pierson disowned us all, changed her name to Molly Morgan Miller, and disappeared. And that Mom's uncle John Trumbull Robinson Jr., known as Wassa, turned on his sons in a manic rage in the parking lot of a drive-in restaurant near their home in Wayne, Illinois, sending Donny fleeing into a cornfield and leaving David holding on for his life in the open back of the family station wagon as his father gunned off, pursued by demons that would hound him into the electroshock ward. And that Wassa's oldest son, Johnny, went even further astray. (As children, all we knew was that if he rang up collect from an institution, we shouldn't accept the call.) One night in the late 1970s, Johnny showed up at Donny's apartment in Manhattan and belligerently demanded money for his cab fare. When Donny refused, Johnny darted for the knife rack in the kitchen. Donny tackled him, and Johnny clamped his teeth on Donny's forearm and didn't let go until Donny punched him repeatedly in the head, breaking his own finger. When the police arrived, Donny went to Lenox Hill for the bite, and the cops took Johnny to Bellevue and then to Ward's Island, where he kept declaring, "I am John Trumbull Robinson the *Third*," incredulous that the storied name didn't precipitate his immediate release. He died in Baton Rouge, in 1996, broke, crazy, and alone.

They were us, too. That you must carry everyone with you, swelling the ranks, is a hard-ridden Wasp hobbyhorse. My father remembers (with dismay) his prep school class at St. Paul's being charged by the rector to have lots of children and go into politics, lest they be overwhelmed by the outsiders massing at the gate. Charles W. Eliot, Harvard's president from 1869 to 1909, boiled that imperative down to "produce and reproduce," observing that: "The family, rather than the individual, is the important social unit. If society as a whole is to gain by mobility and openness of structure, those who rise must stay up in successive generations, that the higher level of society may be constantly enlarged, and that the proportion of pure, gentle, magnanimous, and refined persons may be steadily increased."

For generations—the three centuries when Wasps ran the country—my family rose and stayed aloft. After my various forebears came to America in the mid-seventeenth century as weavers or constables or tavern owners, it was their descendants who made good: signing the Declaration of Independence (the trembly penned John Morton) or leading the Union Army (the shilly-shallying George McClellan). The branches of my family tree were bowed with squires, judges, ministers, senators, and colonial dames. Yet no one grew really wealthy until the turn of the twentieth century, when the Friends made enough from steel, coal, and banking to become—briefly—smashingly rich: chauffeur rich, yacht rich, $350,000,000-in-today's-money rich. On the whole, we were attendant lords, the seat-fillers in historical paintings who look on approvingly as those whose names are taught in school read a ringing speech or charge a well-garrisoned hill.

My great-great-grandfather Henry Cornelius Robinson was in this way typical. An eloquent and energetic mayor of Hartford in the 1870s, a man who greeted male friends by gripping their shoulders and crying, "Comrade!" a passionate man moved to tears by stirring music, a burly man with a scimitar nose and sideburns that swept into a forked beard worthy of ZZ Top, he was also a man who liked to lie on his red sofa after a hard day and have his daughter rub his forehead with a sponge dipped in bay rum. He wrote Christmas carols—"Exult, ye sons of men, 'tis clearest morn! / Exult, ye sons of men, the child is born!"—and kept two Union flags from the Civil War draped over his piazza and a huge American flag above them. When Ulysses Grant died, Robinson consoled Hartford's citizens with a speech recited from memory: "It is a great thing to have lost such a man; it is much greater to have had such a man to lose," he declared. "He was a child of the people, he was a type of the people, and the hearts of the people are keeping sad time to the funeral march of twenty thousand soldiers. The nation pauses in its activities. The reaper and the loom are at rest, and even the money-changers have locked their vaults." Yet when President Benjamin Harrison asked him to serve as minister to Spain—a step toward becoming such a man himself—he declined: "What, leave Hartford?"

In latter years, as the money that had buoyed flotation

leaked and then flooded away, my family, like many others, tried to caulk the seams. In a country built on growth and transformation, on the appetite for *more*, the ambition to preserve things as they were is peculiar to the modern Wasp. All we ask is to maintain. So success, while vital, came to be understood not as blazing a trail but as waging a culture- or comfort-preserving rearguard action. Prep school faculties teem with Wasps who majored in English or history, as brokerage houses do with Wasps who majored in finance. Wasps serve as the caretakers of tradition in publishing, foundations, university administration, lexicography, antiquarian societies, nature conservancies, and trusts and estates law. Nearly empty of Wasps, however, are electric-car manufactories, Internet start-ups, and the X Games.

Figures like Henry Cornelius Robinson saw their duty as leading without fanfare. Wasps continued to see this as their role even as they began to follow, and even as, shortly after I was born, they fell so far behind they lost touch entirely. Their accelerating crack-up was like a sonic boom: you heard it only after the Concorde was gone.

I NOW see that the charged moments I prized, my earliest memories, were always linked to those distant family constellations. When I sat by our kitchen sink in Buffalo and my mother touched me lightly in passing, like the Holy Spirit, I felt the cool linoleum below and the ensuing solitude but couldn't know then that my ancestors, and the amassed weight of their expectations, had crowded the room to keep Mom intent on her chores. What her parents thought and felt and did was alive in her, and so alive in me. Or mostly it was; not everything connects. Sifting through our over-stuffed attics and well-guarded memory banks, I try to fit the pieces together in time, hopscotching among decades and mashing up friends and mentors, girlfriends and grand-parents, in search of a larger design. Love enters into it, too, muddying everything.

Life is a scavenger hunt run backward as well as forward, a race to comprehend. But with Wasps, the caretakers lock the explanatory sorrows away, then swallow the key.

TWO

Mud

S PRING, STRUGGLING NORTH, comes late to Vermont. As we returned from the funeral Mass for Baba, my grandmother's cook for sixty years, our boots sank into ground soaked with snowmelt. We shucked our coats and mucky boots in the mudroom at PineApple Hill, the family seat of our friends the McDills. It was the end of April 2006 in Woodstock, a covered-bridge beauty of a town whose steeples house four of the surviving eighty-seven church bells cast by Paul Revere and his sons. PineApple Hill is a half mile down the road from Maplewood Farm, three hundred acres of alfalfa and clover long owned by my maternal grandmother and her second husband. Timmy and Tom Bourne had a four-story farmhouse, four tumbledown barns, and four spring-fed ponds, until their picturesque herd of Holsteins finished ruminating through all the money, and Timmy died, and Tom died, and the farm was sold to the CEO of Monster.com.

The McDills' mudroom is a handsome place, with large

brown washtubs and coats slung neatly on hooks, its linoleum shining and expectant. As we passed into the house, I
was thinking how Wasps love their mud. Grandma Tim's
family, the Robinsons, staged Thanksgiving dinners where
everyone would play football barefoot in their dress shirts
and trousers, then retire to a white tent, a hundred mud-
footed relatives strong, to sing songs like "Daddy Is a Yale
Man" ("When they reached the sticks / This brave mother
of six / Took a drink and began to explain: 'Your Daddy is a
Yale Man; We may be married soon' "). Members of Yale's
legendary secret society, Skull and Bones, used to plunge
naked into a mud pile during their initiations. (Sadly, they
don't anymore.) And members of the Porcellian, Harvard's
most exclusive "final" club, sing "The Hippopotamus Song"
at club functions, booming the chorus:

> *Mud, mud, glorious mud*
> *Nothing quite like it for cooling the blood*
> *So follow me follow, down to the hollow*
> *And there let me wallow in glorious mud.*

Wasps love mud because it—along with beach sand in the
sheets—is their only sanctioned form of filth. You are allowed and even encouraged to get dirty on a birding ramble
or in a game of touch football. Such stains are dueling scars,
noble marks of privilege and leisure. It's discretionary mud,
clean mud. (Identical spatters from a job would be something else entirely.) And you can absolve yourself of it all in
the mudroom, stripping off the soiled clothes knowing
someone will slip in presently to clean them.

That someone at Maplewood, my grandparents' farm, was

Baba, who had just died at ninety-two. Orphaned young in Naugatuck, Connecticut, Margaret Dunn had come to work for the family as my mother's baby nurse in 1933 and was swiftly rechristened with Mom's baby-talk name. She was just nineteen. After Mom's brother, Paddy, was born, Baba gradually became the family's cook and majordomo. She knew which cows had calved and what the milk tester had been worried about and where the checkbook was, and kept encyclopedic track of what my many cousins and stepcousins were up to. She held the family together.

An exceedingly round, exceedingly short woman, Baba had abandoned learning to drive because her feet didn't reach the pedals. She wore a blue apron over a white housedress and a necklace blessed by the pope, and kept her hair in a wreath fixed with bobby pins and a hairband. Her forte was comfort food, and her hugs smelled of starch and dough. There would be Baptist cakes for breakfast; chicken aspic, tarragon-sprinkled homemade bread, and fresh-picked lettuce for lunch; and roast beef, roasted potatoes, and corn for dinner, which was served to the children at the oilcloth-covered table in the kitchen and to the adults in the dining room around the corner. I still make a hearty tomato soup of hers that clearly originated in the rationing of World War II: the recipe calls for Uncle Ben's rice, six stalks of celery — none of this fussy nonsense about inner stalks or discarding the leaves — and a can of evaporated milk.

Though her cooking evoked groans of happiness, Baba so feared making noise when she ate that she'd nibble at toast like a mouse, having first sucked the edges to dampen their crispness. She was almost always cheerful, and she loved having the grandchildren underfoot, just as we loved watching her put date-and-nut bread into the oven or settle with a hop into her white rocker to watch *General Hospital.* At night, we'd vie for that rocker when we watched *Star Trek* reruns. She sent us Christmas cards with twenty-dollar checks inside, routing my grandmother's money to us in a kind of low-stakes generation-skipping trust, and she gave me her old transistor radio so I could listen to the Red Sox in bed, as she did. I would fall asleep to Ken Harrelson describing the drowsy arc of another Carl Yastrzemski fly ball.

Though Baba emanated abundance, her rooms atop the back stairs were spare as a nun's. I would go in sometimes when she was at work downstairs and examine her possessions without touching anything, like a detective, looking for—what? She had only a low bed, a Naugahyde easy chair, two hooked rugs, a shelf of condensed novels from Reader's Digest, and a crucifix on the wall between the windows that overlooked the Revolutionary War graveyard and Cloudland Road beyond. Her storeroom, under the eaves, was where we gathered in the evenings to watch her Super 8 footage of our previous visit.

Her area was the opposite of the room belonging to Harold Ricker, the genial hired man who worked for the Bournes for thirty years. He had a saggy bed and a wastebasket overflowing with empty Bud cans, and one afternoon when I was about twelve I glided his door open and was wonderstruck by the centerfolds on the wall. Barely breathing, I moved in only to be confounded by a caption that mentioned "muff diving." The muff part was clear, the diving a great mystery, and there was no one I could consult. In some intuitive way, Baba caught wind of all this and chewed Harold out (her dressing-downs happened often enough about neglected calls to the vet that I can picture it: Baba puffed like a pouter pigeon, Harold bent dolefully over his soup). When next I tiptoed into his room, the walls were bare.

She was superb in a crisis. When my cousin Johnny Robinson would call and say, "I'm coming up to kill everyone with my sixteen-gauge shotgun," Baba would reply, "Everyone's out right now, Johnny, but I'll give them the message!" When my stepcousin Lizz Greene, Tom Bourne's granddaughter, was struggling with how to leave her volatile husband, Baba listened to her for hours. She listened to Lizz's husband, too, when he'd call to give his side. But when he showed up at the farm to demand that Lizz come with him, it was Baba who stepped out, her hands working a dishcloth: "It's time for you to leave, *now!*" And when my mother telephoned, in 1958, to announce her (soon to be dissolved) engagement to Richard, a diffident grad student in philosophy, it was Baba, on the extension in the kitchen, who cried, "Oh, no!"

Baba's funeral Mass was a surprise; the eighteen of us Protestant Bournes and Greenes and Piersons and Friends were a little blizzard-bound at Our Lady of the Snows. Mom's brother, Paddy Pierson, heraldic with his blazer and bird's nest of white hair, had carried the urn holding Baba's ashes up the aisle, and the rest of us followed to the front pews. There we were bracketed by a few ancient parishioners known only to Baba, and not even to her at the end, as Alzheimer's carried her out. When the priest took up the ewers of wine and water, he told us the Communion sacrament was for Catholics only. We sat in silence, denied the memorial service we were accustomed to and therefore the family specialty: the droll recitation of recollections that probably should have been shared with the deceased while she was alive.

Timmy Bourne had loved Baba dearly and was in most respects a passionate liberal—she was a leading fund-raiser for the Vermont ACLU—but, like many Yankees of her generation, she viewed Catholics as Jesuitical schemers. The Protestant Reformation, as refined by the Puritans in the seventeenth century and the Transcendentalists in the nineteenth, had surely settled the proper approach to religious observance: hymns and chiming bells. "Going with Catholics in my day was a dirty job; they weren't quite the thing," Grandma Tim would say over morning tea on the porch. "Uncle Billy married one. He told the priest he wasn't going to sign any papers, and they said no, that was all right, and just as they were about to begin the ceremony the priest handed him some papers to sign. The bride fainted dead away, as well she might. He *signed* them, and they raised the children Catholic, but it was a *dirty business.*"

JANE MCDILL Smith, who put us Friends and Piersons up at PineApple Hill that weekend, is a brisk, handsome woman in her seventies, with cornflower blue eyes and a scratchy voice. Jane wears down vests and cardigan sweaters over turtlenecks, layering herself like an old-time skier to compensate for setting her thermostat at sixty degrees. Chilblains aside, she is a consummate hostess, making visitors feel not merely welcome but lordly as she shoos them from the stove and sink.

Jane is part of the family, too, or close enough. She was one of my mother's closest friends; Mom and the three of us children often spent lazy summer weeks with Jane and her three daughters at Line Farm, a McDill house on the back side of their property, while my father and Jane's husband, Tom, worked away down south. What lingers in memory from those summers is the evening Jane's eldest daughter, Julia, and I—both of us about six—decided to hide from our mothers. In our version of running away to join the circus, we lay in the high alfalfa thirty yards up the hill from Line and waited, gleefully, for the search. They came out and called a few times, then Mom tossed her head and murmured something and they laughed and went back inside. The grass felt itchy on my neck, suddenly, and the crickets tuned up mockingly under the dimming sky. After waiting until it was truly night, we went in.

Jane's father, John McDill, was in my mother's father's class at Yale, and they became friends; John later became a father figure to my mother, and a grandfather figure to me. My mother received a proposal from Jane's cousin, and Paddy Pierson dated Jane's sister. When I was born, three months after Julia, John McDill wrote my parents: "Would you consent to a contract of marriage between the two infants? Maplewood and Line Farms *must* be united or the neighborhood will fall apart." Instead, Mom became godmother to Julia, on whom I had a hapless schoolboy crush, and Julia—who weathered the crush calmly, returning a proper thank-you note for each wretched poem I sent her—later made me godfather to her son William.

Such clannishness is comforting to Wasps, who strive to compact the world into the old-boy network it once was. I play golf and poker with a man named Adam Platt, a friendship we arrived at seemingly by chance. But if I meet a Wasp more or less my age and mention Adam's name, odds are that he or she will reassure me, "Oh, *God*—I know Adam Platt." My father, it turns out, went on a date with Adam's mother in the 1950s, later briefed Adam's father when Nicholas Platt became America's ambassador to the Philippines, and still later became his occasional squash partner. And so it's no great surprise that the architect of PineApple Hill, a Colonial Revival tour de force that sits its hill like a diadem, was Adam's great-grandfather.

Jane and her sister inherited the house and its nearly one hundred and fifty acres from her parents, who inherited it from Jane's mother's parents; it's been in the family for a century. It is a high church of the old way of life, complete with speaking tubes for calling the servants, should any reappear to fetch a coddled egg; foodstuffs that can be carbon-dated, such as a box of Reagan-era raisins about which Jane remains optimistic ("A little chewy, but good for the jaws"); battalions of whiskey-colored furniture; a Short and Mason barometer in the front hall whose brass arrow is stuck on "Fair"; and bathrooms, floored in curling linoleum, that feature medicine cabinets with hexagonal glass knobs, all slightly loose, as well as comfortingly rickety toilet paper holders and plastic night-lights shaped like the Duchess's headdress in *Alice in Wonderland*. The chains on the table lamps have been mended and rethreaded with window shade pulls; the desks are accessorized with dry pens from defunct banks, postage meters for sending first-class letters in 1971, and a classroom's worth of wooden rulers. The guest rooms feature hand irons for doorstops, ladder-backed chairs with suspect caning, and change dishes inscribed with French sayings— *"Ne parlez pas d'amour—faites le!"*—and filled with safety pins and bobby pins and orphaned screws. There are Talbots catalogues here and there and the faint scent of Crabtree & Evelyn soap.

When Jane moved back to Woodstock from Washington, D.C., some years after her parents' deaths, a representative from Chubb came by to calculate her insurance premiums. He moved through the rooms, jotting in his notebook and whistling about the house's sizable dimensions, to the growing annoyance of Jane, who was brooding about how the basement floods every spring. Finally, he looked around the front hall and muttered, "Designer wallpaper."

"Excuse me!" she said. "This wallpaper has been here at least fifty years. It probably came from Sears, Roebuck. I have more rolls in the attic and we patch the walls when necessary. It is *not* designer wallpaper."

I like Jane very much without having any real idea what's going on in there. Naturally merry, even larksome, she keeps her high spirits under firm rein and never discusses her dreams or her health, believing, as many Wasps do, that imposing oneself is a form of trespass. I recognize her tactic of forestalling inquiry by initiating it, because I use it myself. I once arrived at PineApple Hill after having called to let Jane know I was en route, and was chatting with her daughters in the dining room when she came in, not having seen me in years, and said, "Why do you introduce yourself on the phone? — I know who you are!"

"Why do you always start conversations with a complaint?"

When Pym, the family's ailing thirteen-year-old Welsh terrier, died in Nigeria, where Tom Smith was the American ambassador, Tom and Jane didn't discuss the matter with their children. "They just came back without a dog and never spoke of it," Julia Smith recalls. "Once someone asked Daddy, 'What happened to Pym?' and he said, 'He went to a better place.' I don't know if he died there, or was put down, or eaten by a lion, or what. None of us had the courage to ask." When Tom was stricken with cancer in his mid-fifties, he chose not to burden anyone with that, either, so his death came as a shock not only to us, but also to Julia and her sisters.

AFTER BABA'S funeral, Jane served roast chicken for dinner, with pineapple upside-down cake for dessert. We sat around her dining-room table chewing in silence until someone mentioned our exclusion from Communion, which seemed so un-Baba. Pier's wife, Sara, who is Catholic, said, "At our church, everyone is invited to Communion." There were nods around the table. We were united in this, though otherwise somewhat sundry: the Friends devoted to competitive games and propriety, my Pierson cousins gentler and more likely to shop for vintage clothes or dye their hair pink.

From the end of the table, my father remarked, "Our disinclusion from the sacrament today is of a piece with the worldwide rise in religious intolerance."

"Oh, and when did that begin, Dorie?" Karen Pierson, Paddy's wife, asked. A talented photographer, she likes to draw people out.

"To give it an arbitrary date," he said, "in 1979, when Jerry Falwell and Pat Robertson came to prominence, and Juhayman bin Seif al-Uteybi took over the Grand Mosque in Mecca, bringing with him a supposed Mahdi, or messianic deliverer of Islam, and about two hundred men." He tipped back in his chair, a habit Mom could never break. "They held out for two weeks against the Saudis, until French commandos got them with nerve gas. Almost all the survivors, about eighty, were beheaded, but jihadism is the result. Fundamentalism is not merely a wave in religion worldwide; it is a tide."

"Why?" Karen asked, after a silence.

"As a historian, I merely assert the fact of it, and that that tide is sweeping the world," he said, his baritone reverberating like plainsong. He looked around the table, seeming to want to say more, to break through our polite attentiveness, but added only, "There will be a subsequent tide, but as to its nature, I cannot speak."

It was the kind of meal where I particularly missed Mom. She would have nudged my youngest cousin, Bella Pierson, to talk about her boat building, or reminded Jane that the house really needed—had *always* needed—a cozy little sitting room (and Jane would have replied, oh, yes, but she, Jane, could do without more easily than the house could withstand change). Then Mom would have suggested we sing one of those nonsensical Robinson songs that Baba liked to hear but refused to join in on, such as "Down in the Diving Bell" or "Clam Chowder" ("If you were like clam chowder, and I was like a spoon / And the band was playing louder and a little more in tune / I'd stir you 'til I spilled you; I'd kiss you till I killed you / If you were like clam chowder, and I was like a spoon"). She'd have gotten us going.

Of course, it was always Paddy who started us on "Down in the Diving Bell," rising in a cheerfully twitchy way to commence the sacred song:

Come listen to my story
Some truth to you I'll tell
About the pretty sights I saw
Down in the diving bell . . .

Even as a child, I sensed in Paddy a kindred spirit: a whimsically funny fellow who would purse his lips and sigh, seeming to hate to have to disagree with your remark—before launching into a spirited refutation. Mom and Grandma Tim were fiercely proud when his work as the White House correspondent for the *Wall Street Journal* landed him on Nixon's "enemies list." Paddy gave me one of my favorite novels, *Bang the Drum Slowly*, and later wrote me encouragingly about my magazine articles. After he left the *Journal* and moved to Maplewood to try farming with Grandpa Tom—he and Karen turned the old sugarhouse up the hill into a warm and comfortable home—and after that move began, perhaps, to strike him as problematic, his letters grew more cautionary. In 1994, he observed that for my writing to achieve its potential:

> *you need at least another decade of very hard work, preparation. The kind of hours of solitude that no wife and children ought to be made to put up with. And let's not kid ourselves: a wife means children.*
>
> *Your dear mother says: "Tad just needs to work a few things out with his shrink, things about his mother and father. Then he'll get married." We all have such things to work out, and I admire your willingness to take on the task. But I trust there might be more to your unmarriedness than pesky things*

about your parents. A better reason is your career as a man of letters.

He'd written on this same theme a few months earlier, concluding, "Greatness seldom cohabits with nippers—they take so much time and energy to bring up right." It began to feel as if he were writing to a younger version of himself.

I HAD last seen Baba a few years earlier, on a cold Saturday afternoon late in winter. I went to the nursing home with Amanda, then my fiancée, and we found Baba, a lifelong teetotaler, drinking a Dixie cup of red wine with slightly anxious pride. She explained that she'd been diagnosed with a lazy esophagus, and the wine was medicinal; the word "esophagus," which she took a while to come out with, struck us all as very funny. Baba was smaller than ever, if possible, and her eyes swam behind giant glasses as she searched my face in growing apprehension, pleased to see me but unsure exactly who I was. As night fell she was prone to sundowning: growing anxious about Baby Bella, my youngest Pierson cousin (then in her mid-twenties), she would venture outside to find and protect her. When I showed Baba a recent photo of myself with Pier and Timmie, she clutched my arm, remembering her news: "And Tad is finally getting married!"

"Yes," I said. "Yes, isn't that wonderful?"

Mom and Paddy had sold Maplewood not long before, so after we said good-bye to Baba I drove Amanda to the farm to show her what once was. The Monster.coms were gut-renovating the farmhouse, the core of which dated to 1780;

the house had been jacked up on its foundations but still looked much the same from the road, white clapboards and dark green shutters out of Currier and Ives. We entered through the porch door, lifting a blue tarp that flapped in the wind, and walked into what had been the dining room. Turning toward the pantry, where we'd inked in our heights twice a year on the door frame, I stopped, stricken. Nothing familiar remained.

There had been such smells: maple logs burning in the small and long living rooms, Baba's bread in the oven, milk whirling in the kitchen pasteurizer, napping dogs. And sounds: the chorus of creaks as someone descended the steep, crooked back stairs; the snick of a door's hand-forged thumb latch; enameled tin cups clinking in the sink following afternoon lemonade; the brown plastic cuckoo clock in the kitchen exploding on the hour with idiot glee; the smash of icicles from the gutters; the hiss of the radiators; tractors coughing to life; my cousins tapping the walls, searching for the hidden room where runaway slaves were secreted when Maplewood was a stop on the Underground Railroad. During cocktail hour we'd lie on the floor upstairs and tickle open the black iron louvers on the old stovepipe dampers to eavesdrop on the gossip below.

The dampers were caulked over, the interior walls gone. A barn from elsewhere had been appended to the back of the house as a "great room." And the only smell was cold sawdust. You no longer had to bow your head to honor the sagging dining-room ceiling, which Tom had stabilized when the center beam broke by stripping a steel hoop from his silo, straightening it with his blowtorch and a sledgehammer, threading it through the beam, and anchoring it to the clapboards with a steel plate that graced the house's exterior like a wart.

I tried to explain to Amanda that across from the front staircase, here, was the long living room, and the Christmas tree stood in that corner. We would come down the stairs in a train, youngest to oldest, chanting the Robinson marching song from the Revolutionary War:

> *Hayfoot, strawfoot*
> *Belly full of bean soup*
> *January, February, March!*

The procession would break apart when we saw all the presents by the tree. After a few rounds of gift-opening, Grandpa Tom would drop himself into the chair by the telephone like a chunk of granite dynamited from Mount Rushmore. A charismatic figure to everyone but his relatives, he would prop his thick canes against his knee and nibble on ribbon candy as he began a series of bellowed phone calls: "How's that cow? I *know* it's Christmas morning—what's the matter with you? How's about you bring her on by?" Grandma Tim would be jabbing me with the butt of one of the flyswatters that lay around and saying, "That's the way Tom's phone conversations start: 'How's that cow?' It could be Jaysus Christ on the line, or Ronald Reagan. 'Ronnie, how's that cow?'" And then she'd be off, singing, "Butlers were suspected of going wee-wee in the sink / Or so the rich used to think . . ."

But soon I stopped even believing myself and had to get us out.

BACK HOME in Brooklyn, I dug out the videotapes my step-cousin Lizz had had made from Baba's home movies. The video service had stitched the clips together as the film had tumbled from the boxes, so the tapes were as ruptured as a Tarantino film, cutting at random between summer and winter, between the mid-1970s and the late 1950s, in brief silent vignettes.

There was Mom, playfully holding a silver baby spoon above my head as I tried to rise off a red towel to grab it. This was the period when Mom wrote to Jane Smith, "Tad is large (I look at him asleep and think, too large), vocal, + suddenly (after 2 years of aloofness), affectionate." As I watched the tape I seemed to remember this sequence: the sun dappling through the overhanging elm, the grass tickling my feet as I lunged off the towel. I was surely re-membering some subsequent afternoon, but now that after-noon becomes this, a late deposit of capital in the bank of memory.

Paddy dances in winter with me on his shoulders in a gray jacket and hood; he is slim and dark haired, twirling jauntily as Grandma Tim, seated on the bench outside the kitchen window, encourages him. He tightens his grip on my calves and jumps up and shoots a leg sideways, clicking his heels like a Cossack. Timmy plants seeds in the garden as Tom hoes around her, both wearing mucky boots and smiling. A one-horse sleigh coasts down the driveway, the black pony wreathed in bells, with Timmy striding alongside in a rac-coon coat like an emissary from Turgenev. My father sports a white Lacoste shirt with the collar up, in the mid-sixties now, looking as if he might suddenly invent the frug. Baba's face peers down at the lens from the sky like God—is this thing on? (I suddenly recall the heft of her camera and its machining purr, the sound-track of memory.)

Lizz Greene and her older sister, Anne, do cartwheels down the front lawn and I fake one—I never could do a cartwheel—and fall, and all of us roll sideways down to the white rail fence. Mom and I dance around each other in the driveway when I am three, she sporting a Jackie-style bouffant and a green sweater with white daisies. Baba again, frowning down at her lens. I am five, sitting on the blue tractor, glowing with pleasure as I turn the iron steering wheel and pat the tires' dusty tread bars; my father stands behind on the tow hitch, smiling.

My parents pose near my mother's Volkswagen Bug in February 1960, inward young lovers made shy by company. They are just days from being married: my father, with a short haircut, grins bashfully; my mother has an air of *noli mi tangere*. The hopeless nostalgia for the life before. A slow pan establishes winter: a lap robe of snow unfolding over the meadow below the dirt road, across the pond and the brook and the island beyond, down to the frozen Ottauquechee River. I always imagined, when I was a boy, that I would grow up to live in a cabin on Woodstock bottomland.

All of us are on the front porch, about 1971, my step-cousins Anne and Lizz and Brett, too. Mom, her hair frosted blond, urges two-year-old Timmie down the hill toward Baba; Timmie, short and round in a corduroy sundress, picks up speed, a smiling bowling ball, and the camera flares up and cuts off. Pier and I lie on the lawn in blue pajamas, wearing baseball mitts; Timmie stands in a long yellow dress nearby. I rise and fling a ball aloft to myself, stagger around and catch it, then throw my arms up. Pier, left out, raises his arms too, smiling sweetly. We all lie in a heap on the ground, wiggling.

We Friend and Smith children are dancing on the porch, hopping around Grandma Tim, who cradles the fireplace broom to her cheek and begins to do the Charleston. Later, years later, she leads me and Pier and Timmie and the Smith girls up the hill, all of us in rubber boots: the seven of us composed "the Muskrat Club." She'd tap our shoulders with the long stalk of a witch's candle and declare, "Arise and take survey of your domain!" And when we went over the top of the hill to the Secret Valley beyond, there was a brook couched in fern and mint and hemlock: our domain.

I always thought of Maplewood as where our family was at its best, but on film it seemed an Eden. If only Baba's camera had always been on. As I fell asleep that night, I saw myself again through her lens: I am three, in a bulky blue snowsuit, stepping off the porch into the cataract of winter sun and sinking into a drift where I wave my arms in comic distress.

THREE

Chimes

I N THE LATE summer of 2005, Timmie, Pier, and I staged a kind of intervention with my father. We were concerned that with Mom gone he was becoming isolated: he'd forgotten my birthday the prior two years and neglected to tell us for five months that a family friend had died. Sleepless at three a.m., grieving still, he would search the *Oxford Book of Prayer* for redemption. Though he had a new girlfriend, as well as hundreds of deep acquaintances and dozens of people around the world he exchanged letters and e-mails with, he had few truly close friends, and his invitations to dinner from Mom's friends had begun to drop away. The three of us had extensive discussions beforehand about how to broach the matter, both because he was not at his best—none of us were—and because we knew his sensitivity to criticism, which we share. Any suggestion of blame or delinquency rankles. Grievances in my family are like underground coal fires: hard to detect and nearly impossible to extinguish.

Having told my father we wanted to talk, we gathered one afternoon over iced tea on the porch of the family's summerhouse in Wainscott, on the south fork of Long Island. The wind was up, stirring the chimes in our cousin Norah's flower garden across the way. I began by saying that there were many things we had relied on Mom for, and among them was being the family's hub, the one who made the phone calls and asked about that interesting dinner party and kept every milestone and deadline in her head. "There's a hole there, Day," I said—when I was young, I couldn't pronounce "Daddy" and called him Daya or Day, which stuck. "And we need you to do some of the imaginative thinking and coordinating that Mom used to do so we start filling it. We all have to be better about, well, being a *family*."

Timmie went next, thanking my father for all the time he'd spent with her in San Francisco earlier that year when she underwent a liver transplant precipitated by an autoimmune disease. We'd all gone out for a week, rotating our visits to the hospital to spell Timmie's husband, Scott, as she came out of intensive care. Bracing herself, she went on, "But sometimes I felt that you were present but absent, Daya—that there were places you'd rather be. I sometimes felt that I, in my hospital bed, just out of intensive care, had to take care of you. That I had to make sure you knew what time the cafeteria closed and what to take for your cold."

Pier spoke last. He'd been the least inclined to have the meeting, disliking conflict and the possibility of giving pain. The most prudent of us, a Goldman Sachs vice president, he was also the most like my father. Quietly, looking out to sea, Pier observed that his children, Wil and Eve, wanted more time with their grandfather, and that their childhood was an opportunity that was already passing and wouldn't come again.

Day breathed in deeply through his nose, his habit when beset, but seemed surprisingly gratified. "Well, if I'm hearing you correctly—and it is a pleasure to hear you all express yourselves so articulately—you feel as if you haven't been kept up to date on what's going on with me, the kind of news that Mom used to convey. You want to hear more about my life with Mary French." Mary was his girlfriend, a lively widow. We glanced at each other: *No, we want you to pay closer attention to us.* We were also secretly amused: Day always used her full name, Mary French, preemptively distinguishing her from any other Marys who might fight their way into the conversation.

None of us had the heart, or the nerve, to correct him. It occurred to me that what we wanted might not be something he'd been raised to do. As I wondered if that meant we hadn't been raised to do it, either, he went on to mention a conversation he and I had had the year before, when I'd told him I thought he might benefit from psychotherapy. He had done a fair amount of Jungian analysis, but I had meant something that was less about myths and archetypes and more about personal examination. "At this stage of my life, I am not interested in delving further inwards," he said now. "I am interested in growing outwards, connecting with the wider world through the filaments of religion and philosophy. Therapy may work for you," he said to me, "as a sophisticated resident of Manhattan, the capital of therapy. But I'm unsophisticated, a provincial man—"

"Oh, come on!" I said. "You're an extremely sophisticated man with a PhD in history who's run large organizations and traveled the world. Don't be ridiculous." Startled to be challenged in his favorite rustic pose, he clammed up, sheepishly. And I did, too, annoyed at myself for challenging him only on the less vital point.

Afterward, in the kitchen, Pier and I shrugged and exchanged a look; it was not an easy house for private conversation. Timmie came in and murmured, "Well, it could have been worse. He didn't get that consternated face that makes me shut down completely."

I said, "But how he could have gotten the idea that we just want more updates about Mary—"

"Mary *French*," Timmie said, and we all grinned.

"It is what it is," Pier concluded after a moment. This is what he often says after a market reverse: his way of suggesting that further postmortems would be fruitless. All we can do is bear up.

FORTY YEARS after my father first caught sight of my mother outside Sterling Library at Yale, where she was getting a master's in English, he wrote her a poem recalling the moment:

> *. . . As if defense were required*
> *To giant unseen forces.*
> *Your hand was on*
> *A broad-brimmed hat,*
> *And your eyes cast down*
> *For pitfalls in the sidewalk.*

In those days, Mom wore Peter Pan collars and walked leaning forward with her head tucked, as if breasting a gale. Day's

poem went on to suggest that he had "waved away the tornado," so "you might raise your eyes to others', smiling."
Mom never acknowledged the poem, but she kept it in her
desk. She was a saver.

In the spring of 1957, they had a few modestly promising
dates. Then, after he returned from a long research trip to
Southeast Asia (where he got engaged, briefly, to a Filipina),
they reconnected. One Sunday afternoon in January of 1959,
she gave him some Coricidin for his cold and they settled
down in her apartment with cups of tea and the photo book
The Family of Man—and suddenly the link was forged. She
heard an internal chime and he felt a kind of decisive purr.

That July, he wrote her from his family's summer-weekend
retreat east of Pittsburgh, the Pike Run Country Club. "I
wish you had been with me," he confided, about having left a
party to walk the golf course. "Far out of their sight and far
from the sound of them I would have taken you, until, under
a great tree in the open we could have disrobed, and on the
wet grass walked, in our innocence, with only the moon and
God to see us." In September, he invited her to Pike Run for
a weekend, feeling it only fair to show her the cocktail souls
whence he came.

To keep everyone straight, Mom drew up a family tree
of Friends, Holtons, and Walkers—my father's paternal
cousins—and took notes on the club members she met: "She
is plump, jollyish, wears Bermuda Liberty dresses; he drinks";
"Playboy, 50, puts head on women's bosoms, gin"; "Mono-
tone voice, discouraging"; "70 but doesn't look it, white
jacket with signal flags, vociferous kisses"; "She has a horse;
his proposal accepted because horse liked him"; "Dark, plays
croquet, difficulty about job which he's quit + Sheila whom

he hasn't married." "I dismissed that world as of no importance," Mom told us years later. "Now I know better."

At dusk on their last day, my father drew my mother outside and proposed. After spending a weekend with the couple in November, Uncle Pad wrote Grandma Tim that "Lib is wonderful, happy and smiling. She and Dorie constantly embracing." My mother reported by letter to Jane Smith: "Being utterly unable to express it to him (never have I felt the poverty of language so acutely) I suppose I will fail miserably in telling *you* how lovely he is. For the first time in my life I am met—confronted by, responded to—in all the ways that are important. For the first time *everything*, not just part of me, is exercised. I've never known what it was like to feel SO WHOLE."

My father wrote her often from Buffalo, where he'd begun work as an assistant professor, expressing joy in their love but also loneliness and the occasional hangover from Benedictine on the rocks. He was troubled by the abstraction inherent in his work of the mind and bewildered by the sort of debilitating wrangles he got into when someone swerved into his lane. He would remain mistrustful of the world's impinging malice, of its oversupply of low-hanging eaves and claw-footed desks, treacherous objects that waited till he was deep in thought to inch into his path and leave him thumped and aggrieved. He had difficulty expressing his underlying boyishness and humor, fearing a loss of dignity; one of Day's colleagues wrote of him, in his journals, "There is much sweetness in him, but the sap doesn't flow." In a letter to Mom from Buffalo, Day observed, "I think that I should like to become an Hasidic Jew, for to such, a rustic's cry of joy is as valuable to God as the ten-volume Talmudic commentaries of the learned legalist. But it is so difficult to become a Jew from a standing start, so to speak."

Mom was a Democrat who came from Democrats; Day a Republican son of Republicans. Mom was airy and anxious; Day earthbound and embarrassed. Mom had at one point thought of becoming a Congregationalist minister; the Filipina Day had been engaged to later became a nun. Neither of my parents was naturally ebullient.

Together, however, they struck people as a golden couple. Everyone was charmed by the elegant way they served tea to each other, and by their vibrant, intuitive connection, so noticeable in games of charades. If Mom received an impossible phrase to act out, such as Mrs. Patrick Campbell's observation that "marriage is the result of the longing for the deep, deep peace of the double bed after the hurly-burly of the chaise-longue," she'd think a moment, then windmill her arms furiously with a sly look—and my father would shout the answer, leaving everyone else to cry, "What? What?!"

At their rehearsal dinner at the Woodstock Inn in February 1960, Grandpa Tom stood to toast Mom, his stepdaughter, and maundered tipsily toward his point: "I never met anyone who was perfect before, but Lib is perfect." Tom's daughter Nicki, a bridesmaid, remembers that "I was so embarrassed for her, and for him, but I wasn't jealous. I thought she was perfect, too." My father had been dreading his own father's toast: at Day's younger brother's wedding, in 1955, Grandpa Ted, still handsome then in his big-shouldered jacket and spectator shoes, had risen to muster a few benevolent but fuddled remarks before sliding into his chair. But in Woodstock, Ted got plastered early. My mother's uncle—a classmate of Ted's at Yale until Ted got kicked out for gambling (he would return the following year, then get kicked out again)—shepherded Ted back to his motel before the end of dinner.

In the morning, when my mother arrived at the Woodstock Episcopal Church, teary and radiant, my father turned to his best man, Ted Terry, to say, "This is going to be for a lifetime." As the reception at Maplewood wound down, my parents stepped from the porch into two feet of fresh snow. The driveway had been shoveled enough to allow them to slip away in Mom's Volkswagen. But two of my father's Williams College fraternity brothers had planted a wrought-iron table in front of the getaway car, and sat with their feet up on it, swigging champagne like lords. Life was going to be like that, a long wassail. Everyone was so young.

A HALF century earlier, in an Edith Wharton novel, there'd have been trouble with the proposed match: my mother's Hartford and New York mandarins would have sniffed at my father's Scotch-Irish Pittsburgh steel family. But by 1960, postindustrial cities such as Pittsburgh and Buffalo, and even the palmier outposts of California and Florida, fell within the cartography of acceptability. (Indeed, my father's great-aunt Rebekah was the only relative who looked into the question of suitability—"Who is this Libby Pierson? Who are her people?"—and after canvassing her sources in Hartford, she reassured my father that "the young lady came out well.")

My parents were both members of a class that believed that its right to govern had been proved by history, by America's crashing success as an experiment in freedom, free enterprise, and power. Members of the class tended not to trumpet that power, but their occasional fanfares now sound both smug and antique. The president of the Philadelphia & Reading Coal Company, George F. Baer, believed his authority derived from a covenant: the world would be "protected and cared for by the Christian men to whom God in his infinite wisdom has given control of the property interests of this country." In the prior century, Robert Walker, secretary of the treasury under President James Polk, declared that the Bible foretold that "a time shall come when the human race shall become as one family, and that the predominance of our Anglo-Celt-Sax-Norman stock shall guide the nations to that result." When my mother graduated as the eighth-grade valedictorian of the Putnam Avenue School, she gave a speech entitled "The Spirit of America" that likewise yoked duty to belief: "It was this same faith that sailed the tiny *Mayflower* to our Eastern shore—which saw the hardy patriot through the grueling Revolutionary War—this courage that led the pioneer ever westward when his heart cried out for rest. . . . Are we to let them down?" No, apparently. On to the ninth grade!

As the twentieth century sped up, the old order absorbed heavy blows. First came the Depression and the perfidy of Franklin Roosevelt, who in his inaugural address declared that the elite had been poor stewards of the country's interests, giving "to a sacred trust the likeness of callous and selfish wrongdoing." Then the Second World War conscripted the servant class. Only by long habit did the aristocracy maintain its assurance. In his memoirs, Thacher Longstreth, a lanky, bow tie–wearing Philadelphia councilman who spent an enthusiastic afternoon when I was fifteen teaching me an abstruse baseball board game he'd invented, wrote that one day in the mid-1930s, his grandmother Gah, first cousin to Herbert Hoover and president of the Women's Christian Temperance Union, marched out of Thacher's parents' house over a fancied slight. They assumed she would return shortly, as she'd left her car keys behind—as well as her chauffeur. Some time later, however, Gah called from her house and in a chilly tone asked that his parents send her car and driver along. How did you get there? Thacher's father asked, dumbfounded. "Well, I went out and stood in front of a car, and the driver stopped, and I told him I was Mrs. William F. Thacher and to take me to Locust Street. And he did."

Gah and her set knew who they were, and so did everyone else. All they lacked was a descriptive name. If pressed, my fathers' fraternity brothers at Williams College would have said that those who didn't fit in weren't "shoe," shorthand for the white bucks they all wore. Then, in 1964, two years after I was born, the sociologist E. Digby Baltzell popularized the acronym "Wasp" in his book *The Protestant Establishment: Aristocracy & Caste in America*. But as with many historical forces and periods—the Ages of Iron, Steam, and Reason, say—Wasps received their enduring name only as they were about to pass from relevance.

That long good-bye began the following year. Nineteen sixty-five marked the beginning of the social upheaval that would sweep away so many certainties and batter so many Wasp redoubts. It was the year that the Immigration and Nationality Act abolished the national-origin quotas in place since 1924, which had confined immigration, in great part, to those from Western Europe, thereby keeping out most of the sorts of people (Eastern European Jews, Hispanics, and Asians, among others) likely to be ignorant of—or to challenge—the traditional order. It was the year Buck Henry wrote his screenplay for *The Graduate*, the movie that deflated the Wasp culture of Southern California with one word—"plastics"—and that foresaw how the emerging generation gap would leave everyone stranded. (The script noted that the characters' clothes should suggest "California Contemporary Sport Style: the adults in styles infinitely too young for them, the children in styles infinitely too old for them.")

Nineteen sixty-five was the year my parents' friend Franny Taliaferro stopped wearing white gloves to lunch, and that my father, Theodore Wood Friend III, truncated his name on his first book to Theodore Friend (after his cousin John Hay Walker III, who as the director of the National Gallery of Art went by "John Walker," told him only yachts and racehorses should carry numerals). And it was the year my father's best man, Ted Terry, a welcome, rather acerbic presence in our lives, realized he'd bet wrong on the future. "I wanted very much to be a partner at a prestigious law firm, and the day I became a partner at Sullivan & Cromwell, January 1, 1965, was the day the Wasp establishment began to collapse," Ted, who went on to head the firm's trusts and estates practice, says. "I had my hand on the brass ring, and then the ring began to melt away. There had been a time when if you're John Foster Dulles, because you've been head of Sullivan & Cromwell, you're going to be secretary of state. You were tapped, like Skull and Bones." (Dulles's grandfather John W. Foster and his uncle Robert Lansing had been secretary of state before him.)

Nineteen sixty-five was the year of the Watts riots—the first significant racially fueled rebellion of the modern era—and the year that Lyndon Johnson both coined and instituted a new mode of national redress, issuing an executive order requiring government contractors to take "affirmative action" with respect to minority employees. And it was the year that two computers first communicated with each other over the phone, as well as the year that the "mouse" was conceived and the first minicomputer was built, all of which laid the foundation upon which the information economy would rise. That economy, now led by Microsoft and Google, would enable a technologically savvy elite gradually to replace the technologically unsavvy Wasp aristocracy.

Nineteen sixty-five was the year my maternal great-uncle Wassa Robinson, who'd captained the hockey team at Yale and been in Skull and Bones, got divorced from his wife, Diddy—a series of breakdowns having removed him, off and on, to the Institute of Living, Hartford's retreat for the scions of privilege. It was the year Wassa's oldest son, Johnny, second in his class at Yale, had his first manic episode; the year Wassa's youngest son, David, began planning his escape from Hartford and his family's "elitist mentality"; and the year Wassa's middle son, Donny, another hockey-playing golden boy and a shoo-in legacy to Yale, was shockingly denied admission.

The university's new admissions director, a Wasp named R. Inslee "Inky" Clark, who came to be loathed by a generation of Yale alums, suddenly increased the public-school share of the freshman class by 9 percent and cut the allotment of alumni sons from 20 percent to 12. "Dad expected me to go to Yale and be something between the president of Bankers Trust and president of the United States," says Donny, a tall, handsome, gregarious man. Occasionally he'd play catch with me at Maplewood, limbering up easily and then grinning across the lawn—ready?—and really burning them in. After attending Rutgers instead, Donny never quite made it as an actor in Los Angeles—"My type was the blond surfer, the ultra-Wasp, and these Jewish casting directors didn't get me"; started a boutique shortbread company with his wife that entailed his wearing a Scottish kilt to distribute samples; got divorced; struggled with depression; staved off financial embarrassment by selling the family's letter from Abraham Lincoln to his friend John Franklin Trumbull (my great-great-great-grandfather); and moved to Maine, where he house-sits for old friends. When Donny lived in Manhattan he'd often walk by the Ralph Lauren store on Madison and glower at the windows' horsey homages to the world the Robinsons once bestrode. "If Ralph really wants to get to the heart of Waspdom," Donny says, "he should do a whole window full of beakers of lithium and patients in white gowns."

The prepossessing sanity of the old ruling class was everywhere in doubt. Nineteen sixty-five was the year Lyndon Johnson irreversibly escalated the war in Vietnam, deploying the first American combat troops in the South and dropping the first bombs on the North; and the year, too, of the first widespread protests against the conflict. It was the year when it first became clear that the Wasp elite running the war hadn't a clue. As David Halberstam suggests in *The Best and the Brightest*, his devastating portrait of the president's advisers, they were led astray both by their class-based fear of Communism and by their implacable certainty. Of national security adviser McGeorge Bundy, the Groton- and Yale-educated Skull and Bones man, Halberstam observes that he "was the finest example of a special elite, a certain breed of men whose continuity is amongst themselves. . . . In their minds they become responsible for the country but not to it." Of Bundy's identically credentialed older brother, William, the assistant secretary of state for East Asian and Pacific affairs, Halberstam writes, "He had such good manners and came from such a fine tradition. . . . [But] he was the classic civil servant really, who believes he has succeeded if he meets the demands on him from the top of the matrix, and does not represent the bottom to the top." As for the secretary of defense, Robert McNamara, who toured Vietnam but saw there only what he expected to see, Halberstam concludes, "He was, there is no kinder or gentler word for it, a fool."

And 1965 was the year that the country's most famous and exclusive clubs stopped updating their look and feel and promise. If you go to these clubs for dinner on a Saturday night, you get scotch-plaid-upholstered furniture in the Vintage Cherry or English Tavern finish; accordion-folded napkins in the water glasses and sourdough rolls on the bread plates; Dover sole and oysters Rockefeller served up by an Irish waitress with dyed auburn hair; and, for company, an elderly gent in the corner in a striped three-piece suit with pocket square who eats his meal and drinks his three Manhattans, sips Sanka with Equal on the advice of his doctor, then lumbers into the night. His demeanor forbids you to notice, let alone trespass upon, his immense loneliness. In

his will the club will receive a small provision for a larger
umbrella stand.

AND SO my parents' generation was the last to grow up with
servants who took care of the meals and the children and the
bother, and so the last to require laundry chutes and dumbwaiters and foot bells under the dining-room rug. It was the
last that had Sunday lunch at Grandmama's and cut the
crusts off white-bread sandwiches and employed silent butlers (the silver clamshells into which you dumped cigarette
butts from your wedding present silver ashtrays); the last to
drink old-fashioneds and wear fox furs and consult the *Social
Register*; the last to grow up with calling cards and the gentlemen separating from the ladies after dinner; the last to
believe that the only colleges available to them were the Ivies
or the little Ivies or, for women, the Seven Sisters and the
junior colleges known as the Three B's; the last that ran
down to New York on the train to meet a certain someone
under the clock at the Biltmore or by the birdcage at Lord &
Taylor; and the last that took ship for Europe with stacks of
monogrammed luggage as a reward for their gentleman's C
or to salve the memory of a fickle beau.

My generation was the last to receive silver christening cups and to be taken shopping for the chain mail of
adulthood—camel hair coats and Brooks Bros. suits and
Lloyd & Haig shoes. And the first to abstain from church,
to give God a rest.

My twins, Walker and Addie, in addition to forgoing all
of the above, will have to make do somehow without chris-

tenings, mint jelly slathered over every roast, and even the faint expectation that a maiden aunt or doting grandparent might bequeath them a few shares of Con Edison, bought in the 1824 IPO. All they'll certainly have, of the old dispensations, is their Waspy names, which Amanda and I bestowed both casually (we just liked them) and as a half-ironic assertion. So Walker and Addie may not even think of themselves as Wasps. This seems to me at once sad, exhilarating, and inconceivable.

Often, in New York, I've had people ask, "So, are you really a Wasp?" as if they had stumbled on a black truffle. At a time when fewer than one in five Americans have any British ancestors, Wasps increasingly doubt their wider currency. Once the most American of people, we failed at the American necessity: assimilation. So we gaze out from the old game preserves—Bar Harbor, Watch Hill, Jupiter Island—and wonder how it all came to this.

Many younger Wasps deny their heritage, instancing a Catholic grandmother or insisting that they belong to the Union Club only for the athletic facilities and don't drop in very often, anyway. The nation's once-most-prominent Wasp, George W. Bush, learned that his past was a losing story when he first ran for Congress, in 1978; his opponent won by reminding the voters that when he was at Dimmit High School and Texas Tech, Bush was swanning about at Andover and Yale. So Bush recast himself as a brush-cutting, "ain't"-spouting populist, leaving Skull and Bones off the résumé. In any ethnic group, some are proud of their background, some are embarrassed, and some just don't care. Wasps, marinated in self-consciousness, lack the freedom of indifference.

Firmness of character requires either a considered affirmation of my heritage or a determined repudiation of it, yet I find myself ambivalent. I am drawn to what we had in great part because it's gone—drawn to the ruinous romance of loss.

FOUR

Sand

As we were driving home from a dinner party in Sag Harbor one recent summer night, Amanda said, "So what was that with the house?"

"What was what with what house?" I said.

"That vague, mumbly thing you did when Glenn asked about our house."

Over drinks in the backyard, our friend and host, Glenn, had proudly itemized the improvements he and his wife had made to their second home: the new kitchen, the spacious back wing. Even the septic situation, the Achilles' heel of old houses on the South Fork of Long Island, had been rectified. Then Glenn asked where we were staying. "In Wainscott," I said.

"It's Tad's family's house," Amanda said, shooting me a prompting glance.

"North of the highway?" Glenn asked.

"South," I allowed. South is better.

"So you come out every weekend?"

"Usually just the two weeks before Labor Day."

"Because . . ." Amanda said.

"We rent it out through mid-August to pay for all the up-keep," I said. "Right now the roof leaks everywhere, so we have to reshingle the whole thing."

"Why not come in the fall and spring?" Glenn said. "It's lovely then."

"Yes," Amanda said, "we spent our honeymoon there, in mid-September, and played golf in Montauk and had lobster rolls practically every night. It was amazing!"

"The house isn't winterized, so we just shut it down," I said.

Glenn and his guests might have gotten the idea—I might in a vague, mumbly way have intended that they get the idea—that the house was a pokey shithole, which it is not. But as Glenn is a rare-books dealer who can price any commodity, I avoided certain details: that the house is not just in Wainscott, but in the Georgica Association, an enclave of two dozen houses on the western shore of Georgica Pond that faces houses owned by Steven Spielberg, Martha Stewart, and Calvin Klein on the eastern. That the house has eight bedrooms and two walled gardens and a lawn that runs to the pond, with the Atlantic in view beyond. And that the property, known as Century House, was where my siblings and I grew up every summer, as my mother and her brother had before us, and their father and his brother before them.

I told Amanda that mentioning all this would have given everyone the wrong idea, and that I'd rather be judged not for what I came from but simply for how I am. She snickered. It's true that the Wasp gold-star mentality—the notion that you should never mention your heritage or shining qualities, which in due course will be recognized by the relevant authorities—is hilariously unsuited to the modern world. It's also true that by ducking behind my privet hedge to avoid being perceived as a Wasp, I had ensured that perception.

Talking about the house just then was complicated by its uncertain status. My cousin Norah Pierson, who had presided over the place for thirteen years, had died suddenly that spring of a brain aneurysm at sixty-six. Norah was the older daughter of Wilson Pierson, my mother's uncle and the house's previous owner. She was tall and imperious, with rose-framed reading glasses dangling on a lanyard, and only her soft blue eyes kept her from exactly resembling Sacagawea. Norah had been an outsized presence: a jeweler who made chunky gold rings; an artist who scoured the beach for perfect knobbed whelks and surf clams, painted them with moons and stars or Mondrian-style rectangles, then returned them to the dunes; a contentious ex-hippie who rolled her own blunts on the porch, pot smoke wreathing her gray topknot. She stayed not in the house but in the artist's studio across the way, flying out like a mob of crows to harass anyone who wandered by with a dog, particularly if they were our invited friends. She dominated dinner table conversation by demanding agreement with her dark beliefs about international banking, the estrogen that leaches from Saran Wrap, and our neighbors' criminal reliance on leaf blowers and "the three-footers"—the slight Mexican immigrants who do most of the local gardening. One night we were all discussing why some of the men in the family feared some of the women, and Norah barked, "It's because we have a cunt!"

Her death changed the flow. Norah and her stepmother, Lou—Wilson's second wife—had generously passed the house on to the younger generation, but to minimize tax consequences they had shotgunned their ownership out through a trust, "Honeysuckle," named for the climbing shrubs that bracket the front steps. Family schisms had already appeared. Two weeks after Norah's death, we all got an e-mail from Uncle Pad that began, "We live in a time of post-Norah," and went on to say that a real-estate agent we knew had a buyer lined up: "He said that Honeysuckle should sell for between $25 million and $35 million."

Pier, who had been made the property's manager by Norah and has sole discretion over matters such as a potential sale, fired off a reply: "Thank you for passing on this tidbit. However, my view is unequivocally NOT to sell for reasons too numerous to list here. Love to all." Then, being Pier, he called Paddy and listened to his arguments in favor of a sale: the Association was awash with the superrich; a hurricane could wipe us out tomorrow; and, of course, the money.

Strong arguments. And yet Timmie and I were firmly with Pier on the side of hell, no. With Maplewood gone, Georgica was the last family base, a treasure-house of memories. Henry James was in Lenox, Massachusetts, when he told Edith Wharton that the most beautiful words in English were "summer afternoon," but he should have been here, where the days were all afternoons. We'd sleep deep and late in the low-ceilinged rooms on the third floor, the "Crow's Nest," then run off to the tennis courts and the beach, home for lunch, back to the beach, tennis again, back for dinner, and then play flashlight tag until puberty. In later years there were bonfires on the beach and sandy pairings-off set to the rout of the surf beneath the distant stars.

In recollection, Georgica is always gin-clear. But there were also the low, close days when the wind licked you like a dog's tongue, and the nights of surprising cold, a nor'easter coming in, when you pulled on another sweater and looked about for improving activities. There was no television for the longest time, and when Wilson and his first wife, Letty, finally gave in, their set crackled snow on every channel but PBS. Our way of life there resembled the one advocated by Sylvester Graham, the abstemious Presbyterian minister who invented graham crackers: "hard mattresses, open bedroom windows, chastity, cold showers, loose clothing, pure water and vigorous exercise."

When it was formed, in 1892, the 137-acre Association was intended as a rustic alternative to the overpopular Hamptons. The common areas haven't been spruced up much since: there is a beat-up road and a few unbumpy speed bumps and a dowdy bathhouse by the private beach that was only recently (and controversially) rebuilt and brought up to code. Thickets of swamp mallow and shadblow, of groundsel and pitch pine, still surround a central field and the lawns of the old houses. Our odd sodality sits at the end of an unmarked street, defended by faded "Private" and "Dead End" signs and, in the summer, by a guard plopped on a beach chair who scrutinizes cars for their green "G" sticker and allows them—or really anyone who's white and who waves—to pass.

Much remains immemorial. On Monday nights everyone carries blankets to the beach and spreads out with wine and chicken for a picnic. As the men's tennis final is played on the first of four clay courts, toddlers and spaniels run on the grass beneath the wooden windmill, and the elders Elliot Ogden, in a fedora, and Edna Thornton, in a broad straw hat, lead the applause. The trophies are handed out to the men in their sweaty whites—often to Pier, who has won the singles six times and carried me along in the doubles seven times—and gracious remarks made by the tournament organizer in his natty shorts, who invokes the theme of generations, the rising power of the young and continued skill of the old. It could be any year, really. There is the joy of the game itself, of play, and the power of this way of life: apparently untroubled afternoons, space, air, light, order, and someone else minding the children; a plenitude that would seem to inoculate parents forever against their children's complaints.

White tennis balls from the seventies still turn up now and then in the underbrush surrounding the wire backstops, a scratchy cordon of dwarf sumac, blackberries, and poison ivy where rabbits scooted to and fro but we feared to seek. In the Sunday-afternoon softball games, the tanned, sloe-eyed children of privilege all round the bases and score; Day, as one of two steady pitchers, has become expert at fumbling slow rollers. Crabbers wade in the shallows of the brackish pond, which is fed by five creeks and replenished by the sea, tiding in periodically across the sandbar. Piping plovers pose like decoys, then flutter up and wheel off against the sun, framed in the wet light local artists love. The beach is administered from a high white chair by the lifeguards, a series of lolling, zinc-nosed sentinels whose names are writ on water going back to Carl Yastrzemski, who grew up down the road in Bridgehampton and spent a summer preserving us a half century ago.

As Labor Day nears, a chill grows in the shadows. Canada geese skim overhead and the whistle of the Montauk train grows insistent. The scrunch of bike tires on gravel is like ripped parchment, a contract torn asunder. A few jellyfish pulse their bells alongside us, bodysurfers awaiting one last wave to take us in. The sea surges and closes over.

In August of 2007, after Norah died, we began pruning the touches she had added to the house since Wilson died, in 1993: plastic flowers, plastic porch chairs, plastic rolling carts piled with plastic place mats. (For someone who hated plastic, Norah couldn't resist it on sale at Kmart.) Gradually the culling became a full-on spring cleaning, led by Amanda, who deplored the grease-caked kitchen and general clutter and grime.

Amanda's family are Wasps, too—they've been in eastern Pennsylvania since the nineteenth century—but in comparison to my family they are a practical, roll-up-your-sleeves group, not only willing to mow the lawn but capable of tuning the mower. When the kids asked what was for dinner, her parents would say, "Poop soup," and at Christmastime her father would tote his gun outside to shoot Santa Claus in the ass. Amanda's mother is famous for vacuuming her way out of the house, and without Amanda's naval sense of cleanliness and order as a spur, we'd never have gotten started on Century House, or felt much guilt about stopping.

Into the trash went the slack window shades and gelled cleaning fluids in rusty tins and petrified rubber plugs from the claw-footed tubs and the nearly empty bottle of Dr. Bronner's almond soap left by Janine, our au pair in the late 1970s. Anything merely ugly or useless or otherwise doubtful went into the garage, a limbo from which Paddy and Karen, when they arrived after Labor Day, could rescue items they cherished. Soon the garage was stuffed with a sloppy mountain of mothball-soaked blankets; faded curtains; unmatched dishes; *New Yorkers* from the 1970s; ghost casters; and dozens and dozens and dozens of keys to bygone locks, some labeled with droopy tags—"French hat box," "Old trunk," "New trunk," "Forrestal and Essex"—but most as orphaned as a lost mitten.

Into the garage, too, went items such as the spare handle to the 1930s GE refrigerator—a unit long gone from the house—with its attached note from the plumber, also long gone from the house and indeed from the earth: "It might be wise to save these old parts for another emergency." The Piersons believed in using "materials at hand" for any arising need; in this manner driftwood would serve as pickets for the garden, and a splintered table, with a few ax strokes, for a compost bin. Gradually the magic attic was born: if you stashed a chair with broken caning under the eaves for a spell, in the crawl spaces where the plaster oozes through the laths, might not the seat heal itself? Well, perhaps a few more years . . .

Our delvings in this vast reliquary uncovered Wilson's cocktail shakers; a brass coal bin; an antique Singer sewing machine; wooden tennis rackets in trapezoidal presses, their wing nuts screwed tight against the salt air; and a dozen golfing trophies won by my great-grandfather Charles Wheeler Pierson; as well as a pitted silver teaspoon that belonged to Robert Burnet, an ancestor who served on General Washington's staff (in a surviving etching, he has the vigorous Pierson beak and a glint in his eye that suggests cantering horses and iced punch with the ladies). We put these talismans on display, our refurbishments seeming to make the house even more timeless. And then there were the poignant little envelopes containing milk teeth or curlicues of Wilson's baby hair. Displaying them felt creepy, like ancestor worship; throwing them out felt remiss. So, after a melancholy look, back into the drawer they went.

One afternoon, I tried to bring order to the living room's hundreds of leather-backed hardcovers and humid paperbacks. Churchill's *The Gathering Storm* was next to *In this Corner . . . Dennis the Menace* and the thrillers *Journey into Fear* and *Keep Cool, Mr. Jones!* Curiosities such as *The 1940 Book of Small Houses* and *7000 Words Often Mispronounced* were intermixed with jovial etiquette books like Hilaire Belloc's *Cautionary Verses* and Gelett Burgess's *Goops and How to Be Them: A Manual of Manners for Polite Infants*, which explained:

> *The proper time for you to show*
> *Whatever little tricks you know*
> *Is when grown people ask you to;*
> *Then you may show what you can do!*
> *But sometimes mother's head will ache*
> *With all the jolly noise you make,*
> *And sometimes other people, too,*
> *Can't spend the time to play with you!*

Taking up *The Secret Garden* by Frances Hodgson Burnett
and *The Lives of the Hunted* by Ernest Thomson Seton brought
to mind the rainy days when I first opened those briny pages
and began reading not only into my own childhood but my
parents' and grandparents' as well. So many of the house's
children's books by Wasps and Brits featured dead or absent
parents: they carved out a replacement world where fantasy
stood in for loving care.

When I glanced up to see Walker and Addie taking tot-
tering steps on the lawn, pushing their stroller toward the
birdbath and singing with happiness, I suddenly felt that I
was them, laboring in the grass, or that I was my father,
looking at me. It was all fluid. Everything in view would have
looked much the same on a summer's day in 1965 — or even
in 1915, when Charles Pierson and his wife, Elizabeth,
bought the house. In a file cabinet deep in a closet, I found a
photo from that year: the Pierson children, Wilson and John,
stood side by side on the lawn in knicker suits. Wilson wore
a suppressed grin, having just made a sly remark, and John,
my future grandfather, was cracking up.

When we were young, the wall of photos on the landing
was more disquieting than the mug shots at the post office:
the Pierson men with their high-bridged noses a mighty ar-
mada gazing down on my weathercocking pinnace. As we
framed those portraits now, many of which had curled onto
their rusting thumbtacks, I mixed in some livelier photos
from the cupboards. But Charles Pierson, vigilant of his dignity, resisted updating. His youthful photo with Elizabeth,
not yet become "Goggy," shows her demurely beautiful in a
Gibson girl dress and a flat-brimmed picture hat, and him
regal in a high-wing collar. His eyes dream a little above an

unyielding mouth. In photos with his young sons, who sport pageboy haircuts and matching linen tunics or middy blouses, they resemble the czar's children with an exacting tutor.

Charles planted a red cedar in the yard and told the boys: "You must each jump over this sapling every year." They strove to comply, but time wins in the end—the cedar is now forty feet tall. The competitive atmosphere drove Wilson to follow his father through Yale, where he, like Charles, was the valedictorian, and to join the faculty immediately after receiving his BA in 1926, eventually becoming chairman of the history department and Yale's first director of the humanities. It drove John to surpass Wilson's record the following year—and then to a breakdown.

At Yale, Charles was a gamecock known as "Cootie." When the university received a frozen mastodon from Siberia, he snuck into the lab with some classmates from Skull and Bones, carved off a few mastodon fillets, then cooked and ate them. This escapade proved to be ideal preparation for his later life as a corporate lawyer in Manhattan. Charles represented the famous miser Hetty Green, argued and won a Supreme Court case on Goggy's behalf over her having to pay New York taxes on Ohio rental properties, and wrote a book called *Our Changing Constitution* to demonstrate that it hadn't changed a bit.

After his unexpected death from endocarditis, in 1934, the family was deluged with condolence letters. One correspondent, Charles Sherman Haight Jr., wrote Wilson that he had recently come before Charles Pierson as a member of the committee that vetted candidates for admission to the bar. Haight had heard of the committee's searching inquiries into the candidates' knowledge of American history, so he was quite nervous. "I was among the first to be called, and when I sat down at your father's desk, he looked up with his most serious manner and asked—'Well, how is Charles Sherman Haight the Third?' (The boy was only two months old then.) Then your dad beamed, and asked no more questions, except as to what men I knew on the list." When not upholding the old-boy network, Charles exemplified, in his correspondence with the better newspapers, the Wasp "letter to the editor" mentality, which supposes that Americans can be led to understand what is right and fair. He would not have seen these roles as contradictory.

Charles had delighted in small economies—his transfer of Wilson to nonresident membership at Shinnecock Hills Golf Club, for instance, saving fifty dollars—so he would have been pleased to read the letter one of his partners sent Goggy after her husband's death:

Wilson dropped in the office Saturday morning and spoke of some cigars which Mr. Pierson had in care of the Bankers Club. I called up the Club and they told me that the cigars had been turned into cash and that Mr. Pierson had a credit of $43.50 on their books. I asked them for a check for this amount and have just received and enclose the same herewith.

Frugality, we came to understand, was a virtue, a way of honoring what you had been given. But the famous Wasp parsimony—counterpoint to, and often following a generation after, a notable example of Wasp profligacy—also derived from unspoken and rather discreditable anxieties. There was the fear that if the money went, we would be revealed as having no more culture or merit than anyone else—the fear that we'd retained power not through inherent superiority but through inherited funds. And, of course, the fear of being poor.

Years later, Goggy Pierson suddenly began to be very critical of her late husband. Wilson, who had loved his father, didn't want to hear it. "But Goggy just couldn't seem to keep it down," Grandma Tim, who was for a time Goggy's daughter-in-law, would say. "Victorian wife, I guess, couldn't talk back while he was alive. But who can blame her, the way he worked? Every night, after supper, he'd go into that awful room and work till midnight, that awful brown room, like the inside of a cow's stomach."

Yet Charles also wrote poetry. The women on Mom's side painted beachscapes and the men wrote poetry. His language was Tennysonian and exuberant, his outlook astonishingly bleak. There were gloomy poems about goblins and blasted moors that ended in hope, and lyrical poems about nature that ended in despair. The latter were better. "Twilight," evidently written in Georgica, concludes:

> *Ah hour so hushed, so steeped in reveries!*
> *Not now on flaming dawn, or soaring lark,*
> *Or throb of rushing wings, or opening bars*
> *Of young life's symphony, not now on these*
> *Muses the shivering soul, but on the dark*
> *And the lone road unlit by sun or stars.*

He lived to see only one of his grandchildren, my mother. Looking down at her in her bassinet, he said, "I hope she's a singer"—meaning he hoped she would sing around the house, filling it with the kind of cultivated beauty he feared was fading from the world.

WILSON, who inherited the place, dominated the photo wall: his deep-socketed eyes glinted down from every angle. He was the author of a definitive work, *Tocqueville in America*, and several histories of Yale itself, which led his colleagues to call him Father Yale. Though he often reminded us that our ancestor Abraham Pierson had been the college's first rector, in 1701 (another ancestor, Jacob Hemingway, was the college's first student), he had a pawky sense of humor about his own donnishness. When he heard a historian named Gaddis Smith ask the department secretary for paper clips, he poked his head out and said, "Young man, when I was your age we used to buy the wire and bend it ourselves."

Humor was the main marital link. There was the morning Letty replaced Wilson's hard-boiled egg with a plaster of paris replica, and he kept banging at it with his knife in increasing consternation as we looked on joyfully, until he finally knocked off a dusty chunk and broke into laughter. And the morning, a few years later, when she replaced his fried egg with a plastic replica that he sawed away at for some time before catching on and, unexpectedly, giggling.

Still, coming across their wedding photo from 1936 was a surprise, because they looked so sprightly: Wilson in a morning suit and spats, with a baby's breath corsage, and Letty, her face a perfect oval of pleasure, in a Norwegian peasant's wedding dress with a fluted lace collar and a lace cap—the Sonja Henie look so popular that year. She began the marriage loving to paint and dance and dress up, but over the decades

Pierson rigor tamped some of that down. Letty was the first who had to make do without the three Irish domestics — - referred to by Goggy Pierson as "the majestics" — and by the time we came along she had sturdy arms and wore dowdy hats and canned beach plum jam nonstop. She was brisk and amiable except about the weather, whose vagaries obsessed and depressed her. Over lunch she would crane to peer out the window to the south and then the window to the north, and then remark, "Rain coming" or "Nor'easter blowing in, looks like." When our au pair, Janine, began to snicker at these Eeyoreish forecasts, we all looked at her, mystified.

As a child, I was at ease around Letty and alarmed by Wilson, by the way he immersed himself in nearly impossible jigsaw puzzles — white eggs on a white backdrop, for instance — his fingertips palpating the tiny pieces like a blind man's. And by how he sat on the porch at night with his pipe flaring, impervious to the mosquitoes, a Conrad hero brooding on the crooked timber of humanity. He never raised his voice, but when he led me down the long lawn to consider the birdbath that I had only half-filled before hurrying to the beach, his silence was terrible. His blue gaze bored into me like a gimlet, pinning my writhing fecklessness down for his extended contemplation.

I recalled that piercing look the other afternoon, when Walker and Addie kept climbing out of their Pack 'n Plays in the room that had been Wilson's study. They had begun to hate naps. They strobed the light on and off, bowled beach stones, and — the fourth time I went in to settle them — industriously smeared Vaseline across Wilson's desk. I said "No!" very loudly, and they began to sob. "Daddy shouldn't have gotten so mad," I said, stricken with remorse. I was astonished by how furious they could make me; they had entered the stage, or I had, where I finally empathized with my parents. "But that's naughty, okay? Naughty means no, don't do it: naughty. You should know better"—*Why?*—"Vaseline stays in its jar and you stay in your cribs, okay? Because Mommy and Daddy have to do some work this afternoon, so we can make some money and buy you more Vaseline."

They stared at me, trying to figure it all out. Then Walker skillfully changed the subject. He dropped beneath the rim of his crib and cried, from its depths, "I playing hide-in-seeks, Daddy!" Standing, in order to be found, he repeated "Hide-in-seeks!" with a confiding smile. And I thought of Mom, cheek to cheek with a Sikh.

Near the end of his life, Wilson and I had dinner at a Greek pub down the road, and over a porterhouse steak and several martinis he told me that he judged himself too rigidly, that he had never been able to truly relax. I have his tambour desk in my office at home; the brass handles are incised with blooming flowers and a pollinating beehive and, in small caps, the adjuration "Nothing Without Labor."

NORAH'S MEMORIAL service took place the Saturday after Labor Day at Wainscott Cemetery, presided over by a former classmate and minister named J. J. Lee Wolfe (who proved to be Jane Smith's first cousin). There was a big turnout, including even several of the neighbors Norah had erupted at over the years. The now-white-haired Georgica lifeguard who had dated Norah when she was fifteen was the last to tip a spadeful of earth on her grave. Aunt Karen declared, "First boyfriend!" and Paddy added, "Stone him!" which drew a laugh.

Afterward, everyone came back to the house and drank wine and ate ham and reminisced. The impromptu eulogies continued for hours. We learned that Norah had made earrings for Elizabeth Taylor that were featured on the cover of *Life*, that when male diamond dealers asked for coffee she would serve it to them in a breast-shaped mug that you could only drink from by sucking on the nipple, and that she liked to pee standing up.

I hadn't planned to, but I told the story about the sea bass, toning it down for the occasion. As I was leaving Georgica after Labor Day in 1997, I reluctantly asked Norah for the seventy dollars she owed me for some sea bass. No one wanted to shop for her because she never paid you back.

"I thought I paid you," she said.

"Um, no."

My girlfriends always liked Norah because she'd sit them down to confide that my parents were troubled by the way I lied and stole, which had been somewhat true when I was thirteen. I didn't always like her, but I loved her, mostly. She'd recently told me, "We're the only people in this family who are making a living on the *street*, by our wits," and there were times when I felt we had a lot in common. This was not one of those times. Or maybe it was: we were standing at either end of the kitchen table, tensed on the balls of our feet, and it seemed suddenly, absurdly likely that we'd end up chasing each other around the table.

"Well, you still owe *me* for the sitting-room window you hit a golf ball through *last* summer!" she said. I had skulled a golf ball through the window, fooling around with a sand wedge on the lawn. I'd then given Norah a blank check for it and followed up a month later with a call to remind her to cash the check, precisely so that she wouldn't hold the incident over me forever. "Oh, don't worry about it," she had said. "We were getting a bunch of things fixed anyway." "Are you sure?" I said. "Really sure?"

I reminded her of this extended back-and-forth, trying to keep my temper. "I don't remember any of that," she said. "I've been waiting all this time for *my* money."

"This is why no one wants to deal with you, Norah," I said. "Because you're completely impossible. Keep the money, fine. But you're on your own with me from here on out."

I went to say good-bye to Mom and Day, getting a lot of raised eyebrows as we hugged. It had been an increasingly audible conversation. Norah came and sat on the front stairs, under the photo wall. "All right," I said, going over to her.

"We can't fight," she said. "There are few enough people I like in the world."

"I'm sorry we fought. It wasn't my intention."

"Who knew you were such a fireball?" she said. We hugged once, and then again.

The next day Mom called and worked her way around to suggesting I phone Norah and apologize more thoroughly: "I think she felt bruised."

"Well, she should have," I said. "She was totally wrong, and exactly in that reality-denying way that *you* often complain about."

Mom sighed. "Yes, I know. But we're all the family she has."

———

WHEN NORAH was born, in 1940, Wilson, who had hoped for a boy to continue the Yale tradition, posted a memo at the university's Davenport College that said, "Our maid is much excited and pleased" and circulated a birth announcement noting that "the newest representative of the Pierson and associated families is more interesting than beautiful." Both he and Letty were distraught when the birth of their second daughter, Tisha, entailed complications that necessitated Letty's having a hysterectomy.

When Letty was pregnant with Tisha, Norah, aged two and a half, was diagnosed with a peritonsillar abscess, or quinsy, and Wilson took her to the hospital. In Norah's recounting of the family romance, her case was so grave she was quarantined and written off. "The doctors figured they had nothing to lose, so they operated on me experimentally, *without anesthesia* and *without antibiotics*, which were all being saved for the war," she would say. "I somehow survived. But my parents never visited — they left me there to die." The baby book that Letty kept covers the entire affair with the note: "Abscess lanced, also used sulfathiozole" (an antibiotic). But to Norah the event made it clear "that I was alone in the world and had to make my own way."

She introduced bikinis to Georgica, ran her mouth, broke curfew, fumed. In her junior year at Miss Porter's, a finishing school, she and Wilson didn't speak; he wanted her to go to college and she wanted to paint. In her senior year, he said, "May I see you in my office?" and sat her down to discuss the perils of banking on a single talent, compared to the well-hedged path of liberal arts. "You could go to a place like Smith and study art history," he said.

"I am a doer, not a voyeur!" Norah replied. She had sand,

an old-fashioned term for gumption. We approved of sand. My great-uncle Wassa Robinson was known as "the Sandy Kid" for his courage. When he was fighting the lung cancer that would kill him, he wrote a close friend to downplay having already lost forty pounds and his sight, concluding, "I'm going to make it even if I have to put sand in the lemon juice." And Grandpa Tom told me once about a farmer he knew who'd found himself without a weapon when a bull got into the wrong field and began goring his cows. The farmer had advanced on the bull and pounded it between the eyes with his fists until he drove it away. "That man," Tom said, "had sand."

Norah went to the School of the Museum of Fine Arts in Boston, and at my parents' wedding a year and a half later, the crinoline underskirt of her bridesmaid's dress hid her three-month pregnancy. When she finally told her parents, their response was fury and dismay and then practicality: they urged her to marry the boy, a Harvard undergraduate, but she said she was not in love with him. They urged her to get an abortion, but she refused. Wilson telephoned the father-to-be and asked him to present himself to discuss the matter. He said he would love to, but he had a rehearsal at the student theatrical society, the Hasty Pudding. From then on he was known in the family as "Hasty Pudding," a story Mom whispered to us early on, shaking her head at the lapse but smiling at the salty nickname.

Wilson's subsequent letters to Hasty Pudding commenced in some lingering expectation of a shared sense of duty. After the baby was born in July 1960, but before Norah relinquished him for adoption, Wilson wrote: "Michael is a dark-haired, strong-faced little character, and Norah naturally feels qualms about giving him up. But we all hope she can make it." After itemizing various expenses, he observed, "You therefore owe me $249.64 and I will be obliged for reimbursement. . . . This has been a sad and painful time for all of us. I assume that your family knows the state of affairs hitherto, but have had no word from them. Yours very sincerely, G. W. Pierson." Five months later, after three further dunning notes had gone unanswered, he wrote with a final tally, rage simmering beneath the starch: this "brings your indebtedness to me as of today from $827.50 to $1298.00 (beyond the $99.64 which is all I have ever received from you). Will you please notify me at once how and when you propose to meet your obligation."

Norah's conduct continued to be a thumb in her father's eye for some time. After a brief marriage, in 1963, she lived with various men, had two abortions, smoked pot and snorted coke. She opened a jewelry store in Laguna Beach and later brought it to Santa Fe, where she built a dwelling widely known as "the Flintstone House." She wrapped an ordinary bungalow in ten thousand pounds of polyurethane foam, intending it to look like the surrounding sandstone cliffs, an experiment to prove nature's dominion over man that Wilson ended up subsidizing. She practiced astral projection and reported that when she hooked up with a handsome dead Wainscotter from her youth, their sex in the ether produced mind-blowing orgasms.

Tisha was also out west, experiencing the raptures of youth culture after her own short-lived marriage. When Letty wrote my parents a Christmas card in 1967, she made light of her children's divergence from the expected path: "Whether either girl will marry their present bedmates who can say. Time will tell. In the meantime, back at the ranch old Square Uncle Wilson and Cube Aunt Letty live a rather unusual life of love."

In the early nineties, Norah tried to look for her son but ran into a bureaucratic wall. After Letty died of leukemia, in 1982, Norah and her father had grown close, and in his presence she mused, "Wouldn't it be great if he just knocked on the door some day?" Wilson frowned—not really—and said, "What would you say to him?" "Come in!" she replied. When he drew up a Pierson family tree, Wilson had already written, beneath Norah and Tisha's names, a melancholy but firm "end of the line."

A few summers later, Norah gathered the Friends and Piersons at Century House for a powwow about depression prompted by her happy introduction to Prozac. Out the window behind her a slop of storm waves pummeled the beach as she went through the long list of people in the family who had been depressed or crazy, or depressed and crazy. Her list ended with Tisha: "My own *sister*, who's God knows where doing God knows *what*." Not long before, Tisha, now calling herself "Reverend Tish" and furious that she was not going to inherit any share of Century House—Wilson feared that she would force a sale—began sending her father and other family members the bull's-eyes of targets she'd peppered with her Colt Python. Later she changed her name to Molly Morgan Miller, wrote everyone to say she no longer considered herself part of the family, and offered her services to police departments as a psychic. Then she dropped from sight.

"You've all got the *gene*," Norah continued, "and you better get *checked out*. It's a *time bomb!*" It was another of her dia-

tribes against invading phragmites, Mexicans, or Jews—
except that this time the enemy was us: *the phone call came
from* inside *the house!* Those of us already on medication
screwed up their faces at the airing of these private matters,
and the rest just waited to be released. "Free *sexual* energy is
part of the disorder, too, by the way. Oh, yes!" She glared
around the room, daring us to dispute her.

At Christmastime in 2001, Norah's son wrote her.
Michael Pierson had become a chatty, sports-obsessed,
Pierson-nosed copy editor named Ross Palmer. He and his
wife were about to have a child, and he had tracked Norah
down to learn about potential genetic quirks. Additionally,
he wrote, "I guess, ultimately, everyone wants to know their
'real' mother." Norah and Ross began to visit back and forth,
and when Norah met Ross's wife, Sharon, she asked how
Sharon planned to be delivered. "The normal way," Sharon
said, meaning with an epidural. "What?" Norah cried. "And
miss the orgasm of childbirth?" Sharon and Ross named
their son Pierson, and in 2003, Norah wrote to her forty-
fifth reunion class at Miss Porter's to say that the advent of
her instant family had made her "think I've died and gone to
heaven!"

Norah never expected much from humanity as a whole: a
few years ago she wrote me to ask, "Do you still have faith in
the 'human experiment'? I think I love geology because it
reminds me that 'we too will pass.' " But she began to express a grandmotherly softening toward the humans around
her. It was the end phase of her arc, one traced by at least one
relative in many families: the shooting-star streak from imp
to hoyden to black sheep to family eccentric. The black sheep
jeers at her relatives where the eccentric jeers only at the

world; the vital distinction, in the family, is between anger and mere chagrin. Extraordinary oddities of conduct are tolerated among Wasps so long as you show up for Christmas.

Two WEEKS after Norah's memorial service that September, Paddy e-mailed us all again about the house.

Dear Honeysuckle Trustees,
The passing of Cousin Norah gives us an opportunity to make changes in the Wainscott house. Surely every one of us has problems with some of the decorative and house-hold items that have come down to us.

Nevertheless, Karen and I were horrified at the scope and the manner in which some of you have removed hundreds of items from the house and heaped them on the floor of the garage.

These include an antique model of a sailing ship from Uncle Wilson's desk, a typed manuscript of Grandpa John's, two Steuben glass candlesticks, shells painted by Norah with stars and stripes after 9/11, Wilson's pipes, books on the natural history of Long Island [. . . .]

Unworthy to some of you, these objects are dear to some of us. The discarded items contributed to the look and feel of a house we love. We are dismayed at what seems to us an assault on, a cleansing of, the Pierson family. . . .

As much of a cleansing as your idea to sell the house? I wanted to reply. And so began another round in the bruisingly polite battle over the family's body and soul. There was history here. Some of the Friends felt that the Pierson family's interests lay at least equally with their house in Greece and with Karen's relatives' houses in Ipswich and Saint John; some of the Piersons felt that the Friends were slow to pitch in and weed the garden. And there was a concern in both families, I think, that it was the Friends who during the formation of the Honeysuckle Trust had stepped in to pay the taxes—some $22,000 from each of us. From then on there was an unspoken sense of haves and have-nots, of those willing to suggest change and those who favored maintenance. And surely there were other trespasses felt by Paddy and unguessed by me, the resentments that rankle in any large family.

In response to Paddy's note, Pier called him, and my father and my sister and I all e-mailed replies. We're an epistolary bunch. My e-mail began with an apology for the appalling mess in the garage, tried to explain how it had gradually arisen, then further apologized for causing Paddy and Karen the distress of finding cherished items on the pile. I explained how mistakes were made, or why we believed that Wilson's pipes (fuzzed with mold) and the books on natural history (duplicate copies or volumes long out of date) were ready to go. But I couldn't forbear adding:

> *Our intent was to illuminate the bones of the house, many of them interred in closets, among mothballs, or at the bottom of heaps of bric-a-brac. So the suggestion that we were perpetrating an assault on, or a cleansing of, the Pierson family strikes me as unfortunate. Most of us in genetic fact are Piersons, too; all of us are in spirit.*

Paddy did not reply, but shortly afterward he e-mailed me about this book. There was history here, too. Paddy had been helpful in supplying some details for my *New Yorker* piece about Mom, published the previous winter, and had written me an appreciative note afterward, wondering if there might not be a "curse on the Family Pierson" and "the Family Robinson." But when I subsequently told him I was thinking about writing a kind of family memoir, he said that he, too, had been contemplating a book, a history of the Piersons and Robinsons. I tried Paddy again on the topic after Norah's memorial service, saying I'd really value a chance to sit down with him. He screwed up his face but said he'd think about it. Then came his e-mail, a note that began with compliments and ended with avuncular affirmations, sandwiched around a rejection that had nothing to do, suddenly, with his own prospective book. He said he no longer had the generous feelings he had when he'd written me about my piece:

> *What's missing, for me, is a keener sense of right and wrong. You paint your mother and your grandfather blacker than I believe they were. Gray is harder to mix, but that is the color most of us live with. As I don't care for your treatment of the family in the* New Yorker *piece, I fear your treatment of the Pierson branch in the book will be much the same; so I do not choose to help your current venture.*

Paddy's note called to mind my last conversation with Norah, six weeks before her death. She had phoned from Santa Fe, as she had recently taken to doing, both to chat and to check in on Walker and Addie. She said that she had just caught up with the piece about Mom. "I know some people in the family feel it was too harsh," she said, "but I certainly didn't think so. We Piersons are complicated."

"Thanks, Norah," I said, pleased to have support from an unexpected quarter. "You knew her pretty well."

"Oh, forever!" she said, and laughed. "And you know what?" she continued. "Even if you were wrong, which you absolutely weren't, so what? Fuck 'em! You're an artist; you have to do what you feel is right."

"Yeah," I said. "I don't know. Maybe."

A DECADE ago, John Thornton, whose family has summered in Georgica for nearly half a century, spent $7.2 million to buy five acres of Association scrubland that fronted both the pond and the ocean. Thornton, then a Goldman Sachs partner, was buying the land not to build on but to forestall development and change. Yet still it came. Three years ago a hedge fund manager built an $18 million shingle-style mansion just inside the Association gate. And two years ago a house on the pond that had been in the same family for generations sold for $31.5 million. For years, the look of the beach cottages was pure Wasp: shutters peeling paint, a beater car in a driveway whose gravel bled into the patchy surrounding grass. Now one new family inspired muttering because they had edged their drive with the small paving stones known as Belgian blocks. "It's suburban and not in keeping," the old-timers said. "If you want to be part of this community, how can you not look around and see what the style is?" But which style? The new style, of the past thirty years, mandates trophy architects and postmodern touches—towers shaped like lighthouses, wave crests on the siding—as well as sunken pools and sodded lawns.

Norah was tortured by each erupting house: the bandsawing and nail-gunning seemed to burn inside her brain, overwriting her childhood. She hated that the soaring prices had forced out the teachers and painters she grew up with, hated the increasing pace of change. And she hated that we now had to rent our house just to pay the upkeep. Early on, our renter, Fred Iseman, registered several legitimate complaints—the phones didn't always work; the dishwasher kept breaking; and the plumbing was extremely delicate, or, in the parlance of notes that Letty had long ago Scotch-taped by the upstairs toilets, "gronicky." Then Fred apologized, saying, "I'm trying hard not to be a fussy Jew," to which Norah replied, "Try harder!"

As we sought to keep our footing, the tide was ripping out. Chronicling the place, preservation of a sort, was one possible recourse. That was the path taken by Richard Pendleton Rogers, a documentary filmmaker known as Dick to his friends and Dickie to his friends in Georgica. Dickie was an anxious, balding redhead whose rueful smile immediately put you at ease. Though he was eighteen years older than I am, we played tennis regularly. He looked rumpled and comical in a white bucket hat and had a herky-jerky, silent-movie serve, but his murderous forehand hurtled past you like a skipping stone. Dickie's 1973 film, *Elephants*, featured his divorced parents, Pen and Muriel Rogers. After we learn that Dickie's grandparents had a footman behind every chair, his mother—who disapproved of her son's low-paying career and kept threatening to sell her Wainscott house from under him—speaks to him in voiceover:

I think it is the most sad thing in the world, what has happened to the Rogers family. We have Kitty, who is locked up. We have

*May, taking care of an old companion. We have John, who
shot himself. We have Freddy, who jumped out of a window.
And we have Pen, who is very sad, and with nothing. . . .
I never should have married your father, unfortunately, but
I did.*

Later, drinking scotch on her lawn in a mink coat, Muriel
adds, with quarrelsome insincerity, "I'm not disappointed in
you, as long as you're happy."

The film ends with Dickie's father philosophizing:

PEN: *The old maxim of Nothing ventured, nothing lost is a
pretty sound old maxim.*
DICK: *That's not the maxim.*
PEN: *Nothing ventured* [uncertainly] . . . *nothing gained.*

The only way to preserve the past intact is to walk away,
but Georgica was too lovely to leave. And so Norah's rebel-
liousness brought her, in the end, to strident and embarrass-
ing guerrilla warfare against change. One afternoon, when
she saw a couple alighting from a Range Rover they'd parked
on the softball field for a wedding—she hated the lavish parties that increasingly turned the field into a parking lot—she
ran over and said, "You fucking nouveaux riches! Why are
you parking here? Where did you come from?"

Norah saw herself fulfilling a time-honored role: the pa-
trolling matron. For years, Muriel Rogers, Esther Bromley,
and Bebba Hayes would slow their cars as they drove by the
tennis courts, making sure all was in order. They were the
kind of women who in nearby Southampton used to be called
the "dreadnaughts," the absolute arbiters of decorum and

guardians of a way of life; even as you got on a first-name basis with their husbands, they never invited you to call them anything other than "Mrs. Rogers" or "Mrs. Bromley." When I was young, one local dreadnaught brought the beach picnic to a frozen halt after she slapped her eleven-year-old grandson for having dared to go for a ride on a passing dune buggy.

My father remembers arriving in Georgica in the early 1960s, his third or fourth summer there, and starting up the stairs to the beach, only to feel a looming shadow. Bebba Hayes was barring the path: "Who are you?" A formidable woman with piercing eyes and a sharp though underutilized sense of humor, she would greet me annually with a "Come up here where I can see you!" And then, after criticizing the firmness of my handshake, she'd say, "All right, then, run along."

Like the French and the Chinese, Wasps accommodate and even admire these figures of majestic conviction and bone structure; they call them grandes dames. One afternoon in the late summer of 1994, I left the beach and walked up to the bathhouse, where Bebba and two other elderly women in large sun hats were peering in silence at a young woman who was playing Kadima, the paddle-and-rubber-ball game. "Who is that glorious creature?" Bebba asked. "She's quite spectacular!" The woman, who had grown up in Georgica as an unnoticed baby sister, the tagalong kid, was now lithe and long legged in a black bathing suit.

I gave her name. "She doesn't know it yet," one of the others said. "With most of them, you can tell they know it." She turned to me and said, "You were drooling."

"No," I said, smiling.

"Oh, yes," the third one said, and they stared at me, unblinking. They were like the Graiae, the three sea deities of Greek myth who pass around a common eye. Life in Georgica, an association founded in a desire for privacy, was in fact always social, always being discussed and censured. The lazy freedom of those afternoons—even the feeling of being neglected, at times; the sense that within this larger colony you were a colony of one—was an illusion. Someone was always at the window.

AFTER ONE elegy, a childhood friend of Norah's asked, "Where did Norah get her rebellious impulse?" Both Norah's business partner and her daughter-in-law, Sharon, brought up the epiphany of the peritonsillar abscess. Then Day stood and questioned that story's explanatory power. "I think the impulse was provoked by George Wilson Pierson, her father," he said. "He had a way—while serving cocktails on this porch, looking out on this lawn—of adumbrating and asseverating and illuminating a topic that was fascinating and elegant, but that almost demanded rebuttal, even as it denied it."

Wilson's sangfroid could be infuriating. Like Spencer Tracy, he had an air of pending rebuke. There was that conversation about feminism over dinner in the summer of 1988, a conversation so vigorous I set it down in my journal. When Mom and Karen contended that women had been slighted in the annals of history, Wilson, ferrying the salt shaker about and fiddling with his bow tie, waited for them to finish. He mellowed, later in life, but he still treated discussions as duels: parry, slash, the piercing thrust. "Certainly women are

important to *society*," he said. "None of us would be here
without them"—a head bob to the ladies. I could see Mom
preparing to be vexed. "But that argument fails to consider
that people at the time didn't regard women as particularly
important to *history*, and that what women have done by and
large doesn't leave a documented record. Each of us can go
into the A&P of scholarship and buy the history he or she
wants, but that doesn't change the facts: that what the mass
of men—and women—do is unimportant." He pulled his
nose reflectively, twice. "Americans are wedded to change in
their historiography, as in all things, but preserving the good
from the past is a far harder thing than to invent or popular-
ize something *different*. The traditional view of history as
the actions and beliefs of society's leaders remains not only
the best, but the only, way to make sense of social and political change—which is history's very subject."

"Yes, but isn't that a self-perpetuating point of view?"
my mother said. "As histories have tended to be written
by men?"

He smiled indulgently. "That histories—the documents
of the past—have tended to be written by men proves my
point."

Whenever Wilson sat on his porch, he was affronted by
the changes emanating from directly across the pond. The
offending property was owned by Juan Trippe, the founder
of Pan American Airways. Trippe had been the president of
the Maidstone Club in East Hampton—in Wilson's eyes a
gaudy, footling place—and had single-handedly ushered in
the age of mass air travel, which, Wilson believed, led to too
many people flying to places they didn't belong. More seriously, Trippe had tampered with the divine order. In the

1950s, to protect his beachfront, he convinced East Hampton to authorize the Army Corps of Engineers to build a stone jetty in front of his house, just beyond the sandbar over the way. The jetty stacked up sand on Trippe's beach to the east by interrupting the longshore drift—thereby eroding Georgica's beach and beaches to the west as far as Bridgehampton. Norah wrote her father in 1954 to ask what had suborned this original sin: "Mr. Trippe's influence? (Or his money?)"

I never so much as caught sight of Trippe, but we were given to understand that he incarnated all that was modern, selfish, and dastardly. Wilson acidly referred to the stones not as a jetty but a "groin," a word suggestive of unspeakable nether regions. During our cleanup, I came across a 1952 photo that showed Georgica Pond and the sandbar beyond. No one was visible, but the caption, in Letty's hand, was "Pond out and Trippe works on the bar"—a sentence as ominous as "Man is in the forest" from *Bambi*.

The Wasp impulse to conservation is long-standing: members of the Massachusetts Bay Colony called themselves "the English" and feared novelty as an error, even a sin. As the historian David Hackett Fischer has observed, they viewed true reform not as innovation but as the recovery of ancestral ways. Likewise, in the summer of 1776, Thomas Jefferson suggested that the inspiration for the Declaration of Independence was the ideals of the Saxon chiefs Hengist and Horsa. "Has not every restitution of the ancient Saxon laws had happy effects?" Jefferson asked. "Is it not better now that we return at once into that happy system of our ancestors, the wisest and most perfect ever yet devised by the wit of man, as it stood before the eighth century?"

The consequence of this mind-set is often a failure to catch the wave of genuine or necessary change. In his 1972 book *The Moving American*, published to acclaim by Knopf, Wilson began by describing the country's demographic upheavals in neutral language. But soon the smoldering coals of his instinctive social Darwinism ignited:

Then the newer immigration (1881–1917) floated irresistibly toward the top. Remember Hollywood? Hollywood was (and is) hardly an Anglo-Saxon institution. In sports, always a sensitive barometer, the old English-style gentleman amateur had disappeared, and even the football juggernauts of once Congregational Yale — with stars by the name of Heffelfinger or Corbin, Hinkey or Coy — had given way to Notre Dame, whose "Fighting Irish," under Knute Rockne, soon sprouted almost unpronounceable Polish and Czech names. Again in the great urban game of cops and robbers, the police forces and styles of civility might still be overwhelmingly from the "old sod," but the new warlords of the underworld seemed to have names ending in "o" or "i" or "-one," and to be playing the game by rules straight out of Sicily. Meanwhile, in quiet offices uptown, bearded doctors were beginning to prescribe therapies for the Yankee psyche that had been invented by and for Jews in Vienna. And after World War II, our Puritan sex code gives a helpless gasp as people of all ages, origins, and social positions begin indulging in a license that can only be called pagan, and in a premarital freedom reminiscent of the European working class.

Or, of course, of his own daughter. It is no great leap from this brand of conservation to the behavior of members of

Boston's Somerset Club during the Civil War, when Robert Gould Shaw marched his Fifty-fourth Massachusetts Infantry regiment — the first black regiment in the Union Army — down the street to entrain for the South. The club closed its windows and drew its curtains.

FIVE

Bearings

MY EARLIEST MEMORIES of my mother don't actually include her. I remember resting my head on mullioned blocks of morning light on the floor of the sunporch, tracing their outlines with my finger, square by square. The house felt . . . not empty, exactly, but cordoned off. Between Mom and me, almost always, were the palings of baby gates and playpens. I was the youngest criminal in America, banging my cup on the bars.

Visiting hours were at night, when she would arrange me in the bathtub — bar of soap, red washcloth, No More Tears shampoo — and glide off with instructions to "sing out every once in a while, so I know you haven't drowned." Busy piloting my imaginary friends around in my little red motorboat (Foogin, Dato, Geeshee, and Mr. and Mrs. Bawsbaw relied on my steady hand at the tiller), I would not sing out. There was the joy when she returned to check, her light, pattering step gaining speed in the hall. Often she was cross, but sometimes she would cry "Boop boop!" and gather me up in the big blue towel, kissing the crown of my head. Sometimes.

Though not unplanned, I was unexpected. In a letter to Jane Smith, Mom reported being "stunned, utterly stunned, by the news that I had borne a *son!* We had called him Sophie for so long! I am nursing him still + expect to continue until he's in long pants so cosi + sweet is he." Later, she wrote another friend who'd just had a boy that "most of my friends in Buffalo seem to have girls + even to slightly disdain the possibility of a boy—but I know, and now you do too, the wonderful *pride* that comes from bearing a son. One really does feel one's fulfilling one's destiny as far as the race goes, not to mention the family, and the joy of presenting one's husband with a son. (Then too one shouldn't minimize the pleasures of the Oedipus Complex: don't struggle, give right in.)" After I was born, Grandma Tim wrote Mom, "I am proud of you for being such a good little mother and producer of sons!" (adding, "I may not call for a while as we have just received a tel. bill for $100.02!"). Despite having been absolved of responsibility by modern genetics, Wasp women continued to labor under son-and-heir anxieties like those of Henry the VIII's wives.

As I turned two, Mom wrote of my "acting the classic part. Passionate, suddenly verbal, desolate in separation, fierce in rage. He has marvelous Kabuki rages for no apparent reason: brief, formal, + highly stylized. He beats his stomach, rolls his eyes, + makes hoarse throwing-up sounds. Then it's over." Throughout this period, she meticulously charted my many fevers and illnesses, as well as what she diagnosed as a recurrent "nervous cough." She noted that the doctor "prescribed cough medicine with sedative, which

I didn't administer, feeling problem was psychological." She herself grew gloomy during Buffalo's heavy winters, comparing herself to Persephone, who spent a third of the year in Hades.

I increasingly provided anecdotes for her letters, in which she described me as "nearly a carbon copy of Dorie . . . he loves words (a non-stop talker, which is occasionally exhausting for his parents)." When we lived in Manila in 1967, the year began with my father in the hospital for weeks with amoebic dysentery, unable to commence his research. Disaster brought out Mom's best, though she liked to suggest otherwise: writing her father-in-law, Grandpa Ted, and his second wife, Grandma Eugenia, about the tasks that faced her in that faraway city, she noted that one was "finding a kindergarten for Tad (no easy job: the child psychiatrist in charge of interviews at one school asked T. what was going on between two dolls in a dollhouse and he answered promptly, 'The little girl has just killed her mother')."

Feeling I had failed to delight her, I turned into a wary, watchful child. I began building the internal Wasp rheostat, the dimmer switch on desires. Yet my parents recognized my occasional tempests as their own. Day, from Amsterdam, wrote Mom about my "pride and tears" over having lost a vote for president of the first grade: "He is truly our son, is he not, with a foolish combustible mixture of ambition and sensitivity?" Many years later, in psychoanalysis, I longed for my analyst, Sylvia—who resembled my mother only in her wit—to reach inside me and rip out the rheostat. I told Sylvia about the passage in the Chronicles of Narnia in which Eustace, a lonely scrub of a boy who has been turned into a dragon, is restored to himself by the Lion God, Aslan, who gouges off the scaly exoskeleton with his claws, going deeper than Eustace believes he can bear. The pain seemed a small price for such deliverance.

Having my tonsils out, at three, was a rare happy memory. I awoke in the hospital early in the morning, my throat aching, and saw my mother in a shaft of light. She was asleep in a chair by the bed, her right hand stilled on my blanket in midcaress. I fought sleep to keep my eyes on her, arrested just so. Breaking my leg skiing at six was a similar blessing, as we were two and a half hours from the nearest hospital, over bumpy dirt roads. Mom sat in the back of the car with me, my head on her lap, stroking my hair and murmuring every Greek myth she knew.

Day, too, was good with physical wounds. When I scraped a knee, he'd pour on hydrogen peroxide and swab the wound clean, then announce whether it needed a Band-Aid or simply time "to breathe." He was eager and engaged, a bright young man on the rise; he went to Washington to witness Martin Luther King's "I have a dream" speech and was an early skeptic on the war in Vietnam.

I have a very early memory of watching him shave, considering himself in the bathroom mirror as he glided the safety razor across his Adam's apple. Then he leaned over and swirled a little shaving cream on my cheeks, saying, "Someday." It's something a lot of dads do, I guess. Day tells me Grandpa Ted did the same to him, years before, blooding his cheeks with a badger brush.

Over Christmas in Woodstock Day presented me with gold medals cut from lined yellow legal paper for "Saucer catching and retrieving" on the snowy hill at Maplewood and, two years later, for making sixty downhill runs one day on the baby tow at Mount Tom. He helped coach my soccer team, the Panthers, and my favorite time was our outing for Saturday-morning practice: afterward, we'd stop at a coffee shop and have a cheeseburger and a Sprite. Sodas were forbidden at home, and the bubbles stinging my throat and nose felt like happiness.

Still. When I was four and we moved to Ithaca, where Day was doing research at Cornell for a year, I began to have a recurrent dream. I'd be standing in a field of tall grass that rose to a knoll, and I'd hear a banjo behind a door inset in the knoll and know that it was Day, who had gone there to play alone. After struggling through the meadow to the top of the hill, I'd put my hand on the doorknob—and the music would abruptly stop. I would run among the low rooms inside, seeking him, but find them all deserted. Eventually the music would take up again, only behind me now, and far away.

WHEN MOM and Day married in 1960, new minted with the decade, they seemed to have it all, except what underwrites it all: income. They began with a healthy combined inheritance of $49,000 in cash and securities, and by 1974 that cushion was down to $42,000—an inflation-adjusted loss of nearly half their net worth. In the early seventies, Mom tried to save money by cutting our hair with a snaffle-edged curry comb whose use surely violated the Eighth Amendment, and when we came home for the holidays, later, she would circulate the subsequent phone bill and ask us to reimburse her for the relevant amounts—often a sum like $0.83. In the summer of 1969, Day wrote Mom, who had ensconced us at Line Farm in Woodstock for a few weeks, to report that "we stand lordly with $35.96 in the bank. I am enclosing checks as you asked, one for 'baby-sitter,' one for 'car-fixed,' but none for 'et cetera.' Can you pay for 'et cetera' out of cash in hand? If not, wait till I get there."

When we wondered why we could see the road through the rusted floor of our station wagon, Day would always say that we were upper middle class and better off than 99 percent of the people in the world. But it was hard to get specifics. It is acceptable for Wasps to discuss necessary expenses ($18,000 for a new roof, the shocking price of heating oil) but not elective expenses and never income. The sense that debtors' prison lurked fell hardest on Pier, who was drawn to numbers the way I was to words and Timmie was to colors and textures. Mom would pay him to balance her checkbook, and he'd occasionally discover that she'd run as much as five hundred dollars into the red. When we took our one summer trip to Europe, he was always mentally converting kroner and francs to dollars, and frowning if I ordered dessert.

In Buffalo, once known as "the Gateway to the Future," downward mobility was protective coloration. The city had been fading since Millard Fillmore returned from the presidency to help found the Buffalo Club (from whose ranks Grover Cleveland followed Fillmore to the White House). But it remained a Wasp stronghold, and my parents and their friends worked to keep that world going. They learned to cook quiche lorraine from James Beard, took waltz and foxtrot lessons and dropped by the Palace Burlesque afterward on a lark, joined the Saturn Club and Buffalo Tennis & Squash, threw raucous parties where a local investor swallowed spiders, ran for office, seized the reins.

Mom was soon presiding over the Junior Group at the Albright-Knox Art Gallery, a kind of culturally ambitious Junior League, and in 1965 she organized a costume ball at the gallery that merited an extended article in the *Buffalo Courier-Express:*

> *Mrs. Theodore W. Friend III, ball chairman, gowned in a flowing white dress, represented Daphne, the wood nymph transformed into a laurel tree by her father to save her from Apollo, the Greek sun god. Sprigs of laurel leaves adorned her hair and bodice and circled her arms. Mr. Friend, portraying Apollo, wore a Greek styled tunic of gold.*

Mom wrote a friend that her ball duties demanded that

> *within a frighteningly short span of hours I must: (a) galvanize caterer, lighting expert, gallery staff, 2 bands (b) rush home + spray D. with gold paint (c) rush downtown and have laurel leaves attached to my head (d) rush home + graciously welcome my 20 dinner guests (the number changes hourly, which doesn't precisely add to my peace of mind) (e) dexterously — and despite laurel leaves sprouting from fingers — serve the food (f) seat myself upon shocking pink loveseat (which arrives tomorrow after months of working up courage to get it) for photographs for the morning paper (g) rush to the ball to instruct judges (h) soothe guests who don't like position of their reserved table and (i) blow trumpet at midnight to announce grand march.*

The impression she gave of an overtaxed but omnicompetent impresario directing masses of stagehands was true, as far as it went. Her voice, with its vibrant stresses and schwas, commanded attention like Katharine Hepburn's; Grandma Tim had been a childhood friend of Hepburn's in Hartford, where she attended the same elocution classes, and later in life was often mistaken for her. But Mom always worried that the performance wasn't going over. Her eighth-grade report card at Prospect Hill School observed that "her posture needs continued attention as she has the habit of flexing her knees in standing position, causing mal-posture. This should improve with consistent exercising, and consciousness of this habit." The following year, with no apparent irony, the school observed, "She often seems preoccupied with her faults, and repeats her efforts without a very clear idea of exactly how she is trying to change." Wasps live on the narrow margin between consciousness of their bad habits and preoccupation with their faults.

Early in their marriage, my father observed, "Elizabeth, perfectionism is a sin." She didn't reply, determined to be her own severest critic. At Smith, she wrote in her diary, "God, is everything I do to be mechanized? I am just snatching at life, taking crisp, brief little bites around the edge of a great perfection which I have not time to approach." A few months later, she observed, "Life is futile when one cannot rise above the common mediocrity of every day's existence — but how to attain greatness?"

In Buffalo, her accordion files were bulwarks against catastrophe, stuffed with articles and pamphlets on homemaking, child rearing, fire preparedness, disease, even preventing menopause. She preserved a series from the *Buffalo Evening News* on how to survive a nuclear bomb: when you sensed the explosion, the paper advised, avoid looking at the blinding flash. And "if you have a fireplace, you might try to fling yourself into or very near the hearth." I can see her being amused by the idea of flinging herself into or very near the hearth, even as she made a mental note to do so. She even suggested building a bomb shelter in their first home, a second-floor apartment.

When we finally left Buffalo for good, Mom got a letter from her gynecologist, a Dr. Patterson, with whom she and her friends enjoyed a chaffing, slightly naughty relationship. He enclosed a flier for a body-familiarization class and wrote that "since you will no longer be able to come to me for your twice monthly pap smear and imaginary lumps in your breasts, I thought you might be interested in going to New York to take this course on your body. . . . Think of all the doctor's bills you'd save if you could spot the pre-cancerous cysts and ruptured membranes early on."

Her decision to go to the ball as Daphne was apt: Daphne spurned numerous suitors before she fled Apollo, and Mom had declined a half-dozen proposals from men drawn to her laughing distance. Her boyfriends' letters, in college and after, are studies in perplexity. One said, "I wonder if you have any idea of the confused picture I have of your feelings toward me. I would draw a parallel between you and France relative to recent foreign policy." Being compared to the Suez Crisis is usually a bad sign. A Yale valedictorian wrote, "Should I make a map of your personality, it would look on paper as Africa did fifty years ago — the edges filled with color and lines, and great white areas covering the interior." Another, less scholarly, cried, "Not only am I perplexed by your polar personality, surprised by your sub-zero senselessness, but also I now realize I was fooled by your frigid heinousness. . . . My dear girl, either you are a schizophrenic, or mentally retarded!" After she broke it off with her fiancé, Richard, he wrote, "It is a good thing that I remained firm in the face of all your urging and did not acquire a new toilet seat. Had I followed your advice I would now be reminded of you so many times a day; fulfilling the most natural functions would be associated with great sorrowful reminiscences."

In 1963, Mom wrote to the psychiatrist Dr. Marie Nyswander, who had published a popular book about frigidity entitled *The Power of Sexual Surrender,* to ask for a consultation. Nyswander's book suggested that women were naturally suited to raising a family, and that feminism had led the modern woman into misplaced anger and neurosis, so that she "deeply resents her role [and] conceives of the male as fundamentally hostile to her, as an exploiter of her. She wishes in her deepest heart, and often without the slightest awareness of the fact, to supplant him, to exchange roles with him."

Mom yearned for the power that Nyswander extolled, but had been unable to find it in herself. In her letter she explained that she'd already had an "arduous 2½ year psychoanalysis," adding, "My problem, perhaps most simply described as an inability to fall in love, appeared to be resolved when, in early 1960, I was able both to conclude the analysis and to marry. Since then, I have come to realize that, while much had been accomplished, certain things still remained to be done. . . . I have reached a point in my thinking and in my marriage where I must talk to someone. And—something that has not occurred before—have someone *talk to me.* The birth of our son, and all the circumstances attending it, have brought matters to a head."

I realize now that my family and their set equated sex with a loss of control and reputation, an expenditure rather than a dividend of spirit. The body was not an instrument of pleasure but an ungovernable rump state beset by rebellions—sneezes, farts, climaxes, and tumors. So sex, like sleep, ought to be practiced quietly and in the dark. (When I dated a Jewish coworker, years ago, she observed that I was fairly silent in bed. Yep.) The fifties were famously tortuous, of course: to get laid, my father's fraternity brothers either had to go to Bennington College and seek out two women known as "Sally Screw" and "Sally Blow," or get married. But among Wasps the fifties' atmosphere lingered well beyond the decade's end. A married friend of my mother's wrote her, in the early seventies, "Sometimes I wonder what it would be like to let oneself go and completely abandon responsibility and embroil oneself in one of those summer physical things. But it seems to me that only emotional dwarfs can really do it and enjoy it—at our age and with our experience, I mean. One would not be able to help noticing ridiculous things about the whole affair, such as your beau's poor old sweater."

Mom met with Dr. Nyswander in New York several times that July. Her notes from those sessions brim with dissatisfactions, bracketed under Mom's "martyrdom" and Day's "pampering himself when I can't." The latter list included:

breaking things (chair), T.V. set scraped on window sill
writing in books — plundering, destroying
not knowing geography
wanting ice cream
using lots of cream + sugar

Alka Seltzer
letting me make vacation arrangements, get the Xmas
  tree
= men are brutes.

Underneath, she wrote some conclusions: "I don't believe in marriage *and* children: one must be sacrificed for the other. *I* was by Moth?"—her shorthand for her mother. "Didn't want child, fearing what it would do to marriage. If a girl—jealous. If a boy—in love." In smaller handwriting at the foot of the page, she added, "I'm even now trying to show Mother I am alone." When she returned from New York, she told Day that Dr. Nyswander had said she couldn't help her.

MY PARENTS weren't draconian about manners and social behavior, but they kept after us, believing that if you appeared well brought up it eased the path. So I was urged not to mumble or be "a wet blanket"; Pier and Timmie, who were closer in age and fought over toys, were reminded, "No arguing!"; and if Timmie sounded curt or surly Mom would trill, "Mrs. Sweetvoice! Mrs. Sweetvoice!" (A hundred years earlier, Robinson children were reminded "GV, GV," meaning "Gentle voice, gentle voice.") Dissent, no matter how valid, was precluded.

There were soft promptings to keep elbows off the table and napkins on laps; to look grown-ups in the eye and use their name and remind them who you were, saying, "Hello, Mrs. Ardnambotham, I'm Tad Friend," in a strong, clear voice as you firmly shook their hand. If you remembered only one thing, it should be the firm handshake, the vital first impression. (The male Wasps of my acquaintance who've made a fortune all grip your hand like a bench vise.) But you shouldn't remember only one thing, of course, because you also had to remember to write the thank-you note—and without ever employing the words "thank you," so as to suggest that the duck mug was such a delight that you were simply moved to correspond.

Our TV viewing was limited to two hours a week, so that we wouldn't become stuporous. (In Swarthmore, we were allowed *Little House on the Prairie*, *All in the Family*, and *The Mary Tyler Moore Show*, which the family watched together in a pillow-filled window bay known as "the nest.") Of course, we watched lots of other programs on the sly, trying to keep up; I learned considerably more about sex from *James at Fifteen* than I did from the drawings of labia in the manuals Mom eventually dropped off in my room. When Mom came home, she would feel the set for warmth and give an exasperated bleat audible wherever we had fled. Famously, she once caught Pier hiding behind the door, and he silently pointed to where Timmie was crouching behind the Japanese floor lamp. Fairness—equal punishments for all—generally trumped loyalty.

Day left most of the tutelage to Mom, but when I clutched my fork like a hammer he'd murmur a phrase he'd picked up in Stockholm, *"Håll din gaffel ordentligt,"* meaning "Hold your fork properly." And when he was traveling, he'd write to inquire with humorous concern after my slacker habits: "Are you practicing your hand-writing? August is a good month for small muscle control." Though he'd developed his own ideas on the topic, he'd been brought up in a family that viewed decorum as the means to placing yourself above reproach. His grandmother Lillian couldn't write a thank-you note longer than three lines, but her notes were faultlessly prompt. She once assured my father, "The Friends were *always* known for their manners," leaving him skeptical—*How could you know?*—and obscurely enraged.

For the Piersons, manners expressed deference and gratitude; their use acknowledged the net of obligations that constitutes polite society. Underpinning Wilson's Clean Plate Club was the appreciation of others' labor. And underlying both John's and Wilson's efforts to draw visitors out and put them at ease after a welcoming drink was the duty to privilege guests' wishes. Generosity was relieved of its burden by the suggestion that its beneficiary was doing *you* a favor; Wilson, when we'd picked more zucchini and Kentucky wonder beans from his garden than we could eat, would leave the surplus at the beach in a shallow basket with a sign saying, "Help / Yourself / and Pierson."

The differences in the Pierson and Friend outlooks expressed an abiding tension: are manners about making others feel cared for and at ease, or about perpetuating a comforting kind of order? In colonial Massachusetts, child rearing entailed "breaking the will," subduing sass and spirit beneath God's law, as the hot iron extinguishes every wrinkle. In 1648, the colony established the death penalty for children over age sixteen who disobeyed their parents. That law is no longer in force, probably, but Wasp parental love continues to feel conditional upon conduct—namely biddable behavior that brings credit to the family and that requires no undue head-scratching to figure out what's going on with little Johnny. The resulting veneer of acquiescence may be thin—many's the aging Wasp who turns crusty with resentment—but then Wasps believe in behavior, not motivations. Much of what I'd grown up with cohered when I later read Henry Dwight Sedgwick's elegant 1935 treatise *In Praise of Gentlemen*, in which he argued that facades are all we can—or need—trust:

> *I walk through a village: I see proper gardens, fresh-painted houses, shining windowpanes, polished knockers and door handles — what to me is untidiness and frowziness within? [. . .] I care little for the private lives of my companions, if only their talk is good and the ladies' dresses display the charm of color, propriety, and elegance, and the men's clothes betray that their tailors recognize that the tailor's craft is an art.*

Such a credo esteems the right to be left alone. And if this condemned us each to be an island of seeming cheer in an archipelago of sorrow, so be it.

To OTHERS, Wasp ways often feel like a sanctum door snicking shut. More daunting than mastering the corn scrapers or the proper form for the requested "honour of a reply" is the exclusionary parlance. My tenth-grade English teacher at Shipley, Marianne Gateson Riely, was legendary for her punctilio in small and possibly even imaginary matters: one should say "quotation marks" rather than "quotes," "examinations" rather than "exams," and pronounce both in "pear-shaped tones." For several days running, a new student named Lisa, who was Jewish and unpreppy (and who left the following year), explained that she hadn't done the home-work because her mother had recently "passed."

"Look here," Mrs. Riely said, endeavoring to be kind. "Why do you keep saying 'passed'? She died, did she not?"

"Yes," Lisa said, in a small voice.

"Well then, say so, so you can be understood." Her correction was as much social as semantic; euphemisms were middle class. Though most serious topics were best avoided, if you had to speak of something like death, you learned to use the earliest Anglo-Saxon word available: "coffin" not "casket"; "undertaker" not "mortician."

But it isn't simply that Wasps cling to prescriptive certainties about usage and grammar (an obsession reflecting the Wasp belief that mastery of language is a precondition for governance). It's the whole breathless, hieratic shorthand. My mother and her friends managed to weave into a world-view such seemingly disparate threads as words like "flibbertigibbet" and "hobbledehoy"; the concierge's habit of presenting information as strictly *entre nous* — "it's the most *dar*ling little snowed-in town"; exclamations of secularized but still fizzy epiphany: "Heaven!" "Wonderful!" "Perfectly marvelous!" "How divine!"; outré slang ("threads" for clothes, "pad" for apartment, "beau" for lover); and a salting of *"tout a faits"* and *"en retards."* While British colloquialisms sound pretentious — even Wasps can't say "sod all" or "rumpy pumpy" with a straight face — morsels of French suggest private school and being *comme il faut.*

The other tic is the use of abbreviations, ampersands, and plus signs to speed a letter for writer and reader alike. This elisiveness climaxes in the use of "and so forth" or "etc." to conclude a brief list, particularly a list of pressing complications: "We're *sick* about missing your key party, but that's the weekend H.'s mother comes in to review the troops & of Forbes's horse show, etc., etc." Its deployment suggests the management of untold complexities unbearably tedious to relate. This image—limpid surface, measureless depths—is the one Wasps always strive to present. Sometimes it's even true.

BEFORE SHE had the Villanova place, my mother's nesting fever broke every Christmas in a flurry of wreath hanging and Norway spruce trundling and crèche building—the Christ child's tiny wicker bassinet would, on Christmas morning, be found to have given birth to a carved chunk of walnut swaddled in cotton batting. She orchestrated feasts of turkey tetrazzini and crème caramel or ginger duck with potato gratin and almond cake, made ahead so that the kitchen appeared pristine. (When asked the menu, she would reply, as her mother and grandmother had, "Piffle pudding with wait-and-see sauce.") These exquisite brown meals seemed chosen to be visually neutral, the better to set off the table's gleaming silver and its red Dutch-oven centerpiece, filled for the season with huge pinecones. Though her presentation was not at all Waspy, her birdlike portions were: there was never quite enough.

On Christmas morning, when we came downstairs to "Hayfoot, Strawfoot," Mom's pile of presents was always double everyone else's. She was at pains to find the perfect gift for her friends, and they repaid her in kind. It makes me strangely sad, now, to remember how excited she would get about giving you just the thing, like one of those nifty four-color pens. She believed in gifts, just as she believed in redemption. She almost never spoke ill of anyone and would excuse the worst conduct—embezzlement, philandering, Pearl Harbor—by saying, "He was probably having a bad day."

Yet Christmas was for her a kind of exam, a test of the state of her relationships. When an old friend named Jean didn't show up for a planned visit to Swarthmore, for the third time, Mom wrote her, "Am I so adamant a hostess that my friends choose pretense rather than risk incurring my disfavor with the truth?" Well, yes. She went on to take the ultimate step, excommunication: "I think I could comprehend + accept nearly anything you choose to tell me. Meanwhile, however, I have a proposal to make, which is this: that you not send me any Christmas presents this year." Happily, though, Mom wrote me a week later to report, "Got a nice letter from Jean in reply to my stern one, so called her at once + all is forgiven."

Giving my mother anything was a tense business: though she depended on social fibs, when it came to aesthetics she had an artist's ruthlessness. A mahogany wall sconce I made for her in eighth grade vanished into the attic lickety-split. It was a handsome thing as sconces go, but in Mom's house sconces went. Many of my father's Christmas presents to her didn't measure up, either—I recall her unwrapping a large crystal unicorn in distressed silence. Even Day's engagement gift to her, a Rouault lithograph of a mother and child, wound up in the attic.

And so Christmas Eve, that moment of pure anticipation, was my favorite part of the holiday. We concluded our rituals by reading Beatrix Potter's *The Tailor of Gloucester* aloud, passing the book, a 1931 edition from my mother's childhood, hand to hand. We pretty much had it memorized, though. The tailor, "a little old man in spectacles, with a pinched face, old crooked fingers, and a suit of thread-bare clothes," is making a silk coat for the mayor of Gloucester, who is to be married shortly, on Christmas Day. After laying out the pieces of the coat on his worktable one evening, the tailor goes home, where he hears rapping sounds from a set of teacups overturned on the sideboard: *"Tip tap, tip tap, tip tap tip!"* When he rights the cups, he discovers that each hides a mouse trapped by the tailor's cat, Simpkin. We always chimed the best bits aloud, and our favorite was these distress signals. It must have been Potter's favorite, too, for she repeated it four times: *"Tip tap, tip tap, tip tap tip!"*

Once the mice scamper off, the tailor takes to his bed with a fever and is delirious for several days. On Christmas morning, he creeps through the snow to his shop and is amazed to find the coat fully assembled. The mice have sewn it for him. My mother could never read this passage—"oh joy! the tailor gave a shout"—without tears springing to her eyes, so we would tacitly arrange the reading order to give her the tip taps. Or we could carry her through by chorusing the ending, where Potter discloses that thereafter the tailor becomes famous for his stitchery: "The stitches of those button-holes were so small—*so* small—they looked as if they had been made by little mice!"

ONCE PIER and Timmie came along, four and six years after me, Mom began to get the hang of it, motherhood. After Pier was born, she told friends that he was "just marvelous" and "no trouble at all. The second baby is *so* much easier than the first." It always amazed me—it continues to amaze me—that Pier so rarely got angry or flustered. Nor did he exhibit, as Timmie and I did, an anxious concern about establishing or preserving his identity. (Even now, at forty, Timmie worries that people look at her—a funny, outgoing woman with a great eye for detail—and see only Mom.) In his early twenties, Pier had a crush on a woman Timmie and I both knew, and we urged him to tell her how he felt. "But she has a boyfriend," he said. "It wouldn't be right to try to break them up." Timmie and I stared at him in disbelief: somehow, we'd grown up in the same family but reading different chapters of its playbook.

Perhaps Pier realized that the simplest and most cunning form of resistance to the program was complete acceptance. He looks like a man from an earlier era: six foot four, graying, a buttoned-down commuter coming home to a beer. I often wonder, as Pier gives me financial advice I pretend to understand—"The beta on the stock will keep you up nights, but you could hedge it with put options"—how he can be as even keeled as he seems. Did he sail through or just batten down?

Though Mom became more confident in her maternal role, her house remained a private museum that she kept free of traffic by requiring us to take afternoon naps until we were twelve, thirteen, amazingly old. At last, slowly, she began to relax her admission policies. She would seek us out with birthday and Valentine's Day cards that said only, "Guess who?" signed with a tiny rounded "M," for "Mom," like a gull's wings—she wrote a surprisingly low, scurrying hand. But by then Timmie and I, especially, had taken to burrowing in the farthest corners to escape her, her absence as well as her enormous presence, her inability to enter a room and simply allow whatever was going on to continue. Very often, the first child she saw would be press-ganged into a chore presented as a delightful opportunity: "Who would like to empty the dishwasher?"

When we were in Wainscott, and expected to be particularly winning, Mom would write up an elaborate chore list that encompassed shopping, cooking, table setting, flower arranging, etc., each chore detailed like engineering specifications: "House pick-up includes—Take out trash (garbage, paper, cans after supper for once a week pickup Tues 11:30). Tidy downstairs—games, newspapers, books, shoes, pillows, dust, whatever needs doing including sweeping up sand if excessive, puff up pillows, straighten chairs." The chore list chafed at us all. She, a Wasp who'd grown up with "help," expected help still; we, Wasps ourselves, expected the same. I shared my father's sense of affront when reminded to take out the trash, having better things to do, surely. We all exuded sulkiness as squids squirt ink, trying to get away in the darkness.

In 1974, to entice us into sunnier moods, Mom and Day provided an incentive: Cheerful Money. They set aside three glass jars in a kitchen drawer, and whenever one of us demonstrated good humor under duress or was spontaneously helpful, they would drop a quarter into the appropriate jar. Whoever accrued the most money by year's end would have that sum doubled (and then we were to use our money to buy each other Christmas presents). Cash is a standard Wasp behavioral-management tool: some families have a "child of the week" bonus, and some use disincentives, such as levies on cursing or misbehavior that are dropped in the "spunk box." Yet the whole idea made me even sulkier, if possible. In 1977, I received only three dollars in Cheerful Money, roughly equivalent to getting a 210 on your SATs. Whereas Timmie smiled more in response, and Pier was positively inspired; naturally even tempered, he became even more so, and reminded Mom and Day of his every outbreak of pep. He won each year running away, and now makes more money than the rest of the Friends and Piersons put together.

Adult Wasps pride themselves on their affability, a quality that informs their admirable refusal to engage in public griping and whining: no matter how down in the dumps he may be, my father's friend Ted Terry responds to "How are you?" with a reflexive "Tip-top!" But such cheer can also be coercive. Where the salesman wheedles you to reexamine the familiar (*this* vacuum cleaner will change your life), the Wasp hales you into looking elsewhere (forget vacuuming—let's have a drink!). One seeks to lift the velvet rope, the other to click it into place. My mother's close friend Sally Lilley recalls that when her father was breathing his last, her mother "put her head on his pillow as he died and then declared that that was the most beautiful experience in her whole life. Now, anyone in his right mind knows that couldn't be true, but having declared it so, that was the way Mummy wanted it to be for all of us."

The determination to garland rawer feelings with brio explains Wasps' reliance on smiley faces and emoticons. When I taught at a tennis camp for a few summers in college, the ever-smiling termagant who ran the camp decorated the letter containing her lowball salary offer with five smiley faces. A depressed prep school classmate once sent me a postcard with seven smileys, each surrounded by handwritten "Ha ha ha ha has." Savingly, both Mom and Grandma Tim tweaked the format and speckled their letters with grouchy faces, frowny faces, teary faces, and Peter Arno–like blotto faces, with crosses for eyes.

Though cheerful, Wasps are not optimistic. Mom was particularly suspicious of happiness, believing it not only unseemly to express it, but foredooming even to feel it, or at least to feel it without reservation. And who could be entirely happy when the new carpet was the wrong shade of cream, closer to ivory or even—eek!—*magnolia?* In 1958, when her friend Elsa Barr asked Mom to be maid of honor at her wedding, Mom's telegram of reply was characteristic: "Can hardly express my happiness at your wonderful wonderful news. Am tremulous and honored. Of course will come somehow. Congratulations to Terry and enormous love to you. Lib. P.S. Hope bridesmaids' dresses won't be yellow." They were green, thank God.

One night, Mom divided up a cheesecake for dessert, and Pier said, "I'm not going to complain, but I got the smallest piece." She repeated this, teasingly, showing us how it was funny. Over the years, that non-complaint complaint became a family watchword, usually directed toward Mom, who maintained no barrier between thought—*That's not the way I would have done it*—and declaration. She would come into the kitchen after I'd finished cooking a summer dinner of chicken, corn on the cob, and rice, and remark, "Hmm. Two starches." She just thought I would want to know. The correct, almost formal reply: "I'm not going to complain, but . . ."

Wasp children often keep that sort of remark or gesture at

the ready—phrased not as an objection (which would draw censure) but as a note for the files, a boundary stake. Whenever my friend Rachel's mother begins to gush about something bucolic, her children make a rolling-pin motion. Once, visiting her son in upstate New York, she had remarked of the hard, plain country homes, "I picture everyone inside sitting around the fire and baking bread," making the rolling-pin motion to underscore her pastoral image. "They're all alcoholics," he said, "and they have the worst incest rate in the country."

Such semaphores themselves became heirlooms. When taking on an onerous task, Grandma Tim would cry, "Adrian would *love* to blow up the air mattress." She had overheard her aunt say that on a camping trip, volunteering her son Adrian Lambert for duty—which seemed funny to Grandma Tim then, and to us as we repeated it over the years.

My mother would wryly say, "Smiling the boy fell dead" to call attention to how she was bearing up (a phrase her mother and grandmother and great-grandfather had invoked in the same way). In Browning's "Incident of the French Camp," a young boy, though badly injured, reports to Napoleon that his troops have taken Ratisbon. "You're wounded!" the emperor observes:

> *"Nay," the soldier's pride*
> *Touched to quick, he said:*
> *"I'm killed, Sire!" And his chief beside,*
> *Smiling the boy fell dead.*

Years later, when I was in my thirties, I broached the question of perimeters with Mom one afternoon on the beach in

Wainscott, trying to get at the banked ferocity between us. There was so much we shared: the tone — playful, sometimes acid — the Pierson jaw, the gab at parties, the inconsolability. And yet. I found myself resisting how much *fun* Mom could be, not wanting to give her that victory. And I worried that I was too much her son, that I now saw the world through her eyes, which were acutely sensitive to grace and melancholy and whimsy but blind to the power of sex or jazz or fury or true absurdity. That having been groomed as an insider, I was excluded from originality and the deepest pleasures and discoveries — that I would never be able to rip off my armor and free any underlying talents or passions.

I didn't put it exactly like that, though.

My birth had meant that Mom had had to relinquish work and worldly achievement, that she would now be known only for taste and wit and self-possession, beloved by friends but not, as budding artists hope, by strangers — but she didn't mention any of that. She did acknowledge, working her fingers through the sand, that she hadn't been quite ready for me. "Some mothers like to get down on the floor and fingerpaint with their children and so forth," she said, "but I was more interested in you when you started talking and becoming a person. I'm afraid I left you alone a good deal when you were small." Brightening, she added, "But the result is that you learned to read very early — and now you're a writer!" I laughed, and, after a startled moment, so did she. Her determination to quell my objections with her pride in me was both masterly and oddly endearing.

SIX

Smoke

W HEN I WAS twenty-four, I lived in a Tribeca loft near the lights of Wall Street with my former college roommates George and Pablo. One evening that February of 1987, Pablo brought home for dinner the three Visconti sisters, commencing what promised to be the most hopeful chapter of my life. He knew them from summers at a beach resort in Tuscany. Their name adorned the family's luxury-goods business in shops around the world, so the sisters were free to dress in linen and stay out late, but they were also warm and tactile, linking their arms in yours as they walked, or gravely adjusting your necktie. Alessandra was an affectionate referee between her siblings, who called her "Switzerland"; Tessa was brassy, often at the center of a storm; and Giovanna, the youngest, was a brunette with plum-colored lips that, when she spoke Italian— *"Non parliamone piu, lasciamo andare!"*—seemed to brush my inner ear. She walked in slow motion, bewildered by our local gravity, but her gestures were quick and sure: the glide of thumb over fingertips for a velvety texture; the little finger waggled for something untoward; the sideways chop of finality. She was only eighteen.

Our crush on them was immediate and collective, so after coursing in a larger group of a dozen friends to Area, Palladium, the World, the 1980s dance clubs of boundless possibility, we'd drive the Viscontis home to their parents' apartment on Park Avenue, piled on laps with the top down in George's VW Cabriolet, seeming to fly not through but above midtown's gleaming canyons. On the straightaway up Park, the twin sets of lights were runway lamps guiding us in. We'd stay over and wake late for espresso and the *Times*, the sisters smoking in white robes with their hair damp, the air thick with unsorted radiance.

At a bar called Stephanie's, over sambucas, Alessandra and Giovanna murmured in Italian, discussing Giovanna's boyfriend. What little I had gleaned about this Shaun from Pablo's well-meant warnings was discouraging: a horse had kicked some of his teeth out, yet he had knit her a cable sweater, so he was sensitive, too. Alessandra came over and clasped my hand. "Hey, softie," she said. "Soft hands."

"I know, Ali, doesn't he?" Tess said. Turning to me, she said, "You should let your hair grow out, be less of a spiky *porcospino*." They liked to anatomize us, a game Giovanna didn't enter into.

"Don't you find us interesting, Tadeus?" Alessandra said, half teasing. "You should write about us: the three faces of womanhood."

"Chekhov got there first," I said.

"You probably think we're slobby American girls," Giovanna said.

I shook my head, blushing: wrong and wrong.

I was earning $18,000 a year working long hours at *Spy* magazine—a satirical monthly that became an immediate hit, at which point the editors cut my pay. So I could already see the gap opening with my investment banker roommates. One reason I liked being around George and Pablo was that they took for granted a way of life my ancestors had led—first-class tickets, cases of wine, the tearing high spirits of youth. And there were always beautiful women on our sofa, smoking and jangling their bracelets.

If I wasn't careful I was going to become the shirty, sarcastic one, the envious observer. But for now the gap was small, and I cloudily imagined that Giovanna would close it entirely—her youth and wealth and European vibe would maintain me: a Henry James plot in reverse. She would cut my tethers and we'd soar together somewhere prosperous and carefree.

After months of nerving myself up, I finally asked her to *Spy*'s black-tie first-anniversary party, hoping to shine in the reflected glow of champagne and Malcolm Forbes. The party was such an undeniable smash—paparazzi, swing dancing, gusts of self-congratulation—that it was impossible not to have a good time, whether we were or not. But when I drove her home, she backed out her door with an enigmatic smile.

A FEW days after the party, Giovanna sat beside me at a table her parents had taken at a benefit for cancer research and quietly disclosed that her mother, Paola, had recently had breast cancer. And that she had few memories before age five. And that Paola had suffered such postpartum depression that Giovanna was sent to her grandmother for a year. And that her father, Federico, had affairs and was jealous of his daughters' boyfriends. She considered me after each revelation, assessing. I wasn't sure if I wanted to hear more or less. At three a.m. we finished a pack of Camel Lights at the Odeon—I didn't smoke, otherwise, or drink nearly as much—and she interrupted me to remark that she always had a good time with me and it wasn't just the buzz talking. She was an interrupter, blurting, "But, Taddles—" out of a sudden fear that if she didn't voice her mood then, she never would. She was often silent, secretly amused, a pitcher-inner at dinner parties, a dog lover, a gallant depressive. These qualities shone for me as a dazzle of facets, but I could never get the whole gleaming stone of her in view.

The next night she was off to Italy to see Shaun. Alessandra chided me for keeping her out so late, saying Giovanna had coughed blood before boarding: "She's only barely nineteen." Taking all these advisories as encouraging— opposition means you're at least being taken seriously—I went out and purchased a midnight blue Italian overcoat, very like the roomy coat Matisse wears in those late photographs of him by Cartier-Bresson. I would be an artist in love.

Late that winter she came to Maplewood. Paddy and Karen were in the Caribbean, so I brought Giovanna and George and his Belgian girlfriend and our friend Loli up to their house for a ski weekend. Giovanna and I were in bunk beds in my cousin Bella's room, awkwardly, but the first night, everyone left us alone together downstairs, and we finally kissed, a soft tobacco sweetness. Then she disclosed what I and my advisers had been discussing for months: that she had a boyfriend.

"Yeah, I know," I said. "I'm happy for you."

"What?" Her laugh spread her Roman nose and gave her an inviting, almost chummy look. I killed myself trying to make her laugh.

"Well, anything that makes you happy—"

"He is pretty terrific, though."

". . ."

"I'm sorry. I told myself I wasn't going to say that."

She gave me a blue cardigan of hers, and I would bury my nose in it when we were apart: cigarettes, Keri lotion, a peaty scent that reminded me of the geraniums on our sunporch in Buffalo. The slow underwater pursuit, the march of the starfish.

One sultry night that summer, I stayed for dinner at her parents' and Federico Visconti made an asparagus risotto. He was intense and volatile, a collector of classic station wagons and sedans, cars that embodied his love for America. Sweating a little, drinking white wine, he began lecturing me about his countrymen's mania for consumption. He grabbed a stack of glossy Italian magazines to show me the sensual car ads, the blatant sex and chrome: "Disgusting, no?" Paola, a sweet, unhappy woman who looked like Giovanna, took my arm and tried to speak about Sri Lanka, which they'd been to recently, but Federico interrupted, "No, no! You know nothing!" She wiped away a tear and shakily kept on. When young, Giovanna had told me, they had been very much in love.

Alessandra, fresh from the shower in a white robe, snapped at Tessa for leaving a ring with her wineglass. "Don't yell at me about *that*," Tessa said. "Yell about what's really going on—but no, no one in this family ever does."

Federico laughed theatrically and squeezed Giovanna's nose. Ignoring him, Giovanna continued telling me about an older woman she'd met at a party: "She was so pillowy. I felt I could put her on the floor and knead her like bread." Now I was sweating. Afterward, Giovanna shrugged: "We're these *merchants*, Taddles. Your family is choosy about words and waits till the other person is done speaking, but we have no tradition except rudeness and upsetting conversations."

"We were merchants, too."

"*Dai!*"

Desultory phone calls, plays and premieres, languorous embraces abruptly broken off—"I always end up with you when I drink too much"—keyed-up midnights in a rocketing cab. I had a phrase I consoled myself with riding home alone: "Face the arithmetic." After the carnage at Fredericksburg, when Lincoln realized that the Union armies were larger and that even devastating defeats worked in his favor, he observed, "No general yet found can face the arithmetic, but the end of the war will be at hand when he shall be discovered." There was something addictive about the pursuit, about abandoning myself to a romantic cause. I had been ashamed, previously, to show (or even feel) passion; now I could because the glove thrown down was in no danger of being picked up.

Giovanna was a shocking lash to all my senses—around her I felt alert, giddy, anxious, and weak. Having never been in love before, I had no notion of how to hide my doglike devotion, how to conduct myself. Years later, she told me that my acerbic moodiness had worried her and her sisters:

"They were saying, 'Tad's a grumposaurus, so it's okay if you don't rush into his arms.' " I believed that my cheerfulness in the face of discouragement would eventually be rewarded, that every good boy deserves favor. In fact, I had adopted our family trick of bearing up so conspicuously it was tantamount to a public sulk.

Pablo's friend Billy had a party on the seventy-seventh floor of the Empire State Building, in an office where he used to work, and we sneaked the stereo and the liquor up in gym bags. Giovanna and I sat in a window bay by the file cabinets and the dancers pulsating to "Wishing Well" and "Need You Tonight." This was our moment, our fated youth, and we enjoyed sitting alongside and watching, the glimmer of respite. In those days, I wore hard contact lenses and one of them was killing me, so I took it out and rubbed it like a pebble between my thumb and forefinger as we kissed, seeing with my nearsighted eye her mouth and ear and a loose lock of hair, while over her shoulder my corrected eye saw the blazing and magnificent city: close-up zooming to master shot, the way New York can suddenly lay itself open to you, for a time, when you're young.

THAT SEPTEMBER of 1987, I had dinner with my parents and with Grandma Jess and her third husband, John Merrick, who were visiting Manhattan from Florida. We met at their hotel, the Parker Meridien, and went into its restaurant. The Maurice was the kind of place where great care is given to the impress on the butter pat. John, broad and garrulous, swapped hellos with our maître d', Alphonse, remarking that he looked exactly like that old baseball announcer. "Doesn't Alf look like Joe Garagiola? Alf, people must tell you that every—"

"Let him show us to the table, John," Jess said.

"You sure you're not Joe Garagiola?"

Alphonse winched up a smile. "If I made his money, you think I'd be working in a place like this?"

John gave a raspy belly laugh: "What a killer." He ordered a bourbon stinger and turned my way: "So they tell me you're knocking 'em dead in the magazine business."

"Not exactly," I said.

He lowered his voice and confided that my uncle Charles, my father's younger brother, "isn't going to make it—this is good night. My doctor tells me that having cancer in the lymph nodes *and* the surrounding tissue is very rare—it happens once in a hundred years. A hundred years."

"I can't get any ice water!" Grandma Jess cried. We fell quiet, as she had wished. "Well, it's a second-class hotel, and that's what you get."

"Oh, now, Jess—" John began.

"I don't know why we came. The whole city is filthy, and no one speaks English."

Jess was a beautiful woman still, a Barbara Stanwyck look-alike happiest at the captain's table aboard the *Statendam* or the *Vistafjord*, surrounded by admirers. The Holton overbite and a nose broken playing field hockey only accentuated her flashing smile. My father loved to recall how she came home after a gallbladder operation, showed him and Charlie two gallstones in a jar, then took the boys outside and flung the stones into the driveway gravel.

But she was easily put out of temper. She liked hugs up to the point at which they spoiled her makeup, so you gave her a gingerly embrace and withdrew. When my cousin Daisy was in her mid-twenties, she visited Jess and they breakfasted in silence until Jess asked: "Do you know anything about the stock market?" She followed Merck and Pfizer religiously.

"I don't," Daisy confessed.

"Well, I don't know what we're going to talk about." Silent agitation. "Why don't you have a boyfriend?"

"I'm picky."

"Yes, you're *much* too picky."

Jess's fretting seemed to me a way of cultivating reassurance. When she was a young prom trotter in Bethlehem, Pennsylvania, she would roller-skate up and down in front of the YMCA, waiting for the inevitable approaches; astounded, still, by the stir her beauty and vivacity aroused, she always feared it might be withdrawn. Her mother had had a wayfaring streak—Mrs. Holton ultimately lived in twenty-six different houses—yet was fiercely censorious. Jess's older brother Oliver and his wife, Millie, had a son named Tommy who, at age four, wandered near the private zoo on their property, home to ducks and pheasants and prize bulls and a wolf. Someone had left a door open, and the wolf seized Tommy by the neck. After this shocking event, the mourners gathered in their living room, and Millie invited everyone to walk the path up the hill, each with a lighted candle, and make a circle, as the Quakers do. Mrs. Holton stepped forward and said, "That would be un-Christian, barbaric."

Unaccountably, she sent Jess to a girls' military school, where her daughter became class treasurer, captain of the basketball team, president of the athletic association, valedictorian, and the Gold Star Girl. In Jess's valedictory address, she explored the mystery of greatness that had made Rubens and Shakespeare "the fortunates who every man would wish to be. . . . It cannot be sheer intellect, nor sheer will, which is the solution of this riddle. . . . Somewhere rests that mystical note of personality which, for lack of a better word, we may call an unseen perfection of adjustment." And still her mother refused to let Jess go on to college, though she herself had attended Mount Holyoke.

Jess's beloved father, George Holton, president of the Bryden Horseshoe Company, was not around to countermand these decisions. A smiling, youthful-looking man who brought the first Rolls-Royce to the Lehigh Valley, he was very fond of gaming and got along so well with his colleagues that he was one of eighty-three men indicted in 1911 for constituting a "wire trust" that fixed the price of wire. Shortly afterward, following a gallbladder operation, he died of peritonitis. Jess was four.

In the early nineties, after John Merrick had died of cirrhosis and shortly before my uncle Charles Friend died of cancer, my parents visited Jess at her retirement community in Delray Beach, where she had had a fourth heart attack but still dressed for dinner and insisted upon making an entrance with a man on her arm. They happened to mention a photo in my sister's room at home, a mournful image of a very young Jess cuddling a black kitten. "Yes," Jess said, "that was not long after my father died—I never got over it." And she burst into tears. It takes a lot of heat to run the freezer, too.

I HAD spent my dating life till then backing away from the all too many qualities that I suddenly discovered I didn't really like. I didn't really like Waspy women: the sturdy ones like corncob dolls; the garrulous ones who looked up from lines of coke to cry, "Shit, girl, *I'm* going to be in Greece about then!"; the twinset ones who knew about makeup but who, in bed, steeled themselves for the procedure. I didn't really like the society blonds in netty fabrics by the pool, idle until you got deep into a book, then pettish: "C'mon, Tad, let's go have a drink, let's *do* something; don't just sit around." And I didn't really like the chain-smoking artists with merry smiles who never washed their sheets — or I did really like them until I found out that they were also fucking a guy named Mel. Just speaking generally here.

I was mostly clueless, worrying that women would find sexual aggression alarming (exactly wrong). My notions were shaped by the dopey songs of my adolescence, like Sammy Johns's 1975 hit, "Chevy Van":

> *'Cause like a princess she was layin' there*
> *Moonlight dancin' off her hair*
> *She woke up and took me by the hand*
> *She's gonna love me in my Chevy van*
> *And that's all right with me*

So I courted sleeping beauties who might awaken and take charge, women who smoked and drank and had a boyfriend. I'd flirt from a distant blind, usually via a purple letter that grandly alluded to my pathos and admiration. When I met a woman who was in an eight-year relationship, I followed up by mail:

> *In the ideal metaphorical context I would be a soldier who had*
> *glimpsed you several times in passing as you worked at your*

flower stand in the market. At last, just before I was mustered out to the front, I would go up to you to buy a bouquet, only to return home with acquired tastes for cigarettes and strong brandy and a white bandage over my eyes as a consequence of mustard gas. Passing your booth one day, tapping in front of myself with a wooden cane, I would prick up my nose at the familiar smell of begonias and narcissi and would then cry out your name.

Hard to believe, on this evidence, but I was no longer a virgin.

I really liked these women until they liked me back. My fade-outs resembled the jump cuts of a ladies' man, or so I hoped, but I felt like a raccoon frozen by the porch light, paws deep in the bins out back. The girlfriend of a friend, a woman I'd flirted with for years, finally called it off with him and sent me a letter that ended: "It's time we grew comfortable in one another's presence. The swallows are circling around the tops of the trees. Night is kneeling down. The lilacs are bursting with color and my rice is plump + perfect + ready." I parsed the note cautiously: *my rice is plump*—yes, almost certainly an invitation. When we started sleeping together, she'd ask me things like "Does your desire replace you?" and I'd panic and say, a beat late, "Sometimes." After I broke up with her, she told me I was like a wet linen sheet that had been crumpled up and left in the freezer.

When I came home from work to our Tribeca apartment, in 1986 and '87, I'd often find a dinner plan in place for Two Eleven on West Broadway—a dim, noisy bistro studded with champagne buckets—or two dozen people at our long trestle table and our friend Andy in the kitchen, roasting chickens. George and Pablo's crowd were warm, solvent, a little careless, amused by my background but incurious about it. We all seemed like assholes, probably: interested only in the next party and confident the world would be ours within five years. But it was fun while it lasted, the years of French cuffs without cuff links, of magnums of Domaines Ott rosé: grace notes I admired and adopted or, just as quixotically, rejected as beyond me. From loft to loft we sluiced in a wash of cashmere, among Venezuelan bankers and Spanish guitar players and dark-eyed girls who knew Pablo from Italy and smelled of lilacs and stayed with us for weeks, including the one who broke his heart. We took a photo of ourselves then, the roomies in boxer shorts, our thumbs and forefingers cocked to make L's, for loser—smiling but stricken or about to be.

I wanted to be more like Pablo Keller Sarmiento, a stocky, spaniel-eyed diplomat's son who spoke five languages. Having been taught to keep my hands close to my body, the first position in some lost Wasp art of self-defense, I delighted in the scrum of him, the bear hugs, the arm around the shoulder after pickup soccer in the park. At the weeklong wedding of Pablo's brother, Andreas, on the family's ranch south of Buenos Aires, we rode galloping across the pampas with only a bridle and a sheepskin ruffle, chasing guanacos that fled with a witchy cackle and startling partridges to flight. I bought black *bombachas*, the gaucho pants that buttoned at the cuff over riding boots, and wore them around New York until the seams gave way.

If I could not seem Argentine—and Lorenza, an Italian friend of Pablo's, told me in her syncopated English that I could not, for "You give no inspire to the wounded woman in your First Aid"—then I wanted to attract the kind of women George was always bringing home: slight French stunners with clothes that colonies of silkworms had gratefully died to spin. A chatty, mop-haired beanpole, George liked to rattle his Rolex up and down on his wrist and make sweeping pronouncements: "We should all move to Chile and buy a lodge on the beach." He could strike you as a preposterous brat; he struck me that way at first. But he was the kind of friend who dropped everything if you wanted to celebrate, or talk something over, or just drive among Tribeca's black warehouses and mope.

He, too, was always hopelessly in love with someone who was already taken, but he was better at getting the girl. When one lover told him she had to try to make it work with her old boyfriend, he lunged into her bathroom and threw up, then ran a bath and sobbed in it until she got into the tub fully clothed to console him, and they ended up making love on the bathroom floor before reading Pablo Neruda aloud. I could imagine doing all that, if necessary, just not with someone else present.

On paper, George Washington Polk IV seemed the textbook Wasp—a descendant of President James Polk and a nephew of the CBS newsman George Polk, for whom the journalism awards are named; a graduate of St. Paul's and Harvard, where he joined the Porcellian. But he had spent the formative years of his childhood in Egypt, and his home base, insofar as he had one, was France. When he arrived at St. Paul's, scrubbed and pressed and determined, he was bewildered to discover that many of his classmates seemed indifferent to their grades and appearance.

It was George's first exposure to the trick of effortlessness, to the loosely knotted tie and the feet on the sill, the butt palmed as the teacher goes by. Visible striving or seriousness of purpose is unWasp because it suggests that you aren't yet at—haven't always been at—the top. Everyone was aiming, not always consciously, for attractiveness: a courtier's ideal that threads back five hundred years through the English gentleman to Baldassare Castiglione and his ideal of *sprezzatura*, a perfectly rounded skill with weapons and poetry and courtly conversation that conceals the labor of its own construction. Seymour St. John, the longtime headmaster of Choate, termed this quality of attractiveness "the sheer restfulness of good breeding."

Even at Harvard, George was still perplexed by the seemingly negligent and distrait, wondering how I could smoke my exams when I never seemed to study and spent all my time watching *Star Trek* reruns. For my part, I admired his careless way of kicking off his hand-lasted wingtips as he entered the room, even as I more sneakingly envied his clubmates in the Porcellian, tall, slab-faced, mumchance Brahmins whose fathers and grandfathers had been in the Porcellian, too, and who never remembered my name. One had resolved an altercation with a cabdriver in Hong Kong by declaring, "Look here, you little yellow man, you're to take me where I wish to go." They were horrible, many of them, yet I wanted what they had—that ultimate sanction—so I could renounce it.

Twenty years on, my father still bridles at the memory of being told, by a Philadelphia matron he'd challenged on a passing remark, "Don't speak that way to your betters." Hauteur cows Wasps, too; painfully aware of the chipped dishes and bitten nails beneath their own insouciance, they can't believe the same insecurities nibble at everyone. No matter how inside they seem, Wasps always sense a further circle just beyond reach. My cousin John Walker, who married the daughter of an earl and became the director of the National Gallery, once told my father that it made him very happy that he'd been able to purchase a plot in Oak Hill Cemetery, in Washington, D.C., that would put him near to Dean Acheson.

I WAS studying, though. Nothing was unstudied. After college, I kept a dictionary nearby when I read, and I'd look up unfamiliar words and note their meanings. That summer and fall every new word summoned up Giovanna:

> **eidetic:** *especially vivid but unreal; said of experiences, esp. in childhood*
>
> **cynosure:** *an object that serves as a focal point of attention and admiration*
>
> **anneal:** *to temper (glass or metal); to subject to a process of heating and slow cooling to reduce brittleness*
>
> **ravel:** *to clarify by separating out (threads of cloth); conversely, to tangle or complicate*
>
> **calvary:** *the hill near Jerusalem where Christ was crucified; an experience of intense mental suffering*
>
> **deliquescence:** *tending to melt or dissolve*
>
> **Weltschmerz:** *sentimental sadness from comparing the real world to an ideal one*
>
> **Lorelei:** *German sirens who lure Rhine River boatmen to their doom*

One night, George pondered my dejected expression and said, "I think it's time for an expedition." So we drove up to Barnard, where Giovanna was a freshman, ignored her protests about an overdue paper, and carried her off. Back at our apartment, she and I had a few beers and started fooling around. This was how the relationship should be conducted: by piracy. Suddenly she jerked upright and said that Shaun was arriving the following day and it all had to stop. Our tolerable rhythm—good dates, then bad ones— had accelerated so that we veered hourly from promise to misery, from deliquescence to Weltschmerz. "This only happened because of my negligence," she said, "because I'm young and didn't know how to end it. I'm too young for you, Taddles—don't you just want to smack me sometimes? I mean, what are you doing with this frustrating girl?"

"You think there might be a reason you're in my bed just before Shaun arrives?"

"Even if Shaun dropped dead, that wouldn't necessarily mean I'd be with you."

I determined on a clean break. The market crash of October 1987 had been like the houselights that signal closing time, and by late the following summer we were all straggling off. There were farewell parties for the South Americans every weekend; Pablo was moving to Tokyo and George to London; and I was going to travel the world for a year. I would draw a line beneath that period and its enthusiasms: bonsai trees, Perry Ellis shirts, holes in my jeans, ratty futons, reading groups, drinking with her, dancing with her, her.

As George and I prepared to decamp, we moved for two months into our friend Loli's vacant pied-à-terre in a brownstone on East Ninth. The place was majestic, with a wall of books, but the ceiling lights blew out one by one—they were special bulbs, like Erlenmeyer flasks, and we were lazy—and the building was surrounded by white brick towers, so by mid-afternoon you could barely make out the small pond and its neglected goldfish at the foot of the yard. Sting was on the stereo at all hours as fall came on, the days quick and cold, and I hung there in the gloom like meat in a locker, waiting.

She dropped by one Saturday, Circe in a green sweater, and I wobbled and fell. Drinks led to dinner at Canal Bar with George and his latest girlfriend and our friend Michael, who leapfrogged parking meters on the walk home. A week before my flight out, Giovanna finally spent the night with me on Loli's futon. "I'm glad it's you," she said. "I mean—well, you know what I mean." Days and nights in the dimness. We stopped in on her parents on our way to my good-bye party, and Paola took hold of my arm and gave it a special squeeze. Federico narrowed his eyes and recounted how a doctor and his wife, touring New Guinea, had to suddenly fly out because local custom demanded that the police chief be granted a night with the wives of all visitors. The implicit threat only seemed testimony of Giovanna's esteem.

I flew to Hawaii carrying the compass she had given me to help me find my way home. The following day, Shaun returned to the States for good.

JOHN MERRICK, now nursing his third cocktail at the Maurice, offered me one of his lamb chops, and I said, "No, thanks, I'm full."

"Never say 'I'm full,' dear," Jess said. "Say 'I've had plenty, thank you.'"

Mom and I shared a smiling glance and she drew breath to speak, but Jess tossed her head and carried on: "I wish I hadn't lived as long as I have. It's not fun. I don't have fun. Except staying in touch with your family," she said more softly. "But that's not fun, really. There's nothing fun."

"Tad has been having fun!" Mom broke in. I had? "He's been keeping company with a young girl named Giovanna Visconti, of the Visconti family. She's very nice. Very pretty, and very nice, and young. Younger than Timmie."

"What do you think of her, Dorie?" Jess asked.

"She has a strong sense of wonder," my father said, smiling. He intended a compliment, but I frowned: "wonder," in a family that prided itself on puzzle solving, seemed to me faint praise. It was true that I couldn't imagine how Giovanna would fit in with my family, but that was the point.

John asked: "Are you"—he made a mystifying fade-away gesture—". . . period?" He repeated the question, and the gesture.

"I think John is asking, 'Are you in love?'" Day said.

"Oh," I said. "Well, yes and no."

Jess laughed and patted my hand approvingly. She had kissed the film star Ronald Colman in a taxi before she married Ted Friend, and other men, in other taxis, after. "We all love your mother, don't we?" Ted would say to his sons while mixing drinks for his guests, and they would nod, shamefacedly. Day and his younger brother, Charlie, were determinedly incurious about the whispering at Pike Run; or their father's nickname, "Tolerant Ted"; or their mother's summer escorts at the Seabright Beach Club and Rumson

Country Club on the New Jersey shore—a string of lanky charmers and soft-spoken "Uncle Mac," who gave the boys choice postage stamps.

During my father's senior year at Williams, he and Charlie spent the Christmas break at the St. Anthony Club in Manhattan. They were wakened early on a Sunday morning, after a late night listening to jazz at Jimmy Ryan's, by the unexpected arrival of their father. Ted had taken the night train up from Pittsburgh to announce that he was divorcing their mother. He began pulling slips of paper from his tweed jacket, evidence he had compiled, and reading them aloud: "October 18, 1952. *On the birthday of her second son*, Jessica leaves the house to go see Charlie Kenworthey."

Jess had fallen in love with Kenworthey, a gregarious corporate lawyer, and had asked Ted to let her go. Ted didn't mention that. He said that as *he* had always kept his marriage vows, he was going to initiate the divorce, which would cast her as a scarlet woman. "Your mother is just like *her* mother," he said. "Mrs. H brought her own man in that weekend at Pike Run, sleeping with him in the Lodge." The idea that sexual incorrigibility ran in the Holton family seemed to comfort and absolve him.

"And then," my father told me years later, "he got back on the train to Pittsburgh. It was very sad. It still is very sad."

One evening when I was fourteen and we were visiting Jess and John Merrick in Rumson, my father happened to mention, over cocktails, an article he'd read about British students who worked out a method of tossing eggs into the air so that they would land on their smaller end and not break. "I have some eggs," Jess said, brightening. "Let's try them." I ran to the refrigerator for the carton and met everyone in the backyard, which was soft underfoot after an afternoon of rain. Day took a large white egg, blew on it for luck, and tossed it into the sky. We watched it revolve up beyond the porch light's corona and then reemerge out of the night to bounce and settle on the grass, intact. Laughter and delight. "Let me have one of those," Jess said, stepping onto the lawn in her high-heeled sandals. She flung an egg up and waited, her blue eyes raised to the dark.

IN MY year away, in Bangkok and Kyoto and Goa, I read Giovanna's occasional letters with a cryptographer's care, trying to decipher the underlying message; she had evidently made a similar effort before mailing them, for she would often close with a P.S. in slightly different handwriting: *"Buona notte"* or "You are much missed." As I neared home, she flew to London, where I was staying with George, to surprise me. She stayed with Alessandra, who had moved to London, too. Everyone was there. When Alessandra was on the phone, I pulled Giovanna into the vestibule: "Give me a kiss. No, a real kiss."

"Here?"

"Come outside."

On the street, she asked, sadly, "Do you think we'll keep doing this forever? Sometime you're going to get fed up." She was seeing not only Shaun but also now some Barry.

"Yes."

"And we won't be friends anymore."

"No." She lit a Marlboro, and I took a drag, and we smiled. We kept doing it for seven more years, through a long relationship of mine and several of hers. When life was going a little too well for either of us, we'd meet at Delia's, a supper club in the East Village where our being together seemed wholly plausible. Then, in the cab back to the world, we'd discuss how I was passive and touchy and resentful, and how she lied and blew hot and cold; how she drove by my apartment at night and thought of us living together in Vermont, but needed to be alone. I could never get to the root of it.

We spent weekends upstate at her family's refurbished hunting lodge on a hill above the Hudson. We picked strawberries with Alessandra and Paola, now separated from Federico; we read and smoked and biked down the immense swooping driveway. We took Ecstasy. We slept together after drinking at the Ale House, and three nights later she came to dinner and told me she was seeing two other people, new ones. We slept together after seeing the Lounge Lizards, then she went off to Italy to visit another boyfriend and, when she returned, left a message canceling our plans, concluding, "So call me." Our youthful caprices had become a measure of adult limitations. With an angry devotion now, a mutual self-contempt bound up with fondness, we sought to prove otherwise. Over the years—and it was ten years, a Trojan War—our total hours together added up to at most three weeks. But there endured the hope that she might slip up and fall for me and then I could finally leave her.

In late 1996, two days after Grandma Jess died, I took Giovanna to *Travel + Leisure* magazine's black-tie twenty-fifth-anniversary party aboard the *QE2*, which was docked on the Hudson: Carly Simon and her son Ben playing the guitar and singing "Paper Moon," dancing on decks high and low. Giovanna looked wonderful in a black-and-white gown and a butterfly brooch picked out in diamonds, and she said I looked grand in my dinner jacket. I was wary of this Britishism, a vogue word then to convey sumptuousness and satisfaction. Still, she was affectionate, willing to be pleased. The magazine had considerately booked staterooms for its guests, so we repaired to room 1039 and drank flutes of Perrier-Jouet. There was a moment, there, a grand moment. At four a.m. she fled by cab in the rain.

That afternoon she called to blame me for sleeping with her: "You knew you'd feel vulnerable afterward." After a jet of fury, this made me laugh. When you can see yourself as ridiculous, you have a chance. And so I got sober like a drunk: I didn't call her for a day, then two days, then three. Eventually it was years.

Much later, married now and grown up, having survived breast cancer herself and quit drinking entirely, Giovanna told me she'd often thought about that night on the *QE2*, wondering if staying aboard would have meant leaving her family behind. A Wasp at heart after all, then. Giovanna had felt like a rebellion, but it was a flight to safety, renouncing nothing. The pursuit was as conservative as it was sensual as it was competitive as it was hopeless: the husky voice and yielding mouth, the sheer fizz of youth and money and glamour and desire, all just beyond reach. Her cardigan got lost, in one move or another, but I wore the blue overcoat until it fell apart.

SEVEN

Loaded

ONE AFTERNOON TWO summers back, Amanda and I were running very late to get Walker and Addie, then a year old, to a birthday party. Addie was hiding under our dining table, and Walker crawled in to join her. He began nuzzling his huge blond head, as outsize as my father's, against Addie's, which set off a fit of giggles. Amanda, somehow seeing this as a teachable moment, crouched to inform them, "Your great-grandparents used to eat breakfast at this table every morning." They seemed unmoved.

"And breakfast was far from your great-grandfather's best time of day," I remarked. Still nothing. Well, perhaps they needn't know everything up front. . . .

Grandpa Ted's table—it was his and Grandma Jess's and then, after the divorce, his and Grandma Eugenia's—is a mahogany affair in the Georgian style, a twentieth-century reproduction of the type often found in hotels and banks because it embodies starchy authority. Walker and Addie like to play among its sprawling sabre legs because it's cozy in there—the snug, spandrelly recesses—and also complex: all those brass fittings and casters, the innumerable screw holes, the telescoping undercarriage enabling expansion to accommodate the four leaves nesting in the closet, so that, if we had a bigger room to lodge the table in and many more chairs, we could seat twenty for a dinner that our kitchen is far too small to produce. In my previous, one-bedroom apartment, the table's shining expanse posed an issue: it was too handsome a thing not to keep and display, but you had to edge around it sideways to get to the sofa or the kitchen.

When you hail from families that have lived for generations in houses with dumbwaiters and coal scuttles, your birthright includes a staggering heritage of bric-a-brac that has no bearing on modern life—the junk DNA that gets handed down alongside the useful genes. Wasp tableware is anything that abhors the dishwasher: gold-rimmed chargers, etched-crystal wineglasses, pedestaled fruit plates, egg spoons of translucent horn. My parents' inherited silver alone included mint-julep spoons, bouillon spoons, demitasse spoons, a stuffing spoon, a berry spoon, a pea spoon, sugar tongs, a butter pick, a pickle fork, a lettuce fork, a cocoa pot, salt tubs, and an egg warmer. Most of these antic materials were eventually stored or sold, but a few with strong associations became part of my mother's decorative mix.

Anything that didn't conform to her aesthetic but still seemed useful, she passed on. The table is one of three heirlooms I have from Grandpa Ted, along with a ratty Persian carpet and an unreadable set of books. (That's if you don't count the family's abiding sense of embarrassment.) It was at that table, which rested on that carpet, that I had my last real exchange with my stepgrandmother Eugenia—an exchange that led, in a roundabout way, to the gift of those books.

Eugenia Arnold Friend was an aging belle from Georgia who called people "Sugar" and wore a fixed smile sealed with ruby lipstick; time and the labor of hairdressers had brought her curls to a state of matronly perfection. At Christmas she sent us physically huge checks, so elephantine they evoked the grand prize from Publishers Clearing House, for five dollars. Grandpa Ted privately referred to her as "the War Department" but seemed oddly contented living with her on Pittsburgh's Squirrel Hill in a large house shrouded by velvet curtains. The drawing room, where the Aubusson carpet and Remington bronze were displayed, had a velvet rope across the doorway.

Eugenia and Ted could be relaxed and funny if their companions were drinkers, but children made her eyes narrow. When my cousin Lili was two, her mother, Joan Anderson Friend, then married to my father's younger brother, Charles, brought her to Pittsburgh. Lili dashed around the house patting all the vases and cocktail shakers, and Eugenia upbraided Joan, declaring, "You should tie her hands behind her back!" Joan packed and left, but she later regretted the rupture when her stepmother-in-law cut Lili and Lili's younger brother out of her will. Eugenia didn't fuck around.

My parents took elaborate precautions to avoid this sort of scene. They would stay at a nearby hotel, with Mom writing Ted and Eugenia beforehand each time to remind them that this arrangement would enable her and Dorie to "feed Tad and Pier at no inconvenience to your kitchen and bring them around, scrubbed and happy, at a time of day when they are at their best and you would most enjoy them."

When I was eight, the danger thought to be past, Day brought me to Pittsburgh to take in a ball game—my first—with his father. It was late in the 1971 season, a year the Pirates would go on to win the World Series. We sat in a box at Three Rivers Stadium, and Grandpa Ted bought me a program and kept supplying me with hot dogs. He was a very genial man. As a youth, when he was the center fielder on the St. Paul's team, he had been handsome, jovial, and rich; he retained none of those qualities but was still faultlessly dressed in a gray suit with a collar pin and tie clasp, his wingtips gleaming. Looking now at photos of him in later life at Pike Run, at his harried, almost fearful countenance, brings to mind Sargent's definition of the portrait: "a painting with something wrong about the mouth." I took to him, though, to his kindness, and his knowing praise of my favorite player, Roberto Clemente, and his long-standing love of baseball. He and Jess had had box seats at Forbes Field, and he had known the Hall of Fame shortstop Honus Wagner well enough to sit him down for a gossip. The Pirates won 7–6 in extra innings, and Day recognized Sandy Koufax in the elevator and got him to sign my program, and I almost caught a foul ball.

That night, at the mahogany table, after finishing my two grudging scoops of Sealtest vanilla, I tongued the last of it off my spoon. Eugenia instantly addressed my father: "I cannot *believe* that you would raise a grandson of *mine* to *lick* his spoon!" Day stiffened, visibly trying to master his temper. Eugenia believed that manners expressed not your character—who cared about that?—but your grasp of decorum and, therefore, your fitness for society. She once reproved my cousin Daisy for spooning her vichyssoise toward herself rather than away, and would have keeled right over had anyone squeezed a grapefruit half so its juice fell into the spoon. The less actual eating you did with your spoon, the better.

I fled the table in tears, running into the study and wedging myself up against a consoling wall of books. That was where Ted found me. He stood by the floor lamp, his hands twitching in his sleeves, and seemed to consider crouching down. Instead, he reached into the shelves and pulled out a set of red volumes, spilling them into my lap. "Here," he said, "take these, take these with you—you'll feel better, you'll see." When I examined the books in bed, after Day took me upstairs, they proved to be a set of James Fenimore Cooper: *The Spy* and the five Leatherstocking Tales about Natty Bumppo, the quintessential American hunter who was both paleface and redskin. As a boy, Day had penciled his initials in the flyleaf of *The Pathfinder*; his grandfather, Ted's father, had originally given the set to *him*.

We had planned to stay longer, but my father decided to leave in the morning. As we were about to go, the black butler, Bert, who drank as much as Una the Scottish cook and Eugenia herself, but not quite as much as my grandfather, came downstairs and murmured, "Miz Friend is indisposed." Expert at nursing a snit into a breach, Eugenia would not see us off.

And so Pittsburgh was closed to me. From then on my parents visited the city without us: a series of clenched, best-behavior arrivals and hasty, never-again departures. A few

years after Ted died, in 1976, my parents were having breakfast one morning as Eugenia's "guests"—she always under-
lined the word—when she suddenly asked Mom, "Is it true
your father is a pinko?"

Seeing Mom at a rare loss, Day replied, "It is true that
John Pierson was a liberal economist who favored full employment in the thirties."

"So is he a pinko or not?"

My father wrote a bildungsroman about his childhood,
Family Laundry, which was published to strong reviews in
1986. On his subsequent visit, Eugenia immediately launched
into an attack on "your dirty, disgraceful, disgusting novel,"
which she felt defamed Ted as a drinker and the complaisant
husband of an adulteress. When she called Day later at our
house to continue her harangue, insinuating that she would
disinherit him, he jerked the receiver from his ear and glared
at it, then waved it in front of his crotch as Mom made fran-
tic placatory gestures from the stove. Finally, red faced, he
returned the receiver to his ear.

MY PARENTS never told me what Wasps were, or that we
were they, but I gradually worked out that if you have a fancy
name and you go to a fancy school, you're one. Wasps name
their dogs after liquor and their cars after dogs and their
children after their ancestors. In continuing thrall to the
Puritan conviction that God covenanted not with individuals but with a family, we cream off family names as given
names. This accounts for my brother's name, Pierson Friend,
which Day proposed to Mom using the rationale that two

names had sufficed for George Washington, Benjamin Franklin, and Abraham Lincoln. Ancestral creaming also explains such given names as Ogden, Minot, Mortimer, Deering, Courtlandt, Whitney, Manning, Norborne, Hobson, Prescott, Payson, Baxter, Brewster, DeLancey, Howland, Grafton, Hardwick, Boylston, and Enders—to select just from the list of former governors of one New York club. In this process, names become a marker of status as well as identity—if the two can even be separated.

So the first clue I had to my heritage was my bassoon solo of an appellation: Theodore Porter Friend. On the 1971 trip to Pittsburgh, I began to puzzle over its pieces: Grandpa Ted was Theodore Wood Friend Jr., my father was Theodore Wood Friend III, so why wasn't I Theodore Wood Friend IV? My father only recently told me that Ted and Eugenia had wondered the same thing. His explanation to them then, and to me later, underscored the lesson that my family's names are not merely polysyllabic incantations repeated with subtle variations, like a skein of Gertrude Stein. Names invoke expectations of achievement, claims for inheritance, and seething resentments. Day told Ted and Eugenia that he and Mom had chosen Porter in homage to my great-great-great-grandfather Porter Ridenour Friend, who had outfitted a company, Friend's Rifles, in the Union Army. He further explained that my nickname came from Abraham Lincoln's son Tad. Both my middle name and nickname, then, were yanked from the previous century to stick it to Eugenia, an unreconstructed southerner. Fair enough.

I'm not wild about my full name, perhaps because it was only ever used, by my mother, as a last warning prior to a spanking: "Theodore Porter Friend! You get in that bathtub this minute!" Surely she, too, had been rebuked with the suggestion that her dawdling outraged the very graves of her ancestors: "Elizabeth Groesbeck Pierson! . . ." My middle name also leaves me cold: in a surviving portrait, Porter Ridenour Friend has an expression both pious and constipated.

I do like "Tad Friend," though, its bang bang chime. It sounds to me as if it sprang from the same Hollywood brain trust responsible for Tab Hunter and Troy Donahue. But to most ears Tad sounds thoroughly Waspy. My wife's brother, Dean, hearing about me early on as the new boyfriend, would ask Amanda, "How's *Tad?*" giving my name the la-di-da pronunciation befitting a total twit. Even Amanda, long before we met, imagined from my byline in *The New Yorker* that I came from people who were rich and confident enough—and out of touch enough—to give their child a clubby nickname. She pictured me being tall and lanky with dark-framed glasses, having a slim wife with long brown hair and two children, and driving a Volvo station wagon. (We've pretty much achieved her vision, minus any car whatsoever.)

The usual point of Wasp nicknames is to propitiate the gods, to mitigate the Olympus-reaching thunder of Winthrop Cabot Lowell with a byname like Bootsy or Scrote. A recent article in the *New York Times* about a Newport decorator made me grin—Wasps, sure enough—when it developed that his most formidable clients were named Topsy, Oatsie, and Boop. Many such nicknames, like Baba or Daya or Wassa, come from baby talk. But the use or invention of an infantile nickname can also be a way of keeping the young in their place. In Wainscott a few summers back, Elliot Ogden, an older gent who has worn what appears to be the same seersucker jacket for the past forty years, shook my hand when I got off the tennis court, congratulated me effusively on my (mediocre) play, then sat me down, put his arm around my shoulders, and mused, preliminarily, "Taddy—Taddy baby!" No one else calls me "Taddy," let alone "Taddy baby." "You know, Taddy," he confided, speaking about my magazine writing, "you're showing real signs of turning into a promising young man." I thanked him gravely—I like Elliot—thinking, *I'm forty-four! If I get any more promising I'll be dead.*

IN 1889, Andrew Carnegie set down his famous "gospel of wealth," the idea that those who made extraordinary sums—in an era when extraordinary sums were being made—should distribute their largesse. The rich man had a duty "to set an example of modest, unostentatious living, shunning display or extravagance; to provide moderately for the legitimate wants of those dependent upon him; and after doing so to consider all surplus revenues which came to him simply as trust funds . . . for the community."

That was one view. Another was expressed by William H. Vanderbilt, who cried, "The public be damned!" My great-great-grandfather James Wood Friend held with Vanderbilt. Rather than dispersing his surplus revenues around Pittsburgh, Big Jim, as he was known, preferred to relish those revenues aboard his yacht, the *Rebemar.* A fierce-looking man with blazing eyes and a thick mustache, he wore suits whose lapels flared like manta rays and kept a big pit bull on a short chain.

We heard about him, through Day, as a rumor of vanished potency, acumen, decisiveness, and greed. On the strength of a handshake, Big Jim and his business partner, Frank Hoffstot, agreed to fund each other's ventures unhesitatingly and to split all profits. In this way, they came to control the Clinton Iron and Steel Company, the People's Coal Company, the Monongahela Dredging Company, and four banks, among other concerns. The contemporary *Encyclopedia of Biography* piously attested that Big Jim's life "was a record of undaunted, persistent effort and stainless, unimpeachable conduct," and that, "realizing that he would not pass this way again, he made wise use of his opportunities and his wealth, conforming his life to the loftiest standards of rectitude." Uh-huh. When workers struck for better wages at their Pressed Steel Car Company, in 1909, Hoffstot and Friend evicted the strikers from their houses, brought in scabs from New York, and deployed their own "Coal and Iron Police" to smash any resistance—tactics that killed a dozen people. James Wood Friend also carried on with the celebrated actress and operetta singer Lillian Russell—the longtime companion of Diamond Jim Brady, whose Pressed Steel Car Company Big Jim bought out from under Diamond Jim while the boulevardier was off enjoying Paris.

At home, Big Jim's life was a series of propitiations of his wife, Martha McClellan Friend, known as Didi. Their grandson John Walker described some of these efforts in his sharp-eyed memoir, *Self-Portrait with Donors*, beginning with the remediation of the mess that spewed from Big Jim's blast furnace:

> *In this dirt-filled city cleanliness was an obsession. Maids toiled away, continually dusting and scrubbing, and rooms were re-painted and redecorated almost annually. Money was easy to make but a large percentage went to the war against grime.*
>
> *Floods from the Allegheny and Monongahela rivers were endemic. The resultant damp caused my grandmother Friend to become totally deaf, or so her deafness was diagnosed. Grand-father, who seems to have felt some unexplained guilt for her loss of hearing, spent his life, as did one of her sons who never married, trying to make her happy. Each Sunday evening the entire family dined together, and we were never allowed an animated conversation for fear my grandmother would think we were quarreling.*

Didi, who carried an ear trumpet and wore a pince-nez, was so fearful of drowning that she permitted her husband to cruise his oceangoing yacht only on the Saint Lawrence River. She was even more terrified of fire. So when Big Jim began building a three-house family compound on Solway Street on the city's Squirrel Hill, at the turn of the century, he made "the Big House" for the two of them completely fireproof—a twilit pile of steel, tile, and brick. The decor was proper to the point of funereal: walnut and mahogany paneling, velvet curtains, and any number of urns.

Having moved into his dream house at last, and given it the name convicts give prisons, James Wood Friend soon thereafter died. Alongside the mausoleum he built for the

Friend dynasty at the Allegheny Cemetery stands a tiny, matching Greco-Roman tomb occupied by Lillian Russell.

THE FAMOUS Wasp traits—remoteness, heartiness, lack of interest in food or adornment, and boozing—seem traditionally male. Yet in many families the supposed patriarch potters about while the matriarch sets the tone. Uxoriousness was particularly marked among the male Friends. Big Jim's younger son, Theodore Wood Friend, known as Dorie—my father would be both named and nicknamed after him—showed none of his father's dash. Dorie Sr., who ran his father's grandly named Bank of North America (a single-branch savings and loan), had skinny legs and a careworn appearance that made him look old when he wasn't, and ancient when he was. His one surviving letter to his wife, Lillian, written when she was on vacation in 1902, is touchingly winsome: "It is only since we have been married that I know how much you are to me and how much I need you to take care of me. . . . I dreamt of you and wakened in the night finding myself reaching over on your side of the bed to see where you were."

His one surviving letter to his son Ted, a decade later, is a stilted series of admonitions. "You must remember that everyone has not the opportunities that you have, and you must try and take advantage of them," Dorie wrote. "There are lots of boys of your age that never get a chance to go away for the summer, or get any vacation at all." He mentioned a nicely phrased letter that Ted had written to another relative: "I was very much pleased to hear that of you, and I am also very proud of my son, and hope that I will always be and that you will never do anything to change my opinion of you in any way." I can't help wishing he'd ended the thought with "very proud of my son."

Ted would change his father's opinion soon enough. When the story of Ted's elopement came up, my parents would exchange a look: Mom amused and Day perturbed. And then Day would bat the matter away before we could learn what had really happened. As a result, elopement always seemed to me a romantic gesture rather than a fatal impulse.

Late at night on April 22, 1930, Ted and Jessica Holton left a dinner at the Pittsburgh Golf Club and drove to Wheeling, West Virginia, where they were married by a justice of the peace—in defiance of her mother and his parents, all of whom strongly disapproved of the match, begun as a shipboard romance. He was twenty-seven, she just twenty-one. Ted and Jess then returned to his parents' house for their honeymoon, Dorie and Lillian Friend being on an American Express tour of Shanghai (where, that same day, they dutifully acquired a pair of oversize ginger jars that now rest in my father's living room).

Two weeks later, Ted wrote letters in racy green ink to each of his parents, who were still in Asia, justifying this precipitate step. "I know I promised you I would never elope," he told his mother. "I know you will forgive that when you get to know just what a wonderful girl she is. And you never did want me to be an old bachelor." With his father, he adopted a bluffer tone, cataloguing the people they'd been seeing and giving an update on the markets—before ending, abruptly, with "Am I a very bad boy? Ted."

Another letter went off to Dorie and Lillian from Ted's

aunt Rebekah, who strove to put the best face on the scandal, remarking, "I love it when she calls Ted 'Theo.,' which is rather nice." But she concluded firmly, "Please never go away again for such a long stretch + now mark heathen China off your list."

WHEN MY father was twenty-three, he happened to play golf with an elderly man named Harmer Denny Denny, a former candidate for mayor of Pittsburgh. After a few holes, Denny said, "I knew your grandfather, and he was a fine man. I always respected him. But he didn't have confidence in his golf game." Day realized the same was true of his father: Ted stabbed his putts; he couldn't seem to settle over them and roll the ball. In this way Ted resembled Robert Lowell's father, memorialized in the poem "Commander Lowell," who "took four shots with his putter to sink his putt" and quickly "squandered sixty thousand dollars. / Smiling on all . . ."

Early in their marriage, Ted promised to buy Jess a yacht. And he'd surprise her with notes at Christmas: "The second year was better than the first / If I love you any more I'm sure to burst / Jessica, Dorie, and Theodore Friend / Seems to me like a perfect blend—Teddo loves Byrd." Then the notes, and all mention of yachts, came to an end.

One explanation is that Ted was no longer well-to-do. For years the family overspent and underworked, and then they got blindsided by the Depression. When Day was born, in 1931, Didi and her four children and their eighteen servants were still in the compound, coasting along, with Ted and Jess just down the street. Coasting was common in Pittsburgh. John Walker wrote that "it was customary for the top executives, most of whom had inherited their wealth, to leave their offices between half past three and four; and Father, having spent the morning reading the newspapers, would join them for backgammon, bridge, billiards, and alcohol." The Protestant work ethic, a self-gratifying reading of John Calvin that held that success demonstrated God's plan for your salvation, had for centuries banished Wasp guilt and buttressed the status quo. But the less-advertised corollary to the ethic, which held that if you were born to success nothing further was required, proved a tidy recipe for despair.

When Day was eleven or so, he found a newspaper clipping in his grandparents' library headlined "Friend Will Divides $15,000,000 Among Kin / Widow of Business Man Gets One-Third of Estate and the Rest Is Shared Alike by Four Children." He showed the report of this astounding sum—which now, with inflation, would be some twenty-three times greater—to his grandmother Lillian. "It wasn't that much!" she said, snatching the clipping away. (When Lillian died, in 1976, it came to light in her desk, alongside her Republican Party card, on which she had written in a determined hand, "If you know or hear of a narcotic Pusher call this No., it is free—800 368 5363.")

In the years before Big Jim's widow, Didi, died, in 1935, she fretted about the looming abyss. "Debt, debt, debt," she would croak, like Poe's Raven. The Depression was at its nadir, and Ted, at his brokerage firm, was giving fresh meaning to the economist Joseph Schumpeter's observation that stocks and bonds are "evaporated property." The properties Ted talked up were themselves evaporating, his plunges bearing the sweaty stamp of the boiler room: Nerlip Mines, which would sweep Canada clean of cobalt; Red Rock Cola, which would bring Coke to its knees; and an extraordinary, self-explanatory breakthrough called Hygienic Telephone. Even the stocks he bought as a hedge were bogbound dinosaurs like Pennsylvania Railroad. In his early forties Ted was fired from his firm, and by his forty-seventh birthday he had essentially retired to playing backgammon, rather well, at the Pittsburgh Club.

It turned out that when he and Jess bought their house together, in 1935, he put nothing down. "There are people in Pittsburgh who said I married your father for his money," Jess told my father years later. "I bought the house with *my* money." It seems exceedingly strange that Dorie and Lillian didn't bankroll their son's independence. Perhaps they were worried that he'd fritter the money away—he was always on the phone, sotto voce, to his bookie, Nat—or perhaps they were content to let someone else stake their wastrel. When Ted moved into his next house, with Eugenia, she, too, wrote the check. He had an eye for a shapely bankbook.

My FATHER and his younger brother, Charles, were raised in significant part by the servants, who called them Master Dorie and Master Charlie. Following the theory of the time, Ted and Jess thwarted thumb sucking by encasing their sons' hands in aluminum mittens. Following the theory of their class, they skipped hugs, bathing their children, reading before bed, security blankets, and saying "I love you." My father longed to play the guitar, but his parents discouraged the impulse as unwholesome. The most up-to-date source of information in the house was *The Book of Knowledge* from Ted's childhood, published in 1908. When the boys returned from Sunday school, Ted, barely disentangled from his bed-sheets, would inquire what they had learned and then some-times rattle off from memory the books of the Old Testament, ending in triumph with the thunderous mouthful, "Zepha-niah, Haggai, Zechariah, Malachi!" Years later, my father would write in his novel, about the narrator's father:

> *When I was old enough I sorted out his values. "Success" was praised but never defined or achieved; "congeniality" was ex-pressed constantly but diluted by resentment and belittlement of the successful; "tolerance" was much spoken of with regard to Jews, Catholics, and Negroes, but its selective nature and condescending tone tipped it more nearly toward vice than virtue.*

Ted and Jess never fought in front of their sons. Wasps, living so much in public, have a keen sense of privacy. (When Timmie joined Facebook recently, she was appalled to dis-cover that it invited everyone in her address book to be her friend—as appalled as if the site had rifled through her purse.) The phrase *"pas devant,"* short for *"pas devant les do-mestiques,"* was a reminder to table certain topics in front of the servants. Isabella Stewart Gardner kept the maxim "Think much, speak little, write nothing" above her bath-tub, and J. P. Morgan kept it, in French, over his mantel. The Friends adopted the adage, too, or at least the last two-thirds of it (unlike the Piersons, they were not much for letters). Meals were taciturn affairs, the events of the day often sum-marized with a terse "Nothing to report." Day's grandmother Lillian was the only conversationalist at the Sunday lunch table, with its inviolable meal of roast chicken, mashed potatoes, creamed onions, and ice cream, and she prattled or dropped deadly adjurations like "Curiosity killed the cat."

Day, alone much of the time, invented a baseball game involving five dice and played out whole schedules with eight National League teams, writing up box scores and maintaining running season averages in a set of blue spiral notebooks. When he was eleven he shared the game with three summer friends at the Seabright Beach Club; they'd play two real softball games on the sand during the day and dice baseball at home at night. This monastic spasm ended at thirteen, when Day came up with a better diversion: the Seabright Beach Club Female Rating Society.

When Day was pursuing his PhD at Yale, specializing in Indonesian and Philippine history—countries as far as possible from Pittsburgh, both geographically and culturally— he flunked his oral exams. Part of the problem, he began to realize, was that the absence of family discussion had left him unable to converse, let alone declaim. So he got out his Sunday school Bible, went into the woods behind the house that his mother shared with Charlie Kenworthey, and began reciting Psalm No. 1 to the open air, like Demosthenes overcoming his stutter by discoursing with a mouth full of pebbles:

> *Blessed is the man*
> *who does not walk in the counsel of the wicked*
> *or stand in the way of sinners*
> *or sit in the seat of mockers.*

Day passed his subsequent orals and later in life shone at debate, rising at public forums to pose knotty tripartite questions prefaced by a précis of his qualifications: "I appreciate the rigor of your analysis, but as a retired academic and sometime executive, I cannot help but observe . . ." In his determination to escape, he overshot and indeed repudiated the cultural ideal of bluff, casual intelligence. Not for him the insouciance that made his friend Ted Terry a Williams hero as secretary-treasurer of both Phi Beta Kappa and Kappa Beta Phi, the drinking society he joined by consuming, in one hour, as many ounces of beer as he weighed in pounds — 160 ounces, or more than thirteen beers. Ted likes to say, "If I die at my desk, at least I will have had four good years of retirement at Williams College."

When my father wrote the class report for his fiftieth reunion, he took the step of recalling two gang rapes at fraternities when he was there, events widely gossiped about but never reported. At the reunion, he says, "Nobody spoke to me about it — nobody. Possibly I'd offended by suggesting that our culture of alcoholism and lack of responsibility, of conformity, supported gang rape. Possibly people feared that I would hurt fund-raising. And possibly I'd struck home. But it's very lonely to strike home."

One of his friends later hit the proper fraternal note, saying, "Jesus, Dorie — we had a gang rape? Why wasn't I invited?"

My great-great-uncle Charles Wood Friend, Dorie Sr.'s older brother, was a negligent executive at the Farmers Bank who shut up shop at three. Uncle Charlie never married, choosing to take care of his mother, Didi, and frequent the north side bordellos. Once, he arrived home from such an outing very late for the formal-dress Sunday night dinner in the Big House. Putting his monocle hurriedly in place, he slipped into his chair after the meal had begun. Soon it became apparent that he had slipped from his chair to the floor. "I do believe," Didi observed, "that Charles is indisposed." Day and his brother, Charlie, loved to wake their great-uncle from his afternoon nap: blinking and yawning, he would take a silver brush in each hand and solemnly smooth his thin white hair. Then he would accompany them downstairs, full of jokes, ring the bell for Quinlan the butler, and order what Grandpa Ted liked to call "an umbrella stand" full of scotch.

There was a conspiratorial pleasure in the way Ted spoke of his uncle. In those days, everyone drank too much, so Ted's humid eyes, his controlled movements and marathon runner's pace, his amiable way of treating each shift in fortune or conversation as sufficient cause to signal for another round, disguising his solitary mission in the flurry of troop movements, was easier to overlook. And Jess liked a man who liked his cocktails. During the divorce, though, she told Day that she had been shocked, early in the marriage, when she and Ted and another couple were driving back from a vacation in Rumson one summer night. They had to pull off in Hershey, Pennsylvania, to look for a hospital because Ted was unconscious. The doctor in the emergency room examined him, then took Jess aside and asked, "How long has your husband been an alcoholic?"

As I began to realize when I started swiping Michelobs

from the pantry of the Wainscott house and no one raised an alarm, boozing was permitted, even encouraged, in our world, as long as it conformed to protocols designed to avert that word "alcoholic." There are, after all, only a few circumstances in which Wasps may properly drop their guard: charades or costume parties; roughhousing with dogs, who enact their owner's feelings by proxy; and cocktail hour, the solvent of all care. To make clear that you are not losing control but manifesting it, no one takes more than one drink, or at least one drink that counts. So a host never asks, "Would you care for another drink?" but rather, "May I refresh your drink?" or "Would you like a repair?" or simply "A dividend?" If you don't begin to drink before 5:30 or 6:00 p.m., when "the sun crosses the yardarm," you aren't an alcoholic. Or anyway not before noon. So the relative of mine who popped up to pour herself a "brownie" at 12:01 p.m. wasn't an alcoholic. And binge drinking wasn't alcoholism; it was just "letting off a little steam." Drink occasions an exception to the rule against euphemism: nobody is ever drunk, just "tight" or "loose" or "squiffy" or romantically, nautically, "three sheets to the wind."

You need to establish a pattern—a standard, really—and stick to it. Uncle Wilson, for instance, would have a Michelob at lunch, and several glasses of pinot grigio at dinner, but focus his ingenuity on the intervening cocktail hour, when he would serve up turbid creations with names such as Raising Cane or Ceiling Zero. In the butler's pantry he'd tacked up a typed page of mixological reminders, such as "Martinis: gayety in minimum time and at minimum expense," and after filling a canvas bag with ice cubes from the aluminum trays in the freezer, he'd sliver the ice by smacking the bag with a wooden mallet—instructing our au pair, Janine, to yell, "No, Uncle Wilson, no!" after each smack. The cocktail hour was a full hour, with Wilson and Letty and my parents in blazers and ties and Pappagallo dresses, eating Wheat Thins arrayed with cheese in a slim walnut salver. The dogs, Penny and Charlie, had to do tricks to get a nibble. "Way back, way back!" Wilson would cry, and Penny would inch back on her hind legs, like an outfielder tracking a fly ball, then leap to nip the falling cheese. The ceremony, the pleasing rigmarole, almost disguised the fact that if you had more than one of Wilson's concoctions, it was good night, nurse.

Likewise, Grandpa Ted made cracking the beers that preceded his bourbons into a ritual, teaching my father, at eight, to pour them out, tilting the glass just so. At Williams, Day began drinking bourbon straight, in loyalty. Over lunch at home during my father's fourth year of graduate school, Ted said he would continue to shoulder Yale's fees. After lunch, Ted took his son aside. "Am I a good provider?" he asked.

"Yes," Day said, and thanked him.

"You think I drink too much, don't you?"

Day reddened and, in a low voice, answered, "Yes."

Ted had his answer ready: "I like the taste." My father nodded, and they never spoke of it again.

In the years after my last visit to Pittsburgh, when Ted was falling apart from arterial stenosis, cerebral arteriosclerosis, and Parkinson's disease, he kept drinking. His nurses' notes about his variable temper and acuity suggest that drink was his only constant: "4 highballs, good dinner," was a typical evening's account, terse gestures toward a largely unwritten epic of drinking, not for the taste, but for the oblivion.

When Ted died, in 1976, I remember Day taking the call and sitting abruptly on the stool by the phone, massaging his forehead with his thumb and forefinger as he wrote down the details, Mom's hands on his shoulders. He asked if I'd like to send anything with him to the funeral. I had been writing to my grandfather, trying to help him get well via baseball trivia — "Quicky quiz: What four players have hit 30 homers and stolen 30 bases in the same year?" — so I stuck to that theme. Not without a pang, I gave Day my two most cherished Pirates baseball cards: the manager, Danny Murtaugh, and Roberto Clemente, who himself had recently died in a plane crash while on a humanitarian mission. During Eugenia's open-coffin viewing of Ted in her front hall, my father slipped the cards under his father's pillow. Theodore Wood Friend Jr. and his companions were then chauffeured to Allegheny Cemetery and loaded into the mausoleum James Wood Friend had built for himself and all the family heroes to follow.

EIGHT

Appearances

SOON AFTER MY father's inauguration as president of Swarthmore, in 1973, he and my mother privately agreed that the job—for all its prestige and prerogatives, including Ulverstone, the colossus of a house with its glum, Tolkienish name—was a gilded cage. Six weeks in, Day arrived at his office to discover it smeared with ketchup and cat shit by students protesting the Vietnam War (which he had always opposed). Two weeks later, Mom wrote her college roommate Chrissie about a blowup she and Day had had over attending college events on a Saturday; he wanted to make an appearance at six, she at just five. "So, because this is the one and only hour he can go with the children to get me something for my birthday tomorrow, he's gone stamping out in a rage on that tender errand. That's the thing about this job: there's not even time for a proper argument + its resolution."

They found themselves becalmed in the horse latitudes of Wasp life, the middle passage when duty is all that drives the ship. Day worked from 7:30 in the morning to 10:30 at night, occasionally stripping off his jacket to hit fungoes to me in the late afternoon, now and then taking us to the movies, but mostly absent or preoccupied. At one point, away on a fundraising trip, he wrote Mom to acknowledge his "grumpiness and over-responsibility," promising to mend his ways if she, too, would criticize less and be more optimistic, so that "sunshine can fall abundant upon the children." He was often on the road, wooing potential donors or reassuring alumni groups, accompanied by Malta, the small red bear Mom had given me as a child: she'd hide it in the suitcase of any of us embarking on a long trip. He would send Mom thick, newsy letters, sometimes to complain about not getting letters in return. From Hong Kong, he wrote, "I do my airport exercises freely, i.e. you are not here to be embarrassed by a middle-aged man performing odd stretches in public." (I myself now stretch out my hamstrings in airports, trying not to care if I look peculiar.) Even when home, he wrote notes and dispatched them upstairs or across the bed at two a.m.: "I see you, and in your silences hear you thinking about something you do not seem to share with me. That makes me sad. I feel helpless before that."

The family compass had shifted, the polarities of absence. Mom was at home more, though she was often planning or hosting college events and then—with a faint air of martyrdom—updating her dinner party book, to ensure that no guest ever had to sit beside the same person or eat the same meal twice. Pier and I played lots of Nerf soccer with friends in our end of the house, conscripting Timmie as steady goalie, running up and down the hall—staying out of the way. The phone was always ringing, and no one wanted to answer it, so Mom had buzzers attached to the six extensions so that whoever finally picked up no longer had to shout through the house: one buzz meant the call was for Day, two was Mom, and so on. Ringing and buzzing was continual, as if the house had tinnitus.

In her bread-and-butter letter to Letty and Wilson about our 1977 visit to Wainscott, Mom wrote of returning home to a profusion of problems, among them the lethargy of Timmie's hamster, Sparky: "A few days ago I brought him into our bedroom + turned on the air conditioner; that has perked him up a bit + D. + I can now hear him in the night running endlessly in his little toy wheel in the darkness. Not too different from the rest of us."

In 1994, Pier and I were home for Thanksgiving and we all got into a discussion of those years. Mom said that they had been crazy to try for the president's job, not being nearly ready. Pier, loyally, said that Day was right to take it, and that they couldn't have known what lay ahead. I agreed but added that I thought that period had been tough on all of us.

Day breathed in and said, "I hear your feelings, and pay careful attention because you're very good at articulating your feelings, and I think it's beneficial to till the soil. But it sounds like everyone's saying 'Dad threw us into the cauldron.' "

"Not on purpose, obviously," I said. "Pier and I just said we'd have taken the job, too. But in retrospect I think we would all have been better off somewhere else."

"Yes, well, one thing I've learned as a historian is to beware of fantasies of flight from the past."

I was suddenly so angry that, bewildered, I clamped

up and we let the topic die. His dismissal of "fantasies of flight" had reminded me how for four years I had longed to flee Swarthmore's public schools. Some of Baba's unloveliest footage shows my seventh-grade camouflage: a heavy flannel shirt, clunky horn-rims, and a tan fishing hat atop a Doug Henning–style cascade of hair. Newly aware of my scoliosis, I am trying to tilt my right shoulder up to look even, longing for puberty to kick in and unconsoled by Mom's reassurance that it's better to be a late bloomer, that the kids who were shaving and partying and swaggering through the halls would all end up pumping gas.

My bookish timidity would have made me a mark anyway, but being the son of the president in a college town multiplied my visibility. I lacked the guts to tell my parents about the noogies and Indian burns, but there also wasn't much opportunity: they discussed college matters so extensively over dinner—the professor suing for tenure, drunken assaults at a frat with powerful alumni—that, for a period, we had to raise a hand before speaking. I took out my misery on Pier and Timmie, passing it down.

Each weekday at 6:40 a.m., I awoke in foreboding to Mom's step on a loose hall floorboard. Years later, Timmie would tell me that she, too, awoke to that creak dreading school. On snowy mornings I'd put my ear to my clock radio as the newscaster read off the closed schools by number. If 403 was on the list, I'd fall back on my pillow, washed with relief. I sicked out as much as I dared, claiming to have thrown up in the night. Day would bring the thermometer and sit at the foot of my bed in a three-piece suit, lost in thought as, five feet away, I pressed its bulb to my reading light to kick the mercury to 101 or 102. Once I overdid it, in my zeal, and he frowned, focusing: 109 degrees. "Someone's been goosing this thermometer!" he declared.

But he relished accusation as little as I did; we were careful not to really get into it. So I went off to school hunched with anxiety—sick now, as I hadn't been before. Only near the end of eighth grade did I finally work up the courage to say, "I want to go somewhere else." And Day said, "If you get your grades up, we'll respect your seriousness and take the matter forward." It was Cheerful Money all over again, but this time I snapped at the bait.

PREP SCHOOL is the place where Wasps recognize themselves as such, where they learn their trademark self-deprecation, becoming confident enough of their status to poor-mouth. There they learn what Kipling called "the Law," emerging deeply loyal to school and family, believing that the religion observed in daily chapel knits a class together, and convinced that character is comportment—"Manners Makyth Man," as the motto of Britain's Winchester School has it. Harry Sedgwick, the nephew of Uncle Wilson's Groton classmate and friend Francis "Duke" Sedgwick, described the initiation another way, observing, "Childhood for Sedgwick boys ended when we were sent to Groton."

Groton's motto was *Cui servire est regnare:* "To serve Him is to rule." My father's St. Paul's roommate, Ted Terry, still recalls the telegram the school sent his mother when she requested their application: "We only accept superior boys." "It was a very strict, cold-blooded place, with no nurturing concept," Ted says, "which somehow became part of this strange notion we had that we were better than other people. We made life miserable for anyone thought to be gay or Jewish, and I recall making a lot of fun of a kid with a harelip. The only thing that saved him was when he was joined by a Chinese kid named Kin Tsu." He recounts this with mild remorse but also with bemusement; that's just how things were. New boys had it the worst, because anything new was not old: they were dismissed with a lip-curling "New-boyh!" (Even when Timmie went to St. Paul's, forty years later, "cocky newbs" routinely got "ponded," or tossed in the pond.)

The schools forged their students not in fire but in ice: at Groton boys slept in unheated rooms and washed up in cold water at communal sinks; at St. Paul's the boys poured water across the windowsills in the aptly named Old Upper dorm to caulk them with ice against the drafts. Sports were paramount, the more obscure and self-invented, the better. The craze of St. Paul's in my father's day was a kind of handball or jai alai using a tennis ball and a dorm's gabled roof, a game known as "nigger baby." The ruling idea was to mint citizens rather than intellects; Endicott Peabody, Groton's founder and longtime head, once said, "I am not sure I like boys to think too much." When Grandma Tim attended Ethel Walker, one of the first prep schools for girls, there was one commencement prize for scholarship and a dozen for such qualities as "character and influence," "courage and fortitude," "efforts and development," and "faithfulness and dependability," with four prizes alone for "neatness and order."

This distrust of ideas was particularly pronounced at finishing schools such as Miss Porter's, attended by both

Jacqueline Bouvier and my cousin Norah, who emerged from it somewhat less finished. At Miss Porter's, "Young ladies were expected, if they did not know how to do so already, to learn to play tennis, to curtsy, to pour tea, to remove the finger bowl *with* the doily and place these at eleven o'clock before separating the dessert spoon and fork," Stephen Birmingham wrote in *America's Secret Aristocracy*. "Girls were not permitted to wear high heels because of Miss Porter's arcane belief that high heels damaged a woman's childbearing ability."

I knew so little about the famed "St. Grottlesex" boarding schools that I thought St. Paul's was in Pittsburgh, rather than New Hampshire. They held no allure. Mom enthusiastically threw herself into "finding Tad a school," driving me all over the area to visit campuses, but I knew I wanted to go to the Shipley School, in Bryn Mawr, where my friend from around the corner, David Hunt, had gone. Shipley's faint hope for immortality was a passing mention in *The Catcher in the Rye:* Holden Caulfield, surprised to hear that a girl he liked goes to a school near his own, says, "I could've sworn she went to Shipley." Jane Smith and my great-aunt Diddy and my cousin Lili were all Shipley graduates, but I didn't know that then; I just knew that it seemed a congenial place where I could find my way socially. It had been an all-girls school until a few years before, and I would graduate with merely a dozen other boys in a class of sixty-three.

Though Bryn Mawr was only half an hour north of Swarthmore, on the Main Line, even the weather seemed better up there, the hyacinths budding early and fading late. The Main Line had arisen from the Pennsylvania Railroad's sale of land alongside its line west from Philadelphia; beginning in 1880, the company required its executives to move to these new suburbs and offered lots to owners who would build "homes of more than ordinary architectural interest" and spend at least $8,000 along Montgomery Avenue, where Shipley lay, and $5,000 in the adjacent lanes.

By the late 1970s, the Main Line was a green and leafy land of churches and lacrosse fields and mansions of granite and schist. In Swarthmore, if you wanted to swim or play tennis, you went to the swim club or the public courts, and street hockey was rampant. On the Main Line, there was no street hockey, and many of my new classmates had their own tennis courts and pools—though I wouldn't get to see them just yet. Conditions had improved for the Shipley boys since David had arrived in seventh grade to find his locker booby-trapped with tampons, but we were still viewed as interlopers. Sharing the bottom of the social ladder with us were the boarders, girls from such countries as Nicaragua and South Africa; my first year, tenth grade, we boys spent most of our time with them. A rung higher were late-arriving girls from outlying suburbs like Paoli, and above them were several layers of local girls of newer money or lesser athletic aptitude. At the top were six or eight girls from old Main Line families with legacy memberships in the Merion Cricket Club, girls who had cars that had nicknames ("Betsy," "Thumper," "Stormin' "), rode their own horses, and smoked pot. They dated boys like Bucky Buckley and Chad Chadwick from the all-male Haverford School and Episcopal Academy, and believed they could distinguish an Episcopal guy from a Haverford guy by his manners and tone—- Haverfordians being more athletic but "a little rough around the edges." We didn't even merit a stereotype.

For me, though, being an interloper was a promotion from being a total pussy. I loved the way the in crowd looked, their chubby-faced lissomeness, the Fair Isle sweaters and creamy skin mandated by the Pennsylvania Railroad. I loved how they didn't care or sometimes even know what their parents did, and the way they danced the pretzel—a jitterbug variant featuring lots of back-to-back twirling—to breezy songs like "Brown Eyed Girl." Most of all I loved their casual certainty that they were on the primrose path. They were confident of a welcome from one of the right colleges—the Ivies, the little Ivies, UVA, Trinity, Bowdoin, Bucknell, Colgate, Hamilton—already seeing its stencil on the rear window of their parents' Volvo.

I loved passing notes or flicking them into girls' cubbies, then poring over the scribbled replies, relishing each foothold gained on the rock face of intimacy, from "Catch ya later," to "Bye," to "Party hearty," to "Take care," to "Luv ya," to "Luv," to "Love" with a smiley face, to "Love" unadorned. The promise Shipley held out, down to the handsome young teacher who invited his students to turn in their papers by Friday at midnight, at his apartment, was that the party would continue forever hearty. Spirit was the school's keynote: everyone was always "super" and "getting psyched" and "having a blast." Only a killjoy, noting that the yearbook signatures of graduating seniors so often began "It's been real," might wonder if it hadn't.

I quickly adopted the prevailing look of ceremonial outdoorsiness: Shetland sweater draped over my shoulders, ski tickets dangling from my down vest year-round. We wore duck boots and boat shoes though there wasn't a large body of water for a hundred miles. Docksiders were superior to

Topsiders, and Blucher moccasins from L.L. Bean best of all. These facts were simply evident, incontrovertible.

As I was absorbing social distinctions that originated in Britain, I began, over the summer, to scrutinize the *Country Life* magazines scattered around Century House. The British weekly celebrated landed leisure with columns such as "A Causerie on Bridge" and hard-hitting features on "The Chiddingfold, Leconfield, and Cowdray Hunt." Browsing the full-page real-estate ads, I began to dream of acquiring a Georgian estate with a sunroom, conservatory, staff cottages, fenced paddock, harness room, loose boxes, lily pond, double-bank fishing, timbered gardens, and a cow byre. I asked my parents for a subscription for Christmas and instead, thriftily, received a packet of old issues bundled up by Uncle Wilson and Aunt Letty. They all thought my nascent Anglophilia hilarious, overlooking where I had found the magazines in the first place.

Mom gamely helped me shop to fit in, though her pride in me sometimes made the expeditions a trial: when I was seventeen, she took me to Jos. A. Bank and asked the salesman, "Do you have a pair of pants for a young man who's going to Harvard?" As layering was also de rigueur, once I left home in the mornings I would slip one of my father's way-too-large Lacoste shirts over an oxford-cloth button-down, flipping up the collar points to appear, in theory, studly.

This was the preppy look, regularly confused with the Wasp look. The confusion is understandable, as Wasps and preppies are often visually indistinguishable and can even interbreed, like horses and donkeys, though their offspring are usually sterile. The young of each species favor the preppy look: a vibrant effusion of pinks and yellows and greens blazoned with animal insignias such as the spouting whale. Older Wasps and preppies fade toward the Wasp look: dull, molting colors of khaki and battleship gray, and tweeds. (Though preppy men often have an Indian-summer flowering, in their sixties, into Nantucket-red pants topped by blazers in goldenrod or anise.)

One reason for the confusion is that as Wasps began to vanish as a ruling class, they disappeared not from but *into* the culture, which produced perfect (and therefore imperfect) reproductions of their clothes and furniture, as well as armies of preppies to use them. The Wasp tastemakers of the twentieth century were neither Anglo, nor Saxon, nor Protestant. They were Jews, and to a lesser extent Catholics. This effort began among the heads of the movie studios, who enshrined a vision of American family life that banned immigrant accents, noses, and names—Jacob Garfinkle becoming John Garfield, Issur Danielovitch becoming Kirk Douglas, Betty Joan Perske becoming Lauren Bacall.

The look and feel of an idealized Main Line or Nantucket was later mass-marketed by Martha Stewart, a Polish American Catholic, and, particularly, Ralph Lauren, born Ralph Lifshitz, the son of Jewish immigrants from Belarus. Lauren's determination to obscure what, exactly, he's drawing on is striking. In his book *Ralph Lauren*, he goes out of his way never to acknowledge the Wasp, though what he calls the "dream of America" that inspired him is manifestly that: "families in the country, weathered trucks and farmhouses; sailing off the coast of Maine; following dirt roads in an old wood-paneled station wagon . . ." as well as "images of collegians from Princeton, Harvard, and Yale."

Mom bought Lauren's pricey blue-and-white bedclothes

one pillow sham at a time until she had the full set; she relished getting her heritage — or at least its linens — in implicit quotation marks. In jazzing it up, she was an escapee. Day could never understand her Lauren fixation and complained that she had turned their bedroom into a boudoir. He also felt, as many Wasps do, that Lauren was a parasite on a culture he hadn't lived (though it is a little ridiculous for those who've inherited money to complain about Lauren's profiting off their way of life — to carp about his *unearned* unearned wealth). If Ralph Lauren bought his first new car, he might conceivably buy a red BMW, as my father finally did not long ago, after two years of shopping. He might even choose the station wagon with stick shift, as my father did. But Ralph Lauren would never refuse on principle to get a single option: my father's car is basically a shiny red go-kart.

The real difference between preppies and Wasps is not couture but outlook. Preppies are infantile and optimistic, forever stuck at age seventeen; Wasps emerge from the womb wrinkly and cautious, already vice presidents, already fifty-two.

As I was trying to climb up and out, Mom was, too. Her childhood idol was Wonder Woman, the Amazon warrior also known as Princess Diana — a name derived from Diana, Roman goddess of the hunt and the moon — and she caused a stir at a Swarthmore costume party by dressing as the scantily clad superheroine, complete with the indestructible bracelets and lasso of truth and a tiny Wonder Woman bathing suit (which Mom had bought for Timmie, who hated it).

In the late seventies, determined to be more than just a wife and mother—even as she was devoted in her attendance at Shipley soccer games—Mom began to enroll in weekend career seminars. At one, when she was asked to write down her greatest accomplishments, she put "analysis." She described her fixable weaknesses as "fear of flying (= fear of losing control)," "hyper-perfectionism," and "procrastination." Her unfixable weaknesses, she felt, were "Not a team player (not great at folding bandages for the war effort)" and "Don't like 3's—jealousy + competitiveness." Then she listed her favorite activities:

1. *Get presents for people*
2. *Improve the look of my surroundings*
3. *Wander around Bloomingdale's*
4. *Buy attractive things*
5. *Arrange, organize, tidy*
6. *Paint*
7. *Hit a good forehand*
8. *Eat fruit*
9. *Watch things (projects) progress + get completed (e.g. I-95).*
10. *Talk + think about houses — being built, being fixed*
11. *Be near the sea*
12. *Check things off lists*

Taking that list as itself check-offable, she began to paint more seriously. She started with acrylics, in which she could endlessly rework the plumb lines, adding depth to her eggplants and cantaloupes and her Spode blue-and-white Gloucester tea service, glossing her still-lifes with shafts of afternoon sun. As her confidence grew, she graduated to watercolors, where all plotting must be hazarded on an irreversible act. She was devoted to Matisse, and her titles delineated a bright domestic world he would have recognized: *Blue and White, The Blue Cow, The Blue Colander, The Red Dining Room*. She treated blue and white (and, as an accent, red) the way that Bach treated melody: later, in Villanova, she wove her favorite colors through every set of dishes, every coverlet, every room, so that her house became a spatial partita, a walk-around fugue.

My favorite of her paintings—it hangs just off our kitchen in Brooklyn—is called *Big Lemons*. The title suggests deadpan intent: four lemons bulk like boulders in white ramekins, stunned by their own surpassing tartness. A devotee of color and line, she had more difficulty conveying movement. When she painted people—my brother; my father; the dog, Sam—they were shown asleep. The living, too, suited her best in repose.

IN THE summer of 1978, following my first year at Shipley, Uncle Wilson taught me bridge in the evenings. Bridge is really a game for four, pairs of partners who aren't allowed to consult, so two-handed bridge requires you, when picking up your "partner's" hand, to act as if you had no knowledge of your own. I sucked at this. If I led a spade to myself when a heart was the textbook play, Wilson would look grave as a turnip and say, "Very interesting," leaving me stewing. But I needed to win. In fourth grade, I had made a chart grading myself and my twenty-four classmates from 0 to 10 in categories suggested by Mom: Nice, Smart, Good-Looking,

Good Sport, Good Athlete, and Cooperative. I was, it turned out, the smartest and nicest, tied for most cooperative, the second handsomest, and the fourth most athletic—in short, the all-around best.

That tenth-grade summer, Uncle Wilson wrote us of triumphing in the Sunday regatta: "Then we *demolished* the brash Petrie in his cat." Wilson had been keenly affected by having recently had to sell his back three acres to Donald Petrie, a banker at Lazard Frères. This comedown, and the further affront of Petrie's money and vigor and braggadocio, explained my great-uncle's glee. Games and sports are where Wasps permit themselves aggression, as we take for granted that skill on the court or field forecasts, or at least stands in for, success in the larger world. As the Duke of Wellington was supposed to have said, "The battle of Waterloo was won on the playing fields of Eton" (which weren't yet in existence when he attended the school, but never mind).

My cousins John Walker and his son John Anthony played 140 straight chess games across John Anthony's late adolescence, commencing the next game straightaway because neither could stand to lose. (When Mom found more eggs than John did at an Easter egg hunt, he became visibly upset.) The series ended when John Anthony heaved the set into the fire. Before he dropped out and moved to India, however, he often spoke of the burden of those struggles. "The undercurrent of competition in my family was very, very strong," his sister Gillian, who is now a family therapist, says. "I remember going after my brother with a butcher knife in a croquet game when I was about eighteen because he'd *cheated*, or something. I went to the kitchen and grabbed this knife, really intending to stab him. Then I suddenly realized that perhaps I had gone too far."

For five or six years, beginning in the late 1970s, almost all the letters between Day, Pier, and me were about squash matches we had played or would play, often with each other. Hardball squash was a prep school game played in icebox-like courts with a ball that left a lingering bull's-eye welt on your leg when it hit you, which it regularly did. Like the other Wasp sports—crew, polo, sailing, court tennis, paddle tennis, golf, and skiing—it required a large or intricately carpentered space unusable for any other purpose, expensive equipment, and a willingness to endure cold and/or discomfort. But squash's crisp geometries, the poised pursuit in a cool white box, struck me as particularly Waspy. (Nowadays, squash mostly transpires on more temperate International courts, with a ball of greatly reduced lethality, and so is played by a much broader mix of people, Pakistanis and Egyptians and Australians—who, it turns out, were always better at the game than the American Wasp.)

I learned the game in occasional lessons from Day, who'd sometimes hit with Pier and me after he'd played one of the mustachioed sluggers on Swarthmore's team. I found the game enthralling, a perfect mix of violence (you can whack the ball as hard as you like and it will probably stay in play) and precision (if you don't keep your shots tight to the side walls, you open up the court for your opponent). At its higher levels, it becomes a kind of fast-twitch speed chess.

By the time Pier was eighteen or so, the three of us were evenly matched: Day had briefly been number one in Buffalo in the mid-1960s and had a nifty hard serve; Pier would play number five for a strong Williams team and was rangy and graceful; and I would later win the Harvard Club championship in New York with a combination of touch and focus. A competition-intensifying facet of the game is that both players are moving quickly in the same small space, which provides considerable opportunity for discussion about who got in whose way and whether the point should be replayed, matters known as "lets." So there was a good deal of epistolary chatter about victories and defeats and conduct. In 1985, my father wrote me of a long match with Pier, and how in the deciding game:

> *I drew a nick of blood on his knuckle with my racquet, and he raised a welt on my forearm with his — all unintentional, the slash of fatigue and effort. I was leading 12–3 when he zoomed in under my radar and tied it at 14-all. What do I call? No set? I chose set three. Pier thinks a bit and grins. "Don't you just want to let it go? As it is? Just finish in a tie?" I say "Sure!" What a nice idea. I am as proud of his diplomacy as of his comeback.*

Offering a tie to my father wouldn't have occurred to me; at squash, particularly, I was so zealous I'd throw an occasional racquet in self-disgust. And Day, while notably fair-minded off the court, was worse than I was on it. Even warming up, he'd knock the ball to himself six or seven times before flicking it cross-court to you. After a tight match with him in the mid-1980s, I wondered aloud in the locker room about some of his lets. He began replaying the points in question in his mind and finally, grinning sheepishly, acknowledged that two of his calls had been "overcompetitive."

In squash, the confined space and absence of a net—the tight-shot close-up of it—brings out emotions often undetectable in tennis's panorama. At the Georgica tennis clinic, beginning at age five or six, Timmie and Pier and I had been schooled in playing hard, making no excuses, giving opponents the benefit of line calls, and complimenting their play. This was the Association's codified wisdom, its Deuteronomy. John Thornton, who grew up in Georgica and taught me the game as the resident pro in his summers off from Harvard, where he was captain of the team, says, "Virginia Turner, who taught me to play in Georgica, felt strongly that you were debasing the game if you crossed behind a court while a ball was in play, or served without having two balls. It was a Ten Commandments kind of thing." It's no coincidence that doubles, which is comparatively social and sublimated, is Georgica's preferred game; in ladies' doubles, Mom would apologize as often to her opponents for her booming forehand winners as she would to her partner for her flinching volleys into the net. The linchpin of top-flight doubles is poaching—cutting over to volley balls aimed at your partner—but in Georgica too much poaching is seen as aggressive and unsporting. I have a vivid childhood memory of watching Mom and her partner and their two opponents all racing toward their respective baselines when a lob went up.

Sportsmanship makes sports enjoyable; indeed, it makes them worth playing. And it is certainly more attractive than the aggression it is intended to counterweight. But sportsmanship, taken to its logical end, is a concomitant of the romance of loss. It is preparation for defeat. I always found it telling that the Wasp hero Robert Falcon Scott, in his race to the South Pole, decided not to use the dogsleds employed by Roald Amundsen and his Norwegian party, because Scott deplored the ruthlessness of shooting the dogs one by one and using their meat as food (the Norwegians set out with sixty-five dogs and returned with only eleven). Instead, Scott relied on motorized sledges, which broke, and Siberian ponies, which died. When Scott's party of five, laboriously pulling their sleds themselves, arrived at the Pole in January 1912 to find that Amundsen had beaten them by a month, Henry "Birdie" Bowers wrote in his diary, "It is sad that we have been forestalled by the Norwegians, but I am glad that we have done it by good British man-haulage." The Scott party perished of exhaustion and malnutrition on its return journey.

Apsley Cherry-Garrard, a member of Scott's Antarctic team and of the search party that found the explorer's frozen body, later contrasted the expeditions:

On the one hand, Amundsen going straight there, getting there first, and returning without the loss of a single man, and without having put any greater strain on himself and his men than was all in the day's work of polar exploration. Nothing more business-like can be imagined. On the other hand, our expedition, running appalling risks, performing prodigies of superhuman endurance, achieving immortal renown, commemorated in august cathedral sermons and by public statues, yet reaching the Pole only to find our terrible journey superfluous, and leaving our best men dead on the ice.

A jaunty James Wood Friend aboard his yacht, the *Rebemar*, c. 1900.

The Friend family compound in Pittsburgh, the Big House in foreground, c. 1900.

Wilson (left) and John Pierson with their father, Charles, c. 1915.

The Robinson family with friends, guides, and Blackfoot Indians on a Montana ranch that is now part of Glacier National Park. Timmy Robinson is second from right; her brother, Wassa, is fourth from right; their parents are second and third from left, c. 1922.

John Pierson ascendant in India, 1928.

Timmy Robinson in her wedding dress, 1930.

My mother, Elizabeth
Pierson, as a baby, with
her Robinson
grandparents, her
parents, and her
skylarking uncle Wassa,
in Hartford, 1933.

Century House after the Hurricane of 1938.

My father (left) and his
brother, Charles, with their
mother, Jessica Holton, at
their house on Solway
Street in Pittsburgh, 1937.

My grandfather Ted Friend, glass at his feet, examining his watch like the White Rabbit, c. 1940.

John Pierson in a rare return to Century House, with (from left) Paddy Pierson, Norah Pierson, Goggy Pierson, Elizabeth Pierson, Letty Pierson, and Tisha Pierson, 1946.

My parents' wedding rehearsal dinner. My father (second from right) and his ushers are singing their Williams College fraternity song. His brother, Charles, is standing at far left; next to Charles is Ted Terry, 1960.

Maplewood Farm in winter. (Photo by Karen Z. Pierson)

Tad, Timmie, Elizabeth, Pier, and Dorie Friend in Buffalo, 1970. (Photo by Anneliese Garver)

Daisy, Charles, and Suzanne Friend in Milan, 1975.

Tad, Pier, and Timmie Friend in Swarthmore, 1975. Nice hair. (Photo by Anneliese Garver)

Wilson Pierson at Yale, standing with the statue of his ancestor Abraham Pierson, the college's first rector, 1976.

Tom Bourne, Paddy Pierson, Timmy Bourne, and the golden retriever, Heather, at Maplewood after a load of snow sheared off the porch roof, 1971. (Photo by Karen Z. Pierson)

The "loser" picture: George Polk, Tad Friend, and
Pablo Keller Sarmiento in Manhattan, 1988.

The Playhouse in Villanova. (Photo by Karen Mauch)

Tad Friend and Amanda Hesser walking up the aisle, Georgica, 2002. (Photo by Sara Press)

The family in Georgica, 2006. Front row: Tad Friend (with Addie), Genevieve and Wilson Friend (Pier and Sara's children), Amanda Hesser (with Walker). Back row: Pier Friend, Norah Pierson, Dorie Friend, Scott Haskins, Sara Friend, Timmie Friend Haskins.

Walker Friend, Amanda Hesse Tad Friend, and Addie Friend; Georgica, 2008.

SPORTS WERE the Shipley boys' vehicle for advancement. David Hunt, an intense and meticulous young man who rubbed his forehead wearily when problems arose, was our leader. I was only the first of several decent athletes who followed him over from Swarthmore, and by junior year we formed a doughty corps. We had a good soccer team, cocaptained by David and me, and an excellent tennis team. After we beat Episcopal in tennis, 3 to 2, we swarmed the courts like Visigoths, feeling that we ought now be permitted to carry off their women (their women being our women).

By midway through junior year, we were going to parties at Pam Borthwick's. Her parents' pool house embodied the Main Line as it was in 1978, rather than in Ralph Lauren's ads: a party cocoon with kelly green shag carpeting, a teak bar, orange Naugahyde cushions, orange-and-rust-striped wallpaper, and picture windows that steamed up from everyone smoking and draining beer balls—round mini-kegs— and dancing to the Doobie Brothers and the Grateful Dead and Meat Loaf's teen-sex anthem, "Paradise by the Dashboard Light," or really just yelling along and believing that we, too, were glowing like the metal on the edge of a knife. (Somehow disco, the actually danceable music of the period, failed to penetrate the Main Line's green hedges.) Later, we'd flop into the pool, using the empty beer balls as floaties to keep from drowning.

Pam, a funny, scornful girl just outside the inner circle, was doing exactly what we were: asserting her claim. Once she and I became coeditors of the school paper, she stopped calling me Grasshopper—a dig at my skinny frame—and began calling me Taddeus. Then she wrote in the *Beacon* that at the recent mixer, "most of the Haverford and Episcopal studs refused to dance, although they did do a good job of holding up the gym walls. If it hadn't been for the Shipley guys, who were uninhibited enough to get out there and show up the other guys, things would never have started cooking."

We finally had a stereotype: uninhibited. Of course, the only boy it really fit was Rob Nikpour, whose family had fled Iran with the fall of the shah. Rob was a nineteen-year-old rake with a sparse, pungent English vocabulary, his default expression being "Boy, how did you get so fucked up?" At his attic parties we'd down whiskey shots and put on Nick Gilder's "Hot Child in the City" for some vital truths:

> *Danger, in the shape of something wild*
> *Stranger, dressed in black, she's a hungry child.*

Leaving one of Rob's parties to drive a Shipley boarder home, I backed my parents' station wagon right through his hedge. Danger, in the shape of a Chevy Impala. Then she and I made out until we passed out. There was still the split between girls you could get somewhere with—the boarders and outliers—and the Main Line set, most of whom preserved their virginity for college. It was as if they had continued to heed the school's rules from the 1940s: "Keep away from the windows when boys come singly or in groups. . . . This is for your own protection. Sooner or later it becomes known when boys are trying to get you to talk with them or laugh with them. It is much better for you to report it yourself." After one classmate finally slept with her Episcopal boyfriend, he immediately bragged to everyone, "I banged her lights out." The lesson was evident.

WHAT NAGS at me about the Main Line was how intensely I admired it, and how little thought I gave to where it might take me. It turned out that the Main Line led straight to the Main Line. After "having a ball" in college, many of my classmates turned for home. A Shipley friend who lives a few miles from the school laments: "I didn't learn about Kmart until college, which was kind of an oversight. I am just now learning how to cook. And only this year did my dad give me the money from an account he'd been managing for me, money he'd gotten by suing a woman who hit me in a car accident in tenth grade. I was scared to ask why he hadn't told me about it until I was forty-five."

My senior year, a queen bee explained that a local low-income housing project was a terrible idea because "Water seeks its own level," and another classmate joked: "What are the three things you can't give a nigger? A fat lip, a black eye, and a job." Most disenchanting of all was a realization that began to steal over me after David Hunt started dating Joy Carabasi, who was indisputably inner circle, making us a true class at last. I became privy to the whispers about the girl whose father beat and molested her; the girl whose parents were both alcoholics and who, for mysterious reasons, permitted her only half a glass of orange juice; the murmurs that so and so's mother was Jewish and so and so's father had married a Catholic, making them NOCD—"Not our class, dear"—mothers' shorthand echoed by the daughters, first in irony and soon enough with a little shrug. There was the girl whose father wrote her, when she was date-raped in college, to say, This is what comes of living in the fast lane. There was the girl whose father killed himself then, and the girl whose mother killed herself later. It seemed to me a lot of trauma for our small class, but then privilege doesn't exempt you from affliction; it just makes it less visible.

When I think of Shipley now, I think of Sally Cattone, a golden girl a grade ahead. She had entered Shipley in kindergarten and was a walking brochure for the place: a great field hockey player with a Dorothy Hamill haircut and a billboard grin who drove, too fast, an orange Volvo with signal flags on the door that spelled out her initials. Her parents had three or four houses all over the map, and her parties were legendary. Sally's boyfriend, from ninth grade through college, was Gary Tanner, a tall, blond stiff from Episcopal who was headed for Greg Marmalard's frat in *Animal House*, or so I imagined; her yearbook had a photo of them lounging on a greensward. Beneath it were listed her Pet Hates—"Myself, losing"—and her Destiny: "To be married to a very rich man." Her quote was from Jackson Browne:

> *Sometimes I lie awake at night and wonder*
> *Where my life will lead me*
> *Waiting to pass under sleep's dark and silent gate.*

I wasn't attracted to Sally, initially, so much as to the idea of her. I wanted to be her friend, or to think of myself as her friend—or, really, to be seen as someone who could be her friend. I wanted to escape the mass of "goobers" and "rejects" she floated above. So I'd say hello in the hall and kid around, and eventually we did become friends, probably because I took her so seriously and because I could make her laugh. She laughed full out with her head thrown back, and it felt like a reward. By the end of my junior year we were buying cheese steaks at Mallory's and calling each other "Wife" and "Husband" in a jokey way. I was far too awed and awkward to even try for a meaningful silence, but I began to realize that I really liked her. She was warm and joyful and wildly energetic, crying, "You wussy" if you ducked a challenge and, after turning into traffic on a one-way street, mocking herself with a snorted "Adoy!" That her vivacity was just water lilies atop a pool of sorrow only drew me in deeper.

Sally was a star on the girls' squash team, and we played a few times at the Merion Cricket Club, where she was admirably blasé about signing for a postgame sandwich. At first she beat me handily. But by the end of the year I had figured out that if I kept the ball in play, she'd eventually make an error trying for a kill. She said she let me win to salve my tender male ego, but no way. I remember sitting with her in her kitchen after we'd played squash and then a few sets of paddle tennis on her family's court, having an iced tea, and her father walking in and standing a moment, very still, at the sight. He was a manufacturing tycoon, and Sally referred to him, merrily, as "the King." "Let's get out of here," she murmured. In her car, her grin was back in place: "C'mon, Husband, let's go drive around and you tell me something intellectual."

When Sally married some Jim, in 1987, I went to the wedding—Sally looking radiant and nervous, Jim and his groomsmen surprisingly mustachioed—then, recognizing no one at the reception, slipped out the side door and never saw her again. I heard that she became the first woman to make a hole in one at a famous course, and that she and Jim had moved down South, where she ran one of her father's companies. And I heard that Gary Tanner had bought the Cattones' house for his family, which made me feel for him, suddenly. Before they left, Sally later told me on the phone, she and her father taped copies of a photo of Gary and Sally at the prom on the underside of some of the kitchen drawers, where his children might find them.

When Sally and Jim divorced, in 2002, she got custody of their four dogs: Cloey, Asti, Casey, and Bourbon. Her parents always named their dogs after alcohol—Gin, Chivas—so she did, too: Cloey for Clos du Boi, Asti for Asti Spumante, and Casey for case of beer. "Jim said, 'If you get one more dog, I'm leaving,' " Sally said. "So I got two more." She laughed. "I had liked Jim because he was from New Jersey, and he was humble, and he didn't own a collared shirt, and his parents were like this nest of unconditional love for me. But my dad saw him as trailer trash. Jim ended up working for me, and when I wanted to give Jim a raise, Dad would always say, 'No. Don't take his ideas, don't move him up, don't give him a raise.' So I tried to raise Jim up to my level, I guess, but he eventually, unfortunately, returned to his own." She paused a moment. "Dad kept saying, 'You can't have kids—how are you going to run things if you're pregnant?' I tried to force Jimmy to have a baby with me before he left, but he said no way."

When Sally was at Shipley, she told me, her father would hit the scotch and turn volatile. "It could be six o'clock, and if he came home, we'd run to our beds and pretend to be asleep," she said. "My mom would hide in her dressing room.

And when she was driving us to school the next morning, she'd say, 'I'm going to kill everybody!' Lots of fun, yeah!" She laughed. "Sometimes I wish I were still a spoiled brat back at Shipley. But when I come up to the Main Line now to play golf at Merion, which I'm proud to be a member of, that feeling of having to curb my language and behavior comes back over me, that feeling of being watched and . . . I don't know."

When I graduated, Sally was back for the parties from her college in the Midwest—where she set scoring records in field hockey—and late on class night, after I had surprised everyone except my teachers by taking home a raft of prizes, she wrote a long, sweet, tipsy entry in my yearbook about how I would go far.

Reading her inscription again recently made me sad. Some of Sally's first words, in blotchy blue pen, are hard to read, and eventually she switches to a black felt-tip: "I swear you are one of the greatest guys I've ever met. Of course, you will have to work on your squash, 'cause you know I can't win anymore, 'cause it makes you feel so bad. . . . Tad I really love to be with you and love to do things w/ you, take care and remember I'll always remember you and be w/ you if you need me. Take care and may you enjoy life and what it has to offer. Love always, forever and ever, love forever, love, Sally."

To MY mortification, our class chose my father as our commencement speaker. His speech about clarity and kindness was thoughtful and well received, but I sank into my chair early on, after his preliminary joke about pop music fell flat because the name-check he used—Emmylou Harris—was all wrong. I had hoped to spare us both this sort of tone problem when I asked beforehand if he felt okay about the speech, which was my way of hinting that I'd like to vet it. "Yes!" he said cheerfully.

In 1994, for its hundredth anniversary, Shipley wanted an alumnus as its commencement speaker, and asked me. I had the odd experience of seeing Day beaming in the audience, where once he had seen me grimacing. My speech was basically like his: well-meaning advice about staying out of ruts, none of it positively poisonous, and though I was very nervous beforehand, it seemed to go well. I was feeling rather pleased until the president of the student body told me, in the nicest, most dutiful head-boy way—he just thought I, this Methuselan thirty-one year old, would be interested to know what the kids of today were up to—that the class had really wanted Kelsey Grammer.

After Day's speech, that summer when I was working at the Jersey Shore, he began sending me lots of warm, thoughtful notes about courses to consider and ways of thinking about college. The first note included seventy-five photocopied pages from various biographies about the college years of Teddy Roosevelt, Bernard Berenson, and John Maynard Keynes, background material to help me "develop a personal ethic, and vision of the necessary and the ideal." Day had hit his stride in the job at Swarthmore, learning the patience required to wait for consensus; in a compliment he treasured, one of the college's trustees told him he'd helped the college absorb the period's enormous social change. Yet he seemed to yearn for the simplicity of student life. One of his notes was written at six a.m., after he'd been roused from sleep by work anxieties: "If in dreams begin responsibilities, I'm of the momentary opinion that I've had too many dreams."

Entering his late forties, Day was taking stock, a process spurred when he and Mom read the bestselling *Official Preppy Handbook*. The book, assembled and edited by a Jew, was particularly popular with Wasps, who, never having been the target of ethnic humor, didn't feel stigmatized by it. I not only didn't feel stigmatized by the satire, I didn't even recognize it, reading the book for tips on consolidating my place. My father wrote me about it when I was at Harvard, in a way that felt newly candid:

> *I can't quite tell if* [Mom] *sees it as a Guidebook on What to Do and Be, or a Catechism on What to Avoid at All Costs. In any event she seems pleased to realize that we have track lighting in our living room (non-preppy) and that we don't have a single duck as motif or emblem on anything (ducks apparently qualifying as ultra-prep).*
>
> *I find, to my amusement and chagrin, that I have been at a lot of "preppy" places — St. Paul's, Williams, Yale; a member of a hyper-cool prep fraternity (St. Anthony Hall); and am a practitioner of one of the quintessentially prep racquet games (squash, of course).*
>
> *What rescues me, I wonder, from being a sclerotic example of the prep stereotype (if indeed I have escaped that)? Proceeding with serious study of what interested me most may have been the best decision of my youth — and doing so despite the fact that I didn't know where it would lead . . . and then letting it lead me where still fewer Americans have gone unless required to do so — to Southeast Asia (where prep is so far from being relevant as not even to be a non-category).*

The other major decision, of course, was to marry Momma. Her way of being, and being-with-me, is continuously redemptive.

I read the letter and smiled and tossed it in a drawer, maintaining him precisely where he was trying not to be: in the prep-stereotype role of the distant dad.

NINE

Clubs

M Y FRESHMAN YEAR at Harvard I was inseparable from Bruce Monrad, an affable St. Paul's grad who waltzed into our six-man room late the first night in a seersucker suit, carrying a jug of sherried lemonade. The rest of us—a Catholic from Rhode Island, an African American from Maryland, a football player from Vermont, a gay debater from Wyoming—stared in wonder. Bruce was tall and sleek, and he raised his chin and swiveled it as he spoke, like a seal balancing a ball. His father and brother had gone to Harvard, so he knew what was what: he decanted Cointreau as a digestif, called New York "Gotham," stealthily pointed out the Porcellian Club, shepherded us to football games with a flask in his pocket, and saluted the library on the way to breakfast by chanting the inscription above its lintel: "Harry Elkins Widener Memorial Library, MCMXIV!" His preppy comportment effectively cloaked his intelligence—he took graduate-level economics classes— just as his cast-iron graciousness precluded real intimacy. So

I felt comfortable with him. When I heard his voice on my answering machine recently, after twenty years, it gave me a start: the crisp yet agreeable manner, the breathy cheer, were eerily familiar. He sounded like me.

Bruce joined the freshman squash team, so I joined the freshman squash team. He believed no year complete without a beer-drenched visit to the Dartmouth Winter Carnival, so off we went, staying with Paddy and Karen. He made it clear that after college, one went either to business or law school, so I began to consider law. I skipped only his time-maximization scheme: he started going to bed a little later every night, planning to eventually eliminate sleep entirely. Groggily insisting over breakfast that his plan was working perfectly, he would then nod off at Harry Elkins Widener Memorial Library, MCMXIV.

Bruce's chief goal freshman year was to join the humor magazine, the *Harvard Lampoon*, as his dear old dad had done (the phrase "Dear old Dad" came to his lips so often that the roommies shortened it to "DOD"). You had to compete, or "comp," to get on the *Lampoon*, which was known not only for its distinguished alumni—including Robert Benchley, George Plimpton, John Updike, Doug Kenney, and, in my own time, Conan O'Brien—but also for its fortnightly black-tie parties in its Flemish-style castle, parties that featured dancing on the banquet table and the gleeful smashing of plates. It was a select meritocracy with the perquisites of a club. Each semester a hundred or so would-be writers and artists wrote or drew six pieces that aspired to humor, and five to ten would be elected. Some of those slots went to business board compers: if you sold $1,000 in ads for the magazine, and weren't totally repellent, you made it on.

(Formerly an all-male Wasp bastion, the place was by then a coed mix of New York sophisticates and talented sociopaths; of Jews, Catholics, and Wasps—the Wasps, usually less funny, being concentrated on the business side.) Bruce's freshman comp for the business board didn't work out— "DOD was not pleased"—but he tried again sophomore year.

By then I was comping as well. Despite following Bruce's dicta, I found college passing in an aimless blur. Shipley meant nothing at Harvard, so I wore my blue-and-white-checked L.L. Bean sweater around like everyone else, hoping in some muddy way both to fit in and to stand out. I would be thumpingly rejected by the final clubs I aspired to, including the Porcellian, and accepted only by one I was ambivalent about, the Fox—the one Bruce wound up in, as DOD had. After agreeing to join, I would turn in a panic and gracelessly back out. I wanted to leave a mark, and this—the shabby armchairs, the scuffed pool table, the boisterous leakingly sad mixers with Wellesley girls—was not it.

When my maternal grandfather graduated from college, in 1927, a headline in the *New Haven Evening Register* declared, "YALE RECORDS SHATTERED BY J. H. G. PIERSON." The article noted that he had won nine academic prizes, been president of Phi Beta Kappa, and composed the class poem, while also being a member of the cross-country, rifle, and soccer teams, of the student council, and of the Whiffenpoofs—"prizes and recognitions for almost every form of worthy activity that Yale men admire." Like his father, Charles, and his brother, Wilson, the year before, John Pierson was at the top of his class. What's more, he had achieved the highest average—96.1—in the school's 226-year history. "In the gigantic gathering sat the young man's father," the *Evening Register* reported, "and the envying eyes of hundreds of other fathers were turned on him, as the president made the announcement. The father's eyes glistened as he heard the president's words, and witnessed the glances directed at him by the assembled sons of Yale."

Mentors and classmates predicted that John Pierson would become president. Long afterward, at the urging of a Norwegian mystic, he contemplated a dark horse run for the office to raise the tone of political discourse. But there were also, among his fellow Yale Phi Beta Kappas, those who referred to him as "Poor Johnny" Pierson and didn't take him seriously, feeling he lacked some crucial admixture of grit or mettle: sand, perhaps. While he won the class vote for "most brilliant" and "most scholarly," he ran a distant third in "most likely to succeed" and got no votes at all for "most popular."

John Herman Groesbeck Pierson went on to get his PhD in economics at Yale and to dedicate himself to utopian ideas: a theory of government-sponsored full employment that attracted a number of powerful adherents—Hubert Humphrey, for one—and then, as the political tides shifted, no adherents at all; a project to restore the Greek island of Syros by planting eighteen thousand trees, which the local goats immediately began to veto. But he never quite realized the heroic promise of his youth. He was, as Fitzgerald describes Tom Buchanan's career at Yale in *The Great Gatsby*, "one of those men who reach such an acute limited excellence at twenty-one that everything afterward savours of anti-climax."

My mother, and her mother before her, liked to say that Grandpa John's later frustrations flowed from a single head-waters: his rejection by Skull and Bones, the Yale secret society that "tapped" fifteen juniors each year. These were, in theory, the best and most promising men in the class (the society didn't admit women until 1992), men who would go on to form the backbone of Brown Brothers Harriman, Simpson Thacher & Bartlett, and the CIA. They spent Thursday nights their senior year meeting in a windowless Tomb to discuss their lives and sexual histories, forming a lifelong bond. John, whose father had been a Bonesman, was considered a shoo-in, and he turned down another secret society, awaiting the slap on the shoulder that never came.

When Grandpa Ted was blackballed from the Pittsburgh Golf Club, which Ted's parents and grandparents had belonged to, it shocked Ted and Jess and provoked stricken speculation about who could have done such a thing (Collie Burgwin, perhaps?). The rejection even shocked my father, at ten: what was wrong with his father? Bones was a considerably more charmed circle than the Pittsburgh Golf Club, its verdict utterly definitive. When my great-uncle Wassa Robinson called home to say he'd been tapped, his father, a Bonesman himself, burst into tears and cried throughout the conversation.

When Wassa was dying, his Bones classmates, including Justice Potter Stewart, gathered from all over to toast him at a lunch at the Yale Club. One of those men, Harold Turner—a longtime Georgica Association member whose son, Harold Jr., was the tennis pro there after John Thornton—wrote Wassa beforehand to say how much their conversations over the years had meant to him. "There are very few people who are willing to give us a real listen, not strangers, certainly not acquaintances, not even good friends as a regular matter, not even *family* sometimes," he said. "But a good clubmate by virtue of the original nature of the experience of the association will. He's been bred to it by the experience. And what, Dingleman"—Wassa's Bones nickname—"is more precious in this world than someone who will listen?"

As Ron Rosenbaum wrote in an *Esquire* article, "The Last Secrets of Skull and Bones":

> *The Bones experience can be intense enough to work real transformations. Idle, preppie Prince Hals suddenly become serious students of society and themselves, as if acceptance into the tomb were a signal to leave the tavern and prepare to rule the land. Those embarrassed at introspection and afraid of trusting other men are given the mandate and the confidence to do so.*
>
> *"Why," said one source, "do old men—seventy and over—travel thousands of miles for Bones reunions? Why do they sing the songs with such gusto? Where else can you hear Archibald MacLeish take on Henry Luce in a soul-versus-capital debate with no holds barred? Bones survives because the old men who are successful need to convince themselves that not luck or wealth put them where they are, but raw talent, and a talent that was recognized in their youth."*

Deep in the Wasp grain is a longing for such transformative acceptance. The Massachusetts Bay Colony, which demanded letters of recommendation for doubtful immigrants and exiled misbehaving members to other colonies or back to England, was itself a kind of club, and many Wasps still believe, not always consciously, that one's whole life is preparation for admission to a similar club—to *the* club, wherever it may be.

Hence the Wasp's circumspection, his excessive civility. Sixty years ago, the social chronicler Cleveland Amory observed that to be club material at Harvard one must demonstrate "a healthy respect for the observation of Harvard's social taboos. These taboos have always included, among other things, over-careful dress, undue athletic exertion, serious literary endeavor, rah-rah spirit, long hair, grades above C, and Radcliffe girls." In other words, one should stifle all curiosity or enthusiasm; achievement itself, because distinctive, is threatening. The nail that stands up must be hammered down. This way of thinking turns all sins into sins of etiquette: an off-color joke and murder both suggest poor breeding.

I didn't understand much of this when I was young. I just knew that Grandpa John never spoke of Yale, while his brother, Wilson, spoke of nothing but. When I was seventeen I spent a rainy afternoon with Wilson in his study—after we'd lunched on Welsh rarebit at Mory's, Yale's dining club—listening to his patient, cogent, urgent explanation of why I should come to New Haven: the superb teaching, of course, but also Yale's rarefied, character-molding vigor. (When Wilson retired, in 1973, Letty composed a poem that began "Yale for breakfast. Yale for dinner. / Yale the loser. Yale the winner. / Yale's my pain. Yale's my joy. / Yale's my man. Yale's my boy.") The Robinson family, too, was not rational on the topic, and Grandpa Ted, having twice been kicked out of Yale, was so loyal to it that he told my father he'd pay his way anywhere but Harvard. Such conviction partook of the sacramental. So I always admired Uncle Pad, who went his own way to Harvard—and, going my own way likewise, I followed him to Cambridge.

THE ONLY person who seemed to know what I should be doing at Harvard was my freshman adviser, John Marquand. John was a midlevel administrator who was multifariously involved in college life as secretary of the faculty and of the administrative board and senior tutor of an undergraduate house. A balding man with heavy black glasses and a high, quick voice, he didn't hurry to straighten out any confusion with the late novelist John P. Marquand, his distant relative, and presented himself as if he'd been born standing in Harvard Yard, a telamon in its marble frieze. John's arch, donnish air somehow suited his enormous frame: a ravenous gourmand, he weighed easily three hundred pounds, even in the thick of one of his futile diets. Perhaps as a consequence of his visibility—you could pick him out from a distance, motoring along in his old gray Chevy Impala or slue-footing slowly across the Yard, carrying two canvas tote bags filled with memos and minutes—he was unusually watchful, keeping his arms close to him even when he shook hands, curling the palm upward and giving a fractional nod of greeting and assessment.

Most freshmen were advised by their entryway proctors, but each year John selected a dozen young men to mentor (he had no interest in women at all). He took them to restaurants like Locke-Ober and Durgin Park, where he urged them to try the Indian pudding, and told them where to buy sport coats and how to circumvent the foreign-language requirement. He wasn't overly concerned with making sure you studied, believing that the cream of college life—what would afterward rise in memory—wasn't academic. John's good friend Peter Gomes, the minister at Harvard's Memorial Church, says, "His advisees turned out to be Marquandites. They had a nose for wine, learned to like shad roe, understood the essential differences between gossip and conversation—John approved of both, but he understood the difference—and were, in the best sense, obsessed with people. You could never tell John too much about anybody."

I found out later that John came from Berwick, Pennsylvania, the son of a small-town doctor who drank and a housewife who was often too depressed to make dinner. John would spend his days at the cemetery with a store of books, lying stretched out on a stone marker, then take his younger sister, Ellen, to Bennett's restaurant and advise her on the menu. He attended Wesleyan, and then never quite secured his PhD in medieval history at Harvard. John seemed to view these details as irrelevant, as perhaps they were.

After we got to know each other, John told me that my admissions interview the year before had almost sunk me. "I looked at your file," he said. "The phrase I recall is 'Applicant seems to have lockjaw.'" He giggled. "What on earth did you say?"

I felt myself flushing. "I was trying to explain why I went to Shipley, when it had only begun taking boys a few years earlier, and I think I quoted Frost: 'Two roads diverged in a yellow wood . . . ' and so on." I had been rather pleased with myself about that.

"Oh, dear," he said. "Frost? Oh, dear."

Underneath the gossip and the teasing he was a well-wisher. When I came across Cardinal Newman's definition of a gentleman, it called John to mind:

> *His benefits may be considered as parallel to what are called comforts or conveniences in arrangements of a personal nature: like an easy-chair or a good fire, which do their part in expelling cold and fatigue . . . [the true gentleman] carefully avoids whatever may cause a jar or a jolt in the minds of those with whom he is cast; all clashing of opinion, or collision of feeling; all restraint, or suspicion, or gloom, or resentment; his great concern being to make everyone at their ease and at home.*

John would pick out two or three of his advisees and coach them so that they made a mark in the precincts of undergraduate life he valued, particularly the clubs. (He even gave a friend of mine *Debrett's Etiquette and Modern Manners* to assist with the final smoothing.) He had pondered the realms of concentric exclusion, and one night at Locke-Ober he dryly recited for me the doggerel "A Boston Toast":

> *And this is good old Boston,*
> *The home of the bean and the cod,*
> *Where the Lowells talk to the Cabots*
> *And the Cabots talk only to God.*

The summer after my freshman year, John wrote to urge that I comp for the *Lampoon:* "I think you would find its atmosphere not insalubrious, and it might help you get rid of that lockjaw that you don't have." And so, in the fall, I did. There was a cocktail party to mark the first cut of the candidates, and I was surprised to see John at the castle in black tie, clasping a bottle of Rebel Yell. He wasn't much of a drinker, but he always arrived with a gift, then when the dancing began upstairs, took his solitary leave. Later, when I was elected to the Signet, a literary and arts society wryly known as "the final club for women and Jews," I saw him regularly there, too, lunching with Peter Gomes and Dean of Students Archie Epps. Gomes and Epps, who were black, were sometimes referred to as "Afro-Saxons" because of their bow ties and mysteriously British accents, and all three stepped in as spare men at dinner parties. "We were young fogeys," Peter Gomes says, "three from away who each wrested a certain kind of power, the power of knowledge of the place and its rules, when nobody else from our generation gave a fig. We saw ourselves as defenders of the faith: in favor of civility, manners, a slower pace. We (too uncritically) believed in the Harvard aristocracy, the thin crimson line, and we upheld the Yankee code of rectitude better than the dissolute Yankees who remained."

Marquand was more taken than Gomes and Epps by the clubs and the *Lampoon,* and used his friendships with undergraduates to maintain his invitations. Though he didn't emerge from the closet until later, he was gay, of course, and intrigued by the clubs' sublimated homoeroticism, that male bond (though he never, as far as I know, behaved inappropriately with an undergraduate). His longing for a world barred to him by age, weight, and position contributed to my sense that Harvard never requited the love he gave it.

DURING A postgraduate *Wanderjahr* circling the globe, Grandpa John always climbed the local peaks and monuments, a steeplejack in quest of the definitive vantage that had eluded him. He summitted the Matterhorn, as Charles Pierson had done, and wrote his father afterward to describe how he and some friends began the climb before dawn, "rocks sheer and unbelievably high above you; yourself hanging to the brink of space with hobnails and finger-nails and eyelashes." He noted that the guide had "decided that because we were Americans we were probably in pretty good shape and could make it all right. He says that he never would have taken a couple of young Germans or Frenchmen up under similar circumstances."

In Uttar Pradesh, John killed a tiger with a single bullet. Then he returned home to pursue Timmy Robinson, a gorgeous, large-hearted, headstrong debutante known to some in the Pierson family as "the Hartford Butterfly." She wore her pearls flung down her back, marcelled her hair and tied it in a bun at the nape of her neck—thereby achieving the modern "bobbed" look without having to cut her wonderful tresses—and once, after her mother bought her several ball dresses for a deb party, came downstairs to meet her two escorts dressed, instead, in the lining of an old coat. Mom loved that story.

Timmy had rejected John's first proposal, before he left, but he pressed his suit—already balding, smitten, determined—and she yielded at last. Their wedding in 1930, attended by four hundred of the great from Biarritz, Paris, and Park Avenue, was an event: the union of brains with a beauty whose foamy velvet train made her appear like Aphrodite rising from the sea.

When Grandma Tim gave birth to my mother at New Haven Hospital, in 1933, Grandpa John stayed at the curb with the chauffeur, smoking a cigar. And that, essentially, is where he remained. His signature bit of fatherly business was crawling beneath the rug made from the skin of his tiger and growling at Mom and Paddy. He called her Weenie, sometimes rhyming it "Weenie, weenie, little wahine." He had been to Hawaii and seen the wahines, the women surfers, and would later live in Oahu. There was always a restlessness. After Pier was born, Grandma Tim told Mom, "It's too bad John couldn't really enjoy the babies and the nursing and all that, give over to it. Oh, he thought you children were *great*, but there was something about it—something he couldn't let himself feel. Whatever else, you've got to see that your children *love* each other. John and Wilson certainly didn't."

In September of 1938, when my mother was not quite five, her father vanished. She was vacationing with her parents at Century House when John left a note for Timmy saying merely that he did not love her. I would learn about this only in my late twenties, one summer weekend in Georgica, when Mom mentioned it with a toss of her head and a little shiver.

Days after John left the beach house without warning, the

hurricane of '38 hit it, also without warning. Known as "the Storm of the Century," the hurricane killed six hundred people and destroyed ten thousand houses across Long Island and New England. My mother watched from an upstairs window as the sea surged over Georgica Pond and battered the front porch. There was a violent crash: a shutter outside the middle guest room had banged free and smashed its window, and the suck of inrushing air thrust the guest room door through its own frame and into the hall. (Afterward, Wilson removed all the shutters, which are still stacked in the back of the garage.) Taking this as a signal to depart, Wilson shepherded Letty and Goggy and Timmy and Mom and Paddy and Baba and the three majestics—ten people in all—out the side door and into a Buick 8. Goggy Pierson carefully slipped on her rubber-tipped shoes and then stepped off the side entrance into water up to her shins. (Over the years, as Mom told the story, the water rose to Goggy's hip.) As Grandma Tim ducked into the car, a whipping rosebush raked her face, drawing blood. The road out was swamped, so they drove two hundred yards to the marginally higher ground of the softball field and waited. Only after the floodwaters had lapped above the running boards did the wind finally relent.

Grandpa John remained incommunicado for a year. It turned out that after a lifetime of counting stairs obsessively, he had suffered a nervous breakdown and had been seeing a Freudian analyst four days a week. He came home, but the marriage continued to founder. Grandma Tim went to the analyst's office and pressed him for a prognosis. Annoyed at his reticence, she began to grimace and roll her eyes, and he said, "Stop making those faces." "*You* ought to be analyzed!"

she replied spiritedly. He explained that he had been, of course, during his training. Finally, in response to her pressing inquiries, he declared, "Your husband is incurable," whereupon she stripped off one of her gloves and threw it in his face. Then she moved to Woodstock to be near her friends the McDills, where she stripped off her wedding ring and threw it under the porch of her rented house. She had a gift for gesture.

The split led, awkwardly, to new unions. Timmy decided to marry Tom Bourne, who lived at Maplewood Farm, but she let her children know only the day before the wedding, and then only because Letty Pierson told her that she must. John remarried, too, and informed Mom and Paddy later by letter ("We think it would be fine if you could run down to New York and have lunch with us a week from today"). His new wife was Sherleigh Glad, a fierce slip of a woman who had a Virginia Slims perpetually drooping from her lip. I always liked her because she sent me arresting quotations from obscure books. But she hated sharing her husband, at least once trying to throw herself down the stairs before relatives arrived. At one point in the mid-1980s, Mom drew her father aside in his Greenwich apartment to suggest a visit to Pennsylvania. Sherleigh, ear cocked on the landing above, called down, "That would be impossible, John!" That line became another touchstone for us, invoked—in a rackety, cigarette-scorched voice—to rebuff Mom's suggestions. Sherleigh was the kind of person you might marry in penance.

In the years following, Mom and Paddy suffered under Tom Bourne's hectoring impatience and looked longingly at an austere photo of their father they each kept in their rooms at Maplewood. But they saw him only infrequently. When asked in seventh grade to write her autobiography, my mother did it in rhyme: "For I was born within that month [October] / My father grew the haughter / When he found I was not his son / But only an inferior daughter." Poetry tapped her well of loneliness. As a junior in high school, she wrote "The Damned," about the poor; it was rejected by *Seventeen* magazine, and, given the magazine's charter of practical pep, one can see why:

> *Where do they go?*
> *Home to their flats with the tired paint*
> *And sagging walls and bad smells?*
> *No —*
> *They walk the streets forever,*
> *Sinking lower and lower into the ceaselessness*
> *Of their barren and*
> *Gray lives.*

Trying to get to know her father, Mom wrote him after college to ask whether she might stay with him and Sherleigh for a year in Bangkok, where he was chief economist at ECAFE, a UN commission intended to help Asian countries into prosperity. His reply was a wan rehearsal of the pros and cons that concluded: "The fact that it makes sense for me to accept the various risks involved in coming here is no indication that you should. For me it grew naturally out of a series of past events and just couldn't be avoided, really. But each of us has his own unique track of experience; they're non-negotiable and non-transferable. You have to look at it in your own private perspective. — Daddy."

She went ahead anyway, with her college friend Elsa Barr, buying a round-the-world ticket on Pan Am and planning to teach English to Thai businessmen. Their postcard from Japan confirming their flight never arrived and then their plane was late, and Grandpa John, vexed, greeted her at the Bangkok airport by saying, "You know, I'm not going to be able to spend much time with you this year." A half century later, Elsa could still recall the look on Mom's face.

It was a hard year. Sherleigh was sometimes missing at dinner, but when John didn't remark on her absences, neither Mom nor Elsa dared inquire. Their room had mosquito netting draped across an open doorway, and they'd sometimes wake in the night to see Sherleigh ghosting by in a white nightgown. Finally Mom asked Som, their head servant, about it, and she explained, "Liquor bottle full at night. Liquor bottle empty in morning." Then there were lugubrious UN parties and lectures from John at dinner about development economics. "It was all very impersonal," Elsa says. "The only really fun dinner was when a gecko fell from the ceiling onto John's head and then fell into the soup, and I don't even think he laughed at that."

Where Wilson had command presence, John believed himself deserving of command but was diffident about seizing it. He had a dry sense of humor; a friend of my mother's remarked that John and Mom and I all had the same speech pattern: staccato blur, brief pause, staccato blur again, with the whimsical line buried in passing. But he was always touchy about his dignity. When he retired, in 1966, he wrote a "Note on My Decision to Leave the United Nations Secretariat" to inform his family and posterity what had gone amiss:

I had maintained from the beginning that it was an essential condition for the success of the Advisory Committee on the Application of Science and Technology to Development that the Committee's Secretary should have the so-called D-2 rank. That was the issue on which I resigned three years later. . . . [Also] it was, frankly, disconcerting to witness repeated promotions of other staff members . . . and yet be unable to obtain promotion oneself in spite of periodically receiving unusually high official evaluations of one's work. This personal factor, coupled with the impersonal one, began to create in me an obsessive interest in the promotion question which I did not want to see develop farther.

For decades, Grandpa John fought to keep alive the theory of full employment, which had made his name in the 1940s. His letters to publishing houses grew increasingly stiff-necked yet beseeching, and in the early nineties he threatened to sue *Greenwich Time* because it trimmed two lines from his op-ed piece on the topic. He finally asked me if I wanted to write his life up in a book titled *Long Battle for an Idea*. Guiltily, pleading my own restless youth, I declined.

In retirement, he also began planting trees on land he and Paddy had bought on Syros, hoping to restore its mythic lushness. The project bewildered the locals, who whispered that he must be manning a CIA listening station. In 1973 he published *Island in Greece* about the effort. Its first 136 pages were a meticulous account of the search for suitable land, for translators, for the right fixer in the Greek bureaucracy, etc. Only on the last page did the first trees go into the ground. It was, perhaps, a depressive's way of making manifest all the obstacles he had always had to face, as well as an economist's way of forestalling the suspicion that he was, deep down, a hopeless romantic.

I WAS elected to the *Lampoon* the fall of my sophomore year, largely because of my parody of one of those plucky–Little Leaguer tales. With nine other compers I was suddenly haled into Phools Week, a round-the-clock initiation period. We quickly bonded over the miseries of being hazed, which included, in my case, having to perform a striptease at Lamont Library as I sang "Another One Bites the Dust." We often had to drop to our knees and recite our Phools Name, a filthy limerick, and I remember the delight with which the members made me chant mine to John Marquand:

> *My name, Sir, is, Sir, Phool Friend.*
> *My head's wedged up some fat man's rear end.*
> *But I'm used to the smell*
> *And I eat awfully well.*
> *How I dig that intestinal blend.*

John laughed heartily. But the members were onto the hearty laugh; while most of them liked having him around as an authority-figure-cum-mascot, they also flaunted their knowledge of his need for acceptance. One of the skits we performed for John and the members on the final night was a Phools Week perennial called "The Gravitational 'Quand." The burliest of the Phools, Steve Bernheim, played John, and the rest of us played compers at a *Lampoon* cocktail party, whom Bernheim greeted one by one in John's fastidious manner: "I trust you're having a good time?"

"No," we said in turn, "the party sucks!"

Bernheim roared with belly-quaking laughter, the force of which sucked his interlocutor into Marquand's body—and so forth, until all ten of us were one giant 'Quand. It wasn't very funny, nor was it really intended to be; the *Lampoon* prided itself on meanness couched as fearless candor. Everyone was subject to it, but when I think of John's game giggle, I still feel a prickle of shame.

We had been told, early in the week, that there was a second election held by the graduate members and that only those of us who demonstrated a grasp of the organization's deeper purpose would become members and be admitted to the secret rooms upstairs. Not all of us would make it. Graduate members began drifting in and eyeing us coolly, and on Wednesday night they held Inquisitions. We were taken one at a time into a small room lit by a single candle, and told to kneel before it. As my eyes adjusted, I saw that I was surrounded by some twenty graduate and undergraduate members on couches and chairs. They began asking rapid-fire questions such as "Where does laughter come from?" and "Why is the tragedy of life a comedy?" After about half an hour, my chief inquisitor announced that I could go—but only after giving the name of the Phool, excluding myself, who was least worthy of election.

Later, when I was a member, I watched Phools refuse to sell anyone out even after they were assured that no one cared how they came up with the name—it could be random, it could be alphabetical, we just need a name. During the wait you would hear people smoking, sighing theatrically, pissing in beer bottles. Eventually, though sometimes not for an hour or two, every Phool would cave and then stand, painfully, and go collect his things, avoiding eye contact with the remaining Phools as he left.

It took me no more than ten seconds to say, "Phool Bernheim." Steve Bernheim had been a pain all week. He was surly and aggressive and he bridled when asked to perform humiliating skits—defiance that only made the members mad at the rest of us. Worst of all, he kept telling us that the second election was obviously a hoax, a big joke, and that we ought to just walk out of the Castle and go have lunch somewhere and see what they'd do. So it was clear to me that Doubting Steve didn't belong.

I'd like to report that I went up to Steve later, after we'd both made it on, and told him I'd given his name at my Inquisition, and apologized, and he'd grinned and said, "You know what? I gave *your* name!" and then we'd cracked up and become great friends. In truth, I avoided him. It wasn't so much that I had betrayed him, because I felt then that he was betraying the rest of us. It was that he reminded me how eager I was to be of service, to be accepted whatever the cost.

Bruce was not among the new members. He'd sold $1,000 worth of ads, but the magazine hadn't tallied his sales correctly, so he was rejected by mistake. At least, that was the official story I got when I asked about it later. But I wondered, after I got to know how the place operated, whether Bruce's desire had disqualified him. It worked out better at the *Lampoon*—as at any club—if you didn't need it, if you didn't seem to care.

By then Bruce and I had begun to grow apart, and I was increasingly at the magazine, where people hung out for hours with their legs flung over the arm of a chair, asking ostentatiously mannered questions like "Anybody got a serrated knife?" One party that spring, the Sexual Depravity Dinner, featured hash and coke and a stripper who arrived, surveyed the shattered plates and lobster carcasses, and walked out. The son of a Wall Street financier brought as his date a camel on a leash, its leathery mouth pinked with lipstick. I didn't know then about such Gilded Age parties as Mrs. Stuyvesant Fish's Monkey Dinner or Mrs. C. K. G. Billings's Horseback Dinner, but I dimly sensed that the camel was a harbinger of what could lie ahead—that we were anticipating, with our wit and wealth and decadence, a certain kind of adult misery.

The *Lampoon* left me quicker, funnier, and more defensive, perhaps not the qualities I needed to sharpen, much as I loved the place, and much as I valued the sense it gave me of having potential. (Whenever I hear a song from our party tape—"ABC" or "The Love You Save" or "Crimson and Clover"—I feel suddenly springy.) I later read a remark by Kenneth Tynan that seemed apt: Oxford, he said, "removed something from me, something connected with my origins—and replaced it with a Rolls-Royce spare part. I gained speed and sophistication. I doubt if I shall ever know what I lost."

AFTER DAY proposed, in 1959, he sought the approval of his prospective father-in-law as the two men walked on the stony beach at the foot of Grandpa John's house in Riverside, Connecticut. Approval was forthcoming, but Grandpa John believed it his duty to mention that my mother had been rather indulged and might prove a disappointment. My father, who had some experience with disenchantment, said that that was all right.

Mom never felt indulged, of course; on the contrary. For the rest of her life, the hurricane of '38—and the entwined fear of abandonment—kept whirling through her thoughts. It was her primary organizing event. As a child she had frequent thrashing nightmares; as an adult, when she had a headache or felt bruised by a frank conversation, she dragged around in her nightgown looking wounded. She squirreled away leftovers of her favorite desserts—almond cake, lace cookies; anything Pier or I might otherwise scavenge—in a tin beneath her bed. All her life she lamented that she had never seen a full moon; when my father pointed one out, she would glance up and say, "No, not quite full." And she couldn't simply pass on a compliment: she insisted the exchange be a "TL," or "Trade-Last"; first, you had to dredge up a compliment someone had given *you* about *her*. She understood, intellectually, that people rarely vouchsafe a parental compliment to children—certainly we explained the point to her—but she remained hopeful nonetheless.

When Grandpa John was coming for a visit, Mom would bake for days and polish the silver until it reflected our scrubbed faces. On arrival, he'd hug us children gingerly, as if embraces were a foreign custom that had in all decency to be observed, and he and my father, each in his tweed jacket, would grip each other by the upper arms in a sort of Greco-Roman standoff. Then they would sit and talk politely, knowledgeably, about Zen. When Mom would say, "Do you remember how you used to walk into the surf on your hands?"

Grandpa John would look downcast. He'd forsworn hunting and become an enthusiastic conservationist, but when Day would mention the ibex horns nailed up in the Wainscott garage, one of John's youthful trophies, he would smile, hitch up his pants, and declare, "The three antelopes with trophy horns are the kudu, the ibex, and the Indian black buck." Then, just when you thought the spigot might open, he'd fall silent. His generation seemed to believe that intimacies, if any, should travel from young to old.

Mom always had a starched napkin ready for when the small talk really died. One of her happiest memories of childhood was how Grandpa John would fold a linen napkin into the shape of a mouse and, by flexing his forearm, make it scamper up his sleeve. "Now, Daddy," she would ask, as we looked on eagerly, "can you remember the mouse?" "I don't think so," he'd say, frowning as he bent the napkin this way and that and finally, doubtfully, placed the would-be rodent on his jacket sleeve. There it would sit until he twitched it aside with a cough.

Mom's dressing room in the Villanova house contained eleven photographs of Grandpa John. The hallway bureau upstairs showcased a photo of him in tropical khakis and a topee, crouched over his tiger with a rifle in his hands. Years later, Grandpa John would recall that on safari in India he had smelled a black bear before his guide, and that when their party got lost the following day, it was he who led them back to camp. "Those were two of the highest points in my life," he said. Perhaps because his face in the hunting photo was in shadow, you were encouraged to try to pick out prophetic marks of character. You could imagine that if the photographer had asked him to step into the light, everything would have fallen out differently. A few Christmases ago, my father said that if anyone wanted to take the Grandpa John photos away he'd be relieved.

In 1992, John Marquand was diagnosed with colon cancer. The disease galloped through him in seven months, thinning him out in a way whose irony he appreciated, even as he hated, at only fifty-one, to go. He destroyed the letters advisees and friends had written him seeking help with their problems, and then he planned his funeral, discussing where everyone should sit and ordering the wine as if for a particularly festive dinner party: "I think we'll have about three hundred people, so six cases should do, no?" Then he secretly stopped taking his anticoagulant medication, to hasten the end.

On John's last outing, Peter Gomes took him to where he would rest: the elite Harvard Corporation plot in Cambridge's Mount Auburn Cemetery. Peter had been able to secure John a place there only with great difficulty; finally, he says, Dean Henry Rosovsky told him, "John can have my spot. I'm not going in there with all those goyim." At his gravesite on Harvard Hill, John leaned on Peter's arm and observed with satisfaction that you could see straight through to the Lowell House steeple, and that he would be surrounded by the graves of such university luminaries as Christopher Columbus Langdell and George Alfred Leon Sarton. He was in the club at last.

TEN

Frost

WHEN WE WERE young it was eight hours by car from Buffalo or Swarthmore to Woodstock, journeys that felt heroic. Once we got close, crossing the covered bridge over the Ottauquechee, we'd sing "Almost There," a ditty that celebrated everyone we were about to see down to Mickle, the dachshund. Up the driveway we'd roar, honking, and Grandma Tim would charge out in a way I'd not see again until Addie, at eighteen months, began to do it when I came home: holding her arms wide and stamping her feet: stamp, stamp, stampstampstamp!

Grandma Tim was a carnival. Mom would sleep late at Maplewood, catching up, but we were down early to see what was going on. When you arrived at the table for Baba's Baptist cakes, Timmy would poke you with a hard-boiled egg and say, "Good morning, cornucopia, your face is looking soapier. I've been out to the flower garden and I'm sweating like a June bride, as my mother used to say—it's hotter than

Dutch love." Much of her conversation was scraps and tags that would have given a simultaneous translator fits: if she saw a wandering shrew or vole, she'd hail it with "Thar she blows, and sparm at that"; when skeptical, she'd scoff, "In a pig's valise!"; and when she wanted attention, she'd cry, "I am Sir Oracle, and when I ope my lips, let no dog bark."

She swam nude in her ponds, wore diamonds with Keds, decorated us with tippets and muffs and the contents of her "beadlet box"—a bounty of necklaces, stickpins, and tortoiseshell combs that all smelled faintly of nail polish remover. She had studied painting with Guy Pène du Bois, of New York's Ashcan School, and often spent the morning in her third-floor studio, working up abstract green black slashes or flappers doing the Charleston amid pasted-on biscotti wrappers. Then she'd attach the new canvas, along with a favorite postcard, to the bookshelves downstairs, turning the whole house into an atelier, a bricolage. She was not a surpassingly talented painter—daily life was her true medium—but her work had energy and it sold, often to her friends Mary and Laurance Rockefeller up the road, an elegant couple she called, jauntily, "the Rocks." She was pleased by the stir she caused at dinner there when she set an ear of corn to cool atop her water glass: "With the very rich," she said, "the most you can do is treat them to the pigpen."

After coming to Woodstock to await her divorce from Grandpa John, she'd fallen for the place, as Wasps who came for the piney air often did; in this respect the town was like a British hill station. As early as 1918, a newspaper editor in Swanton, farther upstate, characterized Woodstock as "the favored haunt of the idle rich and the gilded Gotham youth." Though Timmy was rather proud of having been dropped from the *Social Register* in 1944—the *Register* took it amiss when she married Tom Bourne (who was not in the book) without having informed it that she had divorced Grandpa John (who was)—she belonged to New York's exclusive Colony Club and remained very much a Robinson in her self-possession and prankish spirits. Following Timmy's parents' wedding in Utica, in 1905, a cousin recalled later, "Many of us went thence to New York on the same train as the bride and groom and in the same car, though John"—John Robinson, the groom—"strongly advised our taking another train. John bribed the porter to let him and the bride off at the front of the car and make the rest of us get off at the rear end so that they could get a flying start."

One winter's day when I was eleven, I was tossing a balsa wood plane around in Grandma Tim's studio, bored, when she put her brush down and said, "I have an idea." She laid a slick of Elmer's on the plane's wings, then sent me down for juice glasses so we could trap the flies buzzing on the windows. The plan was to glue to the plane a squadron of flies whose wing beats would lift it into the air. It turns out to be surpassingly difficult to get a fly to settle on a glue trap, let alone convince a group of them to beat their wings in unison. But the project took care of her fly problem for a while.

She noticed how children were feeling. When Jane Smith was twelve and my mother fourteen, they were slumped in the McDills' living room one day, round shouldered and lank haired and glum. Grandma Tim marched them to the mirror and said, "Girls! Look at yourselves! You are absolutely beautiful. Put your shoulders back, and your head up, posture!" Her own grandmother was famous for never having let her spine touch the back of a chair. Timmy took out her lipstick and made up their lips. Assaying her handiwork, she pulled their shoulders back again and said, *"Bustes en avant!"* Mom and Jane giggled, not having any *bustes* to speak of but aware now of what to do when they did.

Occasionally, a melancholy mood would overtake Timmy, and after dinner she would strike up "The Whiffenpoof Song," which Grandpa John had so often sung:

> *We're little black sheep*
> *Who have gone astray:*
> *Baa! Baa! Baa!*
> *Gentlemen songsters off on a spree,*
> *Damned from here to eternity;*
> *God have mercy on such as we*
> *Baa! Baa! Baa!*

TIMMY AND Tom together were a great puzzle. When not painting and gardening and playing paddle tennis, Timmy lived a life of *noblesse oblige*, teaching art at the Woodstock jail and working for liberal causes. She wrote a letter to the *New York Times* opposing the Vietnam War that began, "Perhaps the American people will not become aroused until they have been bombed themselves." Where Timmy could orchestrate her giddiness, deploying it to create entrances and exits, Tom would sniff an apple and already be gnawing it, unawares. As a wrestler at the Taft School, he was known as "Man Mountain Bourne," and later in life his bad hips seemed only to fuel his powers as he bent over his blowtorch, spot-welding a new cotter pin. He was Hephaestus, the god of fire, whose forge triggers volcanoes. When I was six, one summer morning over breakfast, I waved at Tom from the porch as he chugged up the drive on his tractor, but he never looked over, keeping his gaze fixed uphill. Timmy laughed and explained to my father, "It's not manly! I learned that a long time ago. It's not manly to look at the *house;* you look at the barn and the *fields.*"

When I was thirteen, I remember Tom shaking my leg at five a.m. to roust me to drive the cows in. When I tried to dive back into my dream, he said, "What's the *matter* with you? Men don't sleep in." Once I was up, there was a pleasure in the daybreak, mist rising off the willows Tom had planted round the ponds, the cows snatching mouthfuls of clover as they jostled downhill to the barn. Afterward, Tom took me to the garden and said, optimistically, "We can get these on-ions weeded in jig time." (His favorite thing, he once told his grandson Brett, was being on his knees in his garden.) Two minutes later, he looked over from the tornado path he'd harrowed and roared, "If we had to eat what *you* grew we'd starve to death!"

He had a genius for making you feel first neglected, then small. Nicki Bourne, the youngest of his three children, re-calls that when she was seven, "He took me down to the end of a plowed field. I remember that I was barefoot. Then he said, 'I'm going to be living with another family' "—Timmy and her children—" 'so I won't be with you anymore.' He left me there and went and talked with the farmer nearby, not at all upset. When he came back, I was still crying." He neglected to mention these new arrangements to his older daughter, Nan, who didn't speak to him for two years.

When Nicki was accepted to the Boston Conservatory of Music, Tom told her no, she wasn't a singer. If she really wanted an education, she should work to put herself through college. So she began work at nineteen as a file clerk, making thirty-two dollars a week, and within a year Tom was arranging for her abortion after she got pregnant by a much older man. In the end, Nicki neither went to college nor became a singer.

His son, Tom Jr., says, "I kept away from my father for about thirty years—whenever we got close, I had to end up doing what he wanted me to. When his friends who owned the Yankee Bookshop in town wanted to sell it, he got hold of me and said, 'We'll buy it and you'll come here and run it.' I said, 'There's a difference between loving to read and running a bookstore.' He said, 'No, there isn't—that's the stupidest thing I ever heard!' " Tom was the sort of man the Japanese have in mind when they say there are four fearsome things: Earthquake, Thunder, Fire, and Father.

Yet it was clear from the way he and Timmy clasped hands over cocktails that they loved each other passionately. Tom had broken with his first wife, also named Gertrude, when he'd met Timmy in Woodstock. In private he called Timmy "Mother," which was peculiar, as they had no children together, but his tributes to his "darling consort" remained fervent, particularly when she'd leave Woodstock in the winter to visit her former mother-in-law, Goggy Pierson, in New York. On the one extended trip Tom took without her, in 1970, he wrote home constantly: "I got to thinking of you so in bed that I had to get up and write. Life is mundane and commonplace—really feckless—without you! You are my life. You give me strength and purpose and manhood. You are everything to me. I just had to say these things, dearest. My beloved. Your loving husband." She expressed her love more whimsically, once remarking, as they left a restaurant and passed an iron pillar in the foyer, "Don't pee on the lamppost, Tom." You mostly can't imagine your older relations having sex, fortunately, but with Timmy and Tom you could.

TIMMIE, PIER, and I loved hanging around with Nicki Bourne's daughters from her first marriage: Anne Greene, a placid girl a few years older than I, and her lively younger sister, Lizz. We would all play hide-and-seek in the hayloft of the Golden Cow barn, leaping the manhole-sized gaps in the floorboards, then go for a canter on their horses, Pistol and Parsley. In the afternoon, when we went swimming, our stepcousins would work for Tom, hoisting hundred-pound sacks of grain and feeling jealous of our ease, as Nicki had once been jealous of our mother.

Timmy paid for Lizz's flute lessons and pottery and theater classes, and she'd remind Anne to stand up straight and keep her chin out. Function follows form—*bustes en avant!* But from Timmy's remarks about Nicki's second husband, who was missing a few teeth—"She won't need to buy a jack-o'-lantern at Halloween"—and from the way she'd dance away from Anne and Lizz while whistling "Hoo hoo," it was slowly borne in on me that she viewed these efforts as necessary stopgaps, and that we and they were on diverging roads. We would leave and go to college, and they would stay and have children young.

Such decisions came down to money and expectations. Because of the force of Tom's hugs, real breath-squeezers, it was hard to imagine him losing a battle. But as I got older I began to see that he and Timmy had a kind of morganatic marriage: Timmy wrote the checks and held the purse strings, and she and Tom often had door-slamming fights about expenditures, usually after she'd told him to "Forget it!" about a new tractor, or he'd bought a new tractor anyway on the sly. She believed that Maplewood should be a gentleman's farm, particularly as no one was making a go of dairy farming: in 1960, Woodstock had twenty-eight commercially operated dairy farms; by 1982, only nine.

But Tom had dreams. He had been a successful salesman in Boston, earning $10,000 a year during the Depression and sending his older two children to Milton—and then he'd uprooted his family to buy Maplewood in 1940 and be a landed patriarch, to stand for something. Or rather, he'd uprooted his family and had his first wife buy Maplewood, with her inheritance (he and Timmy later bought her out). Tom would tell his granddaughter Anne, rather proudly, that he'd never handled money his whole life.

Tom saw himself as a man of ideas and believed his innovations would eventually enable him to expand his operations to a kingly thousand acres, giving him the largest and most profitable farm in Vermont. To that end he spent whatever came into his hands: after the new milking parlor and the silage trench, there was the English method of tilling fields and the introduction of round bales (which occasionally began rolling downhill at high speed), and on and on, each innovation certain to reverse the farm's fortunes. I believed it all: he had such confidence, or bluster, anyway. He devised an ingenious belt relay to transport hay from his wagons into the Golden Cow barn's hayloft, then used his bench grinder and blowtorch to weld the necessary parts from scrap. Once in action, the cables broke, the hitches broke, the pulleys broke, and finally the thimbles broke. "None of these was terribly serious, indicating a fault in the idea," he wrote afterward. "The only indication was that the installation was imperfect." Tom was so impatient to try his jerry-rigged tools that he wouldn't even drop his face shield when welding, a habit that burned out his retinas.

As his funds dwindled, Tom turned from dreams of expansion to dreams of auction. Once Timmy's mother died, in 1969, after years of dementia, Tom began selling Timmy chunks of the place that she paid for with her inheritance, beginning with the best 128 acres, which included the house and bottomlands. Then he looked for other investors. My father says, "In the late seventies Tom wanted me to put all the money we had into buying his back land. He was extolling its virtues, saying, 'It'll make you rich, richer.' Tom had this galling assumption that I already was rich." My parents decided to pass. "What I didn't fully understand was that Tom already needed money again. Mom and I began to see him as a kind of massive parasite."

MY FIRST memory of stout, pinkish John Harcourt McDill is of him propping *King Lear* on his chest as we and the Smiths were all reading Shakespeare together one summer, taking the speeches in turn. " 'As flies to wanton boys are we to the gods; they kill us for their sport,' " he declaimed—then laughed with pleasure: "Oh, marvelous!"

Though John wept at the 1812 Overture, his favorite poet was the flinty Robert Frost. We were always meeting up with the Smith girls at PineApple Hill or Line Farm, and though it was our vacation, John would school us in enjoyment by having us read poems aloud and focus on the punctuation, on seemingly transparent phrases such as "before I sleep," and on the vital, linchpin words. When I began "Fire and Ice," he raised his hand. "Don't mumble—read it out, now!" he cried. " 'Some say the world will end in *fire*'—this is about the end of the world!"

Eighth in line to be the Earl of Harcourt, John grew up well-bred but not well-off in Manila, where his father was posted as a doctor, and he tutored rich students to put himself through Yale. Mom loved to talk about how he went on to be a brilliant English teacher there, a Cleanth Brooks in the making. And then, in 1935—her voice would drop, as if, half a mile up the road, he might overhear—John had a nervous breakdown, and with his wife, Julia, retreated to her parents' former summerhouse in Woodstock.

John and his classmate John Pierson were the Barbaro and Charismatic of their age, fragile, mettlesome thoroughbreds who ate up the track before snapping an ankle. But where Grandpa John got back in the race, John McDill remained in Woodstock, sustained by his wife's money. Julia Lee McDill was a descendant of Frederick Billings, the first lawyer in San Francisco during the gold rush, and the family had considerable land in the Woodstock area, including a private nine-hole golf course.

None of the Smiths ever spoke of John's breakdown to us (or even among themselves). And John hardly seemed a shattered recluse: he was president of the Woodstock Winter Sports Association, the Woodstock Country Club, and the local Norman Williams Public Library; a board member of countless other organizations; and a member of the Bridgewater Cellar Hole Club, whose other two members joined him in tramping the woods to map every pioneer cellar hole in the Bridgewater area.

It was all in the admirable Wasp tradition of public service, of the committee for beautification, the panel on good government, the anonymous gift. John did much of this pro bono work alongside his wife, who personally introduced birth control to Vermont, delivering brown-wrapped books on the topic from her Nash Touring car to women in the backwoods. A Yankee who wore a cotton scarf on her head, churned her own butter, and pulled her groceries home from Gillingham's on a sled during the war, to save gas, Julia McDill was often mistaken for a farmer's wife.

John was never mistaken for a farmer. He could type with his eyes shut; was a graceful dancer and loved to call square dances—"Now dive for the oyster, dive!"; made perfect corned-beef hash, flipping it only once; was a beautiful, slow swimmer, backstroking around the island in the pond at Line, his stomach shining whitely like a tiny arctic kingdom; and loved to putter down to Maplewood on his tractor bearing a single tomato ("to-mah-to") from his garden. A Yankee friend of Grandma Tim's who'd seen John gazing at the horizon and very slowly rubbing one of his tomatoes on his shirt sleeve tartly remarked, "It says a lot about a man if he's got time to polish a tomato."

John was charming, though he'd have balked at the word: Wasps admire attractiveness and courtesy but mistrust personal charm, any striving to conciliate. A sort of Thoreau with money, he felt that his talent was for pastoral appreciation. Yet Mom and Grandma Tim, who loved John, would shake their heads about the waste of him. They had a lingering belief in a Calvinist "calling"—the idea that the elect are called by God not only to perform their duties as Christians, but to use their gifts in the world. Wasps have a horror of being at loose ends, believing you could at least be doing needlepoint. (When a Wasp happens on a friend playing tennis or golf, his jovial, cutting remark is invariably along the lines of "Don't you ever work?")

I wondered if John's true calling might have been for serving as a whetstone. He wrote a lovely poem for Julia Smith on her twenty-first birthday:

> *There's a magic in the time of twenty-one*
> *The fuss and fumes of Teen Age left behind:*
> *The blaze, the darks, the enormous inner being*
> *Vast joys, deep hurts, the surging thrill of life,*
> *All these await, patient, for you to find.*

And he made me feel that I had something when I was a lump of a boy, fourteen and lonely. That was when he began to invite me over for tea. I would knock on the front door, and Julia McDill would utter a tart yelp of greeting before remarking, with a private sort of irony, "John is in the library." (John was always in the library.)

I would hear him before I saw him, calling, "Come in, come in!" in his custardy voice. He would be sitting on the couch—or, in later years, lying on the couch under a blanket with his hands pressed atop a book, posed like Wilfred Owen. His circulation was poor. The sun would have lit the wall above him and tea would be steeping under a plum-colored cozy. He'd ask me to pour us each a cup, and he might have a little scotch with his. And then, in a flow of talk that sometimes began with a paean to the doughty men buried in the Revolutionary War graveyard at Maplewood, he would ask what I was reading, thinking about, hoping to do. As I fumbled out my thoughts, the pendulum swings of the banjo clock in the hall, echoing in the high-ceilinged house—tock, tock, tock—made our time together seem strangely urgent.

When I was fifteen, John taught me to drive in an old gray Jeep, the same Jeep in which he'd taught my mother. He was a patient instructor, murmuring, "Slow, slow, no rush," as I learned how to ease out the choke and clutch simultaneously while puttering along his farm's winding paths. Ann Smith remembers driving him into the village once at about fifteen miles an hour, and his alarm: "Too fast, too fast!"

Woodstock was becoming a tourist spot, and John lamented more than once that tins of gourmet maple syrup had appeared in Gillingham's. Gourmet maple syrup! He was a wicked mimic, sticking his chin out and swinging his arms determinedly with his eyes closed to ape the out-of-towners who jogged by below. And he was fond of the yarn about the banker from New York who arrived in the village in the off-season, prepared to buy land and profit from the boom but surprised at the lack of other visitors. He remarked to a local, "Gee, this town is dead." "Yep," the local replied. "And you'd be surprised by how many vultures we see coming in."

This was the age-old anxiety about new money (there are Brahmin families that insist that any money made during or after the War of 1812 is new). The problem Wasps have with the nouveau riche isn't so much the nouveau as the riche. It's envy, felt as disapproval, of what all that unfettered money allows them to do. Old money, having received its money, treats it with custodial anxiety; new money, having earned it, believes it should be used. One of the Smiths, passing Maplewood recently, noticed that Timmy's and Tom's successors, the Monster.coms, had left a discarded Christmas wreath below the road. She retrieved it and put it up on the door of her mother's shed: "It was perfectly good!" And it would serve, in its new setting, to rebuke the neighbors about thrift.

An older Wasp friend remarks, "The new rich behave as if they don't have to deserve spending their money. Whereas when I took my family to Nevis recently, I had to tell myself, 'I'm going to die soon.'" The prospect of a swift and retributive death makes giving yourself pleasure just tolerable. Otherwise it's too close to masturbation.

TOM BOURNE was a salesman above all; he never stopped closing the deal on his own legend, and it explained something when you learned that though he spoke of himself as a Yale grad, class of '22, he'd actually been kicked out his junior year. His biggest sale—his Plan B for greatness—was inspired by the river at the farm's foot. For years, Maplewood's manure ran off into the Ottauquechee like everyone else's, and the river evoked not trout but pigs. Then, in 1967, Tom started the Ottauquechee River Monitoring and Restoration Project. He went door to door to persuade almost one hundred landowners to stop dumping their sewage into the river and hook up to a sewer system. He convinced them, that is, to pay for something they were getting free.

A confirmed atheist, Tom saved the river by promoting

its stewardship as an almost religious duty. I could see that Grandma Tim admired Tom's environmental work—motive enough—and in 1977, when the Ottauquechee was recognized as Vermont's first pollution-free large river, he began to win awards. He also had a gruff knack for turning young men with notions about water filtration into protégés. "Tom was like my father or grandfather praising me, except that I'd heard that kind of thing only about four times in my own family," says Bill Stetson, a Harvard student who worked on the river project and took to dropping by Maplewood for tea. "I could never understand why his family had such a different view—young Tom would express such utter distaste for his father, as if he had been tortured or placed in a concentration camp."

This impulse to conserve, which prompted Tom to deed part of Maplewood to the Vermont Land Trust, was his Waspiest aspect. Though he was Waspily finicky about pronunciation, checking his grandchildren when they said "buff-ay" instead of "boo-fay," the smiley faces in his letters weren't minimalist hieroglyphs but bulb-headed self-portraits. More significantly, he had none of the Wasp's horror of debt. He often told his son, "Don't ever worry about borrowing from the bank, or about paying them, either—just pay the interest." He was MasterCard's dream client.

Yet in the environmental world, he became a burly, shaggy emblem of a nobler time. Tom and Bill Stetson and a third man founded River Watch, with financing from Laurance Rockefeller, and expanded their cleanup efforts to the Hudson, the Mississippi, and even the Danube. "We had a meeting at Tom's house," Stetson recalls, "and we had to shout for an hour because he wouldn't wear his hearing aids." Tom used his deafness strategically, tuning out unwelcome subjects. "We'd planned to continue up at my cabin with the minutiae later, and finally I said, 'Tom, I'm going to excuse myself to light the stove in my cabin and then we'll go over a few final points up there.' Tom sat silent a moment, then burst out, 'For the love of God, you would leave at this point, when we're discussing *the future of the planet*, to go light a stove?' I sat right back down."

ONE DAY in the early 1980s, Grandma Tim said to Anne Greene, "I don't know what's going on, but I can't balance my checkbook." Soon the words were a little funny, too. When I graduated from college, her note remarked, "Your ma says you are off job looking for!" and was decorated with a smiley face out of Edvard Munch. Only her sign-off reassured: "Toujours love." That same year she told Day, "I can't remember numbers anymore, but lines of poetry keep coming back: 'I have a rendezvous with death / At some disputed barricade / When something something something something . . . ' "

When Mom and I drove up for a visit in late 1986, we arrived to find Grandma Tim sunning herself in her Saab in the driveway with her coat on backward. She got cold in the house, as Tom insisted they could get through the winter without fixing the broken furnace. Mom and Day had just gotten them a new mattress to replace the one whose mouse holes were plugged with back issues of *Country Life* and *The Dairyman's Journal*, but everything else was falling apart. As we unloaded our luggage, the Saab began inching toward us, gathering speed. We shouted, but her expression remained fixed and vague. I ran up and reached over her to yank the parking brake. Then we gave Baba the keys. "Now no one in this house can drive!" Baba said with a laugh, or a sort of laugh.

In the afternoon, Mom made them tea as Timmy used to do, scalding the pot. She tried singing "Call John the Boatman," the old round, but her mother just flapped her arms and made strange galloping sounds. Tom turned to Timmy and said in an intended whisper, "You won't ever leave me, will you, dear?" Worried that Mom and Paddy would want to intercede as caretakers and put her in an assisted-living facility, he was increasingly mulish about visitors.

"Of course not," she said, suddenly herself.

"I love you so much," he said. He clasped her hand, his eyes wet.

That night, we couldn't find Grandma Tim anywhere, and finally discovered her in the Saab, half frozen. She had remembered it being warm.

They all flew to Saint John Island and Puerto Rico for their annual winter trip, with Anne Greene going along as their driver. After a few weeks in Mayagüez and San Juan, they ran out of money. When Anne asked, "Why don't you just wire for more?" Tom replied, "No, no, no! I'm going to walk into a bank and say, 'I'm Tom Bourne from Los Estados Unidos, and my brother Jim Bourne worked with Eleanor Roosevelt to start social services here in Puerto Rico—and I need some money!' "

As Tom stumped out of the car and into the bank on canes seemingly hewn from petrified wood, Anne began muttering to Baba about how he made these scenes. Grandma Tim suddenly surfaced and said, "You may not like how rash he is, but in the end he's often right." And then Tom walked out with a big grin and five hundred dollars.

Mom and I had lunch in New York that winter, and she told me Grandma Tim had packed for the trip without including a nightgown, shoes, or sunscreen. When Paddy noted this last omission, she said she'd use Eucerin—the family's balm for dry skin.

"You have to expect nothing, and be delighted by small signs of life," I said.

Mom began to cry, and my scalp prickled hotly; I had wanted to sound adult, and it had come out as unfeeling. "Now that Molly's dead," she said, referring to our family Newfoundland, "I feel that in a way it's time for them all to die—except for Baba. I sometimes think it would be better if the plane returning from Saint John just went down." After a moment, she went on, "That's perverse, of course. But my identity is so tied up with her that sometimes it feels like I'm the confused one, like I'm going down."

"Your grandchildren are going to see you in perfect fettle," I said. She gave me a teary, doubtful smile.

As her Alzheimer's tided in, Timmy still insisted on pulling the rope to peal the church's bell on Sunday mornings, an increasingly syncopated, and eventually Dada, summons to service. Grandpa John came to Woodstock to see the woman who'd divorced him half a century earlier. With Tom discreetly making himself scarce, Timmy led John around the house to see her paintings, now stacked on every chair, pointing urgently at unguessable details as John murmured, "Yes, of course," and "It *is* quite beautiful." When Paddy drove his father up the road to see Julia McDill, Timmy came along for the ride; as John got out of the car, he leaned over and kissed his old love's hand. When he'd gone home, she asked Baba, "Who was that nice man?"

In 1975, Grandpa Tom kept a journal of a year's farming at Maplewood, hoping to make it into a book. I was touched, reading the manuscript recently, by the pleasure he took in planting peas and his euphoria at an emerging parsnip. He doesn't mention people much, but sheep inspire a surprising fund of contemplation. The animals epitomized both the scope of his dominion and the limits of his powers: "When I first brought sheep up here in 1940, I undertook to shear them myself, using old-fashioned scotch hand shears. Those poor sheep! They ended up with what newspapers call 'multiple cuts and abrasions' . . . if I'd been treated that way, I would never recover from the trauma."

This savoring, self-amused narrator was an aspect of his appealing side. "He told us we were going to inherit the farm," Lizz Greene says, "and it was like a rainbow went through my body. Because although we hated his guts some days, he was really our surrogate father. So when he said, 'You, Anne, and Brett: this is your home, and you're going to inherit it all,' it felt like this amazing promise and act of love." Tom wanted someone in the family to keep it all going—to demonstrate sufficient love for him that he could give the farm in return, as King Lear gave his kingdom. Or rather, he wanted everyone to demonstrate that love, and then he'd give (or sell) the farm to each in turn, even if there was no farm left to give.

Tom Jr.'s son, Brett, helped his grandfather run Maplewood for five years, beginning in 1987 and ending when they sold the last thirty cows in the herd. Brett has Tom's fire—he would match his grandfather up the volume knob—but also a saving sweetness and humor. Though he loved trying to wring a living out of the farm's Elysian fields, and saw it as "a shining realm upon the hill," he was skeptical about the inheritance. He'd worked for Tom before, plowing the fields one summer, and Tom had rewarded him with his old Citroën—but after Brett returned from a break in Hawaii, he discovered that Tom had sold the car.

In the waning years of Grandma Tim's life, though it had become evident that the farm would pass to *her* children, Brett and Lizz and Anne still tried to convince Mom and Paddy to let them keep working the place, saying they could turn a profit with small enterprises like mushroom farming, container nurseries, and the "MapleGreen WoodOven Bake Dome." Brett, an admirer of Buckminster Fuller and a sometime stonemason, would build a greenhouse dome around a bread oven, making a combination outdoor kitchen and season-extending greenhouse—a very Tom Bourne sort of innovation. But the Piersons had lost faith in innovations.

ALL JOHN McDill's grandchildren were girls, and he may have seen in me a surrogate grandson. I remember the pleasure I felt when Mom sent him one of my college essays and he wrote me invoking Emerson's famous letter to Whitman: "I greet you at the beginning of a great career." His note made me feel I had a chance as a writer. Wasps are often better at nurturing their children's and grandchildren's friends—at being mentors and friends and houseguests—than their own flesh and blood. There's less at stake. John's daughter Jane, who called him "Grandbother" for his habit of fussing in other people's affairs, says, "There wasn't enough—what's the word . . . *camaraderie* with my parents," adding, of my chats with him, "He never did that with *me*."

In our final teas, John began giving me specific advice. He suggested I take vocal lessons so I would command more attention. He was proud of his own reverberant voice, and when he fell ill, he remarked with distress that he sounded "like an old crow croaking from inside a bag of feathers." Distressed that our family now spent less time in Woodstock than in Wainscott, which he saw as a sybarites' playground, he urged the values of the local gentry: circumspection, forbearance, irony, and distrust of change, change being invariably for the worse.

In our last conversation he recalled the debutante parties when he was young and slim and would leap over walls as a party trick. He would always dance with the wallflowers, making himself indispensable—which was perhaps how he had made the acquaintance of the quiet, rather plain Julia Lee, a student at Yale's forestry school (they never told their children how they'd met). The secret, John said, was this: "At coming-out parties, talk with the *mothers* of the pretty girls. They keep the lists and send the invitations. And you never know which ball will be the truly marvelous one." I remarked that there weren't *so* many coming-out parties, nowadays, but he smiled knowingly. "The final thing, of course," he continued, "is the clothes. You must be handsomely attired. Do you possess a morning coat?"

"No," I said, smiling a little in return.

"Ah!" He asked me to go to the attic and bring down, from the array of hanging wardrobes, his old morning coat, formal shirt, and white gloves. I did, and after he'd touched the shirt's placket, once — it was still soft as a lamb's ear — he pushed it toward me with a little gesture of surrender: "All yours." He wouldn't hear of a refusal.

It hadn't occurred to either of us that I was four inches taller than he — when I tried the suit on later, it was much too small. Yet it remains in my closet even now, in readiness.

THE MORNING of Grandma Tim's funeral, in August of 1992, we gathered in her bedroom. Tom wouldn't let anyone take her body from him the night before, so she lay in her bed still. Overcome by mouth and breast cancer at last, she had essentially starved to death. Her mouth was open, and Day told Mom, who was weeping silently and stroking Grandma Tim's hair, that it looked as if she were singing. When Paddy felt his mother's forehead, he said, "She feels cold." "Not cold," Mom said. "Cool."

In the long living room, my cousin Kate Pierson was hesitantly picking out "The Battle Hymn of the Republic" on the piano: "Mine eyes — have — have — have seen the glory of the co-coming of the Lord . . ." We laid Timmy in the pine coffin. Then eleven of us carried it out the front door and across the lawn toward the graveyard beyond, in time to a fife and drum, as Anne and Lizz's girls ran alongside, catching butterflies under their shirts. We labored across the slanting hill behind Tom, who shuffled so slowly on his canes in the killing heat I kept expecting him to fall.

At the grave we were forty strong. The minister, a hale man with a shock of white hair, boomed out a liturgy at once new and familiar. We come into the world with nothing, and take nothing with us; Timmy has gone where the sun and the moon cannot smite her; grief gropes after love. We sang "O God, Our Help in Ages Past," those piercing words:

> *Time, like an ever-rolling stream,*
> *Bears all its sons away;*
> *They fly, forgotten, as a dream*
> *Dies at the opening day.*

Irving, the local idler, rode past on his three-wheeled bike, then stopped and tiptoed over, taking off his cap with an abashed look. The grave-digger sat on the stone wall opposite, kicking the wall with his boot heel. We lowered the coffin down on ropes, and Tom let a lily fall from his hand onto it, weakly. Then we all tossed down shovelfuls of dirt. The thunk of earth and skitter of pebbles beading down the coffin sides, the finality of it.

Afterward, we ate white lasagna on the porch, and I watched Lizz's seven-year-old daughter, Meghan, splash in a pink wading pool, looking so much like Lizz that time slipped a gear and I felt dizzy. For us, this was an end to Maplewood, or nearly. At the memorial service that October, Grandpa John would surprise everyone by standing, briefly and touchingly, to say, "I'm John Pierson and I loved Timmy, too."

TIM, THE carpenter, already had another coffin ready for Tom in his barn. Yet Tom would live on for more than five years, surrounded, unexpectedly, by his children. Nan and Tom Jr. built houses on their small sections of the farm—

their father had given each of the children sixty acres as their inheritance—and Nicki, who had sold her land to Paddy, lived in a trailer across the road. In the late nineties, Paddy wrote me and remarked that as Tom had so determinedly sought to break his children's spirit young, "The wonder is all three have come home to live within a few hundred yards of their father. (To a lesser extent, one must have the same wonder about me.)" The Bourne children's mix of reasons for moving back was complex: a part of it was that Nan had cancer, and her brother and sister wanted to be near her; a part was sheer love of the place. And a part, perhaps, was the natural longing for their father, or their father as he might have been.

With more than $60,000 a year having gone to Timmy's nurses, Tom didn't have any money left, and the house was fast becoming an eyesore. Yet he began making secretive (though bellowed) plans to return the farm to its imagined glory. He got on the phone to buy, among other follies, a $600 Great Pyrenees sheepdog, a Jersey cow, and a spring lamb for his great-granddaughter. "When we all met with my father to talk about his care, he said, 'If anyone in this room really cared about me, they'd put me up,'" Nicki Bourne recalls. "Turning to Nan, who was dying, he said, 'Look at you; you've got a big empty house, and you've never invited me.' Shame was always a big item for my father." Once, long ago, he'd expressed his own to his first wife, telling her, "You don't know what it's like to look like an elephant and feel like a mouse."

Finally, in December of 1994, his children decided to install Tom in a nursing home. "At a Christmas party, Nan told me, 'We're going to put him in the Old Soldiers' Home on Tuesday,' " Bill Stetson says. "He'd told me he had enough money, so I was shocked. I knew he'd be utterly devastated." Bill and his wife, an IBM heiress, each volunteered to put up $10,000 a year for Tom's care, and Bill asked Laurance and Mary Rockefeller to match them. The resulting trust of $40,000 per annum was enough to keep Tom at Maplewood for his last three years.

Tom's children felt beholden, grateful that their father could stay at home. Yet they still couldn't stand to visit much. For his part, Tom seemed unaware of where the money was coming from. Or at least he never let on, as he adjusted his hearing aid to admit only good news, if he knew that he was being maintained by two legendary American fortunes. He may even have believed that the farm had become profitable at last. In mid-January 1998, Bill Stetson came over for lunch and found Tom slumped in his chair.

"Gramps was a twentieth-century American who was born six weeks into the century and almost saw it out," Brett Bourne says. "He was a full and accurate metaphor for the country, with his strong personality and passions and great charm, as well as his enormous blind spots and oppressive nastiness. By the nineties, his children were all somewhat looking forward to his death. But Nan and Nicki and Tom never got that he was *in* them and in the farm, all around and inside us. I totally understand that inclination to be a salesman, a yeller, an imposer of my will—I react against it, but it's there, the unspoken stuff of who we are as a family. So I always thought, *It's not like we're going to be* free *of him when he dies—we* are *him*."

ELEVEN

Trusts

IN APRIL OF 1989, I spent ten days in a cheap bungalow on Thailand's island of Samui. I was twenty-six and in the middle of my year circling the globe. The plan was that travel would resolve my suit-of-armor problem; that, far away, I'd stop caring what people might think. Instead, I'd lost ten pounds, exchanging them for the drawstring pants and moped-crash scars that signal "world traveler," and for a tenuous self-sufficiency shaken by lonely yearnings for Giovanna or more immediately available women. At my farewell party in New York, a mystical friend named Lisa had told me three things to keep in mind as I went. It was loud, so I strained to catch her murmurings, and heard the last injunction as "You will see whores in trouble and you should help them!" to which I nodded thoughtfully. It turned out that, knowing I'd soon be on an Australian sheep station, Lisa had said, "You will see *horses* in trouble . . ."

At every American Express office there were letters waiting from women back home, unexpectedly intimate letters. And a dark rumination on suicide from a woman I didn't know very well, who said she was writing me "because I have no idea if you will ever receive it and also because you are so far off and the secret feelings of my wandering mind will be safe with you half the world away." Travel makes you a screen for furtive wishes, and that was fine with me. I was willing to go away to be needed.

Over lunch at my guesthouse on Samui, overlooking the Gulf of Thailand, I read *Of Human Bondage* and watched Juanita, the manager, flirt primly with the lodge's other male guests. She was in her early thirties, a pretty, self-contained woman. I could envision settling down with her and helping to run the guesthouse: working the till and the bar, trawling for butterfish, going for evening runs on the white crescent beach.

"Three girls in one week, Chris," Juanita said, bringing him a Singha beer and his bill. "You are new number one stud. If you calculate by number." Chris's nocturnal activities were a running topic.

"Four," he replied. A placid man with mermaid tattoos on both biceps, Chris kept his watch facing inward in the British fashion. "But I love only *you*, Juanita. When will you be my butterfly?"

The Australian, Ross, remarked, "I was drunk as a tick last night." He had the bleared eyes of the blackout drunk and was convalescing from a back infection he'd picked up in a New Guinea mine. His stitch-welted surgical scars looked like a shark's bite.

"You couldn't see, mate," Chris said. "I was worried I couldn't trust you with my girl, that you were going to give me some competition, but then I saw the glaze steal over your eyes. Like fog over the hills."

"I was blind as a skunk. Lost my key, had to crawl into bed with Juanita." Ross gave her a mild look. "Thanks for putting me up, butterfly."

Chris looked at Juanita to see whether there was anything to this, but she was clearing a nearby table. He pulled out his wallet and gazed into it: "Only five girls' worth left. She put her foot onto my throat, by the way. Very limber. This morning she wanted five hundred baht, but I told her I was broke."

Without turning around, Juanita said, "Chris!"

"I thought it would be wrong to *pay* her," he said lazily, trying to catch Juanita's eye. "That encourages prostitution." She bent over the silverware, smiling, probably, and I bent back over my book.

My parents and grandparents had once chased the same will-o'-the-wisp hopes abroad: our attics are stuffed with onionskin envelopes inscribed *"Per Via Aerea"* and *"Mit Luftpost"* by husbands and fathers at the Bay View, the International House, the Hotel des Masques; from Raffles, the White Palace, aboard Pan Am. Yet, like boomerangs, Wasps whistle off only to find themselves back home. In John P. Marquand's 1937 novel *The Late George Apley*, Apley tells his son that their heritage travels with them: "You can leave Pequod Island for Bar Harbor but Pequod Island will nevertheless remain a part of you. You can go to the uttermost ends of the earth but, in a sense, you will still be in Boston." Without quite being aware of it, I was searching, in all those hostels and stupas, for the contentment of Maplewood and Century House.

In Kyoto, I sat through a long tea ceremony, made antsy by its formal simplicities; in the Golden Triangle, I smoked opium but woke up to myself. In the years to come, I would keep returning to the road, still hoping to take French leave in *nostalgie de la boue*. In Manila, covering the presidential election in 1992, I fell in with J.B., a white-haired adventurer from Kentucky who was living at the Mandarin Oriental and placing sizable bets on the outcome. I was fascinated by his monologues as he sat by the pool in a terry cloth robe, drinking Banana Yummies—fascinated, and alarmed, and a little envious. "I tell you," he confided, "I don't use no rubbers, but what I do soon as I pop my nuts, I get up quick and go to the bathroom and pour some rubbing alcohol in and around there good, stings like a red-hot iron but I never had no problems. And if I catch one of my baby dolls peddling her sweet pussy around, I just X her out. We go someplace out of town and I buy her a nightgown and an expensive pair of shoes and then I get her into bed and bare naked and then I dress again like I'm going out for a pack of cigarettes, and I tell her, 'Turn over, baby.' Then I take a red marker and I draw a big X on her ass, and when she says, 'What are you *doing?*' I say, 'I'm crossing you out of my life, sweetheart,' and I walk out the door with all her new clothes and never look back."

Just once did I escape, and briefly. On a horseback trip in Mongolia, in 1997, my companions and I were snowed in high in the Sayan Mountains with a tribe of sixty Tsaatan, reindeer people. We spent our days dozing in their tepees, surrounded by huskies and reindeer and runny-nosed children, and I felt elated to be cut off so completely. Life was reduced to its simplest elements: tea, rice, dogs, a fire. And then the snow melted and we rode down.

In 1933, *Fortune* extolled the financial management of the leading Brahmin families: "The great family trusts stand between the Bostonians and the activities of contemporary life like the transparent but all too solid glass which separates the angel fish of an aquarium from the grubby little boys outside."

But by the 1950s, Wasps had begun to whisper about "the fatal $10,000"—a trust fund that wasn't sufficient to absolutely destroy ambition, but that provided just enough cushion to muffle it. In 1957, as Mom began a career in teaching and her course of psychoanalysis, she wrote Grandpa John to inquire if there was any money being held for her. He replied, aggrievedly:

> *The point that does puzzle me is that you do not in your letter indicate any realization of the key financial facts. I have been paying (until you reached 21) a hundred dollars a month each for you and Paddy, plus 12.5 percent of any net income (after income taxes) above $5,000. . . . You will see, with a little pencil and paper work, that I have very definitely been sharing what I had with you and Paddy, and that there was not much chance of putting any additional sums aside in a savings fund.*

He added, in a footnote: "Aside from my salary, I had a small income, originally about $1,500, on investments left me by my father. In the course of working on full employment and

Voices to America, with little or no pay in some years, I used up the major part of the capital. This, I am afraid, is sometimes the penalty for trying to *do* something in this world, in disregard of more practical considerations." A few months later, however, Goggy Pierson died, and after her large apartment on Park Avenue was sold, John assigned $25,000 from her estate—about $185,000 today—to a trust for Mom (and the same to Paddy).

Mom skirmished with Day about money for years, routinely spending more than he had anticipated on the assumption that funds would suddenly emerge, as they always had, to cover the balance. In 1962, they fought for days over her insistence that they spend twenty-one dollars for a *Consumer Reports*–approved top-of-the-line desk lamp for his study. Twenty years on, once the lamp had proved itself, he acknowledged that she had been right. But he never could convince her that keeping a list of expenditures was not the same thing as making or sticking to a budget. Nor could he forestall her occasional sprees. She knew the one store to go to for just the thing—T. Anthony, Bendel's, Pierre Deux—and those things were always expensive. In 1969, she wrote a friend: "Guess what I've just acquired? A *fur coat*. It's muskrat, which is I guess just one step above caterpillar, but anyway it's *fur*. (It's also just exactly one-half of the total year's clothing allotment for all five of us (!!!)—so if you see me in it at the wedding don't peek underneath—there won't be anything there!)"

Mom's attitude was unusual; Grandpa John's defensiveness about depleting family capital more characteristic. Money managers refer to Wasps as "Wealth Preservers" and put their money into fixed-income investments and cash,

while the freewheeling "Wealth Enhancers'" money goes
into riskier, and more profitable, hedge funds, venture capital, and private equity. Wealth Enhancers like to say that
money is a form of energy, and that if you play around with
that energy—treat it all as a game—it will multiply. Wasps
know that money doesn't multiply; it divides. We understand
our ordained roles: the first generation earns the money, the
second begins the dispersal by aiming (expensively) at social
and civic position, and the third goes in for artistic self-
expression and blowing what remains. So your job as a Wasp
elder is to guard your dwindling hoard against all requests
for food, clothing, and riding lessons, and then to expire at
last, too late, clutching a Byzantine trust document as your
children labor to uncurl your frozen fist. The word "trust,"
so congenial in its associations, is an acute misnomer. To
guard the capital from your feckless offspring, you vest control of it with a trustee, the affable lawyer who will take your
feckless offspring to lunch once a year and charge the trust
for the meal and his time.

The truth is that Wasps fear money and its quicksilver
abdications. That fear informs the rite of passage of the college summer spent "roughing it" on an oil rig, a tuna boat, a
steel-mill floor. The explicit rationale is that working with
your hands, however briefly, is bracing and broadening. My
father, who spent his roustabout summer as a gandy dancer,
or track-maintenance worker, on the Alaska Railroad, wrote
me when I was doing my summer stint as a salad chef and
housepainter on the New Jersey shore to urge that I stay the
course despite my boredom: "You will, in future years, have
a still more heightened sensitivity to the problems of the ordinary laborer: both your capacity to help him or her *vis-à-*

vis that person's boss; and your capacity *as a boss* to visualize needed reforms or decline suggested changes will be morally empowered by your own earlier stamina under laboring conditions."

But most Wasps learn to recoil to safety. That Jersey summer I had a flash of shamed recognition when I read *Stover at Yale*, Owen Johnson's 1912 *bildungsroman* about a bully young man who defies the college's social system yet is nonetheless finally tapped for Skull and Bones. After Dink spends a summer working with his roughneck classmate Tom Regan, he feels rather smug: "He had had a glimpse of what the struggle for existence meant in the stirring masses; and he had known the keenness of a little joy and the reality of sorrow to those for whom everything was real." But later, when he falls for a working-class girl who nobly jilts him, leaving a note that says, "I'm not good enough for you," he realizes how narrowly he has escaped:

> *All the horror and the hopelessness of a life he could not better thronged over him, and he stood a long while looking down the great bleak ways, through the gates that it is better not to pry ajar. Then in a revulsion of feeling, terrified at what he had divined, he left and went, almost in an instinct for protection, hurriedly to the Story home, white and peaceful under the elms.*

EVERY FOUR or five years, growing up, we'd catch a glimpse—a lunch, an overnight—of my father's younger brother, Charles. Charles was the first person I ever saw in espadrilles. He was always on the move in Latin America or

Europe, always several thousand miles from Pittsburgh. Slim and elegant and remarkably handsome in a Jeremy Irons way, he arched his left eyebrow at sentiment. He preferred the mediated view through his Nikon, shooting closed faces and shadowed doorways in Java, Crete, Rangoon, Peru, Leningrad, and Senegal. Possessed of a light voice and strong opinions about food and wine, he was often droll and impulsive—and, like his mother, easily wounded. He spoke Spanish and Italian, though he sometimes conflated them, and signed his brief notes to my parents, *"Tanti Saluti"* or *"Abrazos."* I admired his lack of interest in us and felt he might be onto something. A backgammon player, a gifted mimic, and a dab hand with an orange soufflé, Charles was *Playboy*'s ideal bachelor. Yet even his ex-wives would remember him fondly for his ardent longing to love.

When an attractive Vassar student named Joan Anderson first saw Charles across the bar at Pike Run in 1953, she was smitten: "He was this darling guy, talking and laughing, and you couldn't help wondering 'Who's *that?*' " Charles, a sophomore at Williams, was known there as Bugsy, because he'd somehow taken over a Pittsfield, Massachusetts–based football pool. But with Joan he was doe-eyed and vulnerable. "He hated Pittsburgh and he hated Pike Run, which was the kind of place where people went 'Oooh!' because I wore open-toed shoes," Joan says. "And he felt very, very sensitive about the fact that Jess was considered the loose woman of the club. The whole reason he was attracted to me was that I'd grown up far away, in Mexico." (Charles would arrive for my parents' wedding in Woodstock—in February, in two feet of snow—sporting a white tropical suit.) Yet he also liked to talk about Big Jim Friend's bygone yacht and to assure Joan, "If we can just get through the first few years, I'm going to inherit a lot of money and we'll never have to work again."

They dated for two years and, virgins still, were married a few weeks after graduation. Charles went to business school in Phoenix and was soon out every night as Joan stayed home with their daughter, Lili, and Lili's younger brother — a child Charles felt Joan had foisted on him to keep him in the marriage. The boy was christened Carlos Holton Friend, then renamed, at Joan's mother's insistence, John Christopher Friend. After one fight, Charles told Joan, "I'm not interested in you either physically or mentally." She made a final try at a rapprochement, visiting him in Puerto Rico, where he had started an import company. She had picked out an alluring polka-dotted bikini from Macy's, but when Charles saw her in it, he said, "You look like a *schoolteacher.*" He could pierce your soft spot, a knack he shared with Jess and me.

In the early 1960s, Charles refused to pay his mandated $133 a month in child support and only complied when Jess threatened to disinherit him. Jess told Joan that her son was like his namesake and great-uncle, Charles Wood Friend: someone who should never marry. But Jess would also apologize to Joan and Lili and John Christopher for Charles's absences, explaining that he had been a small, sensitive boy who threw up a lot and cried when my father stole his comic books. Though Charles and Day grew up in the same room, trading stories about cowboys named for states — Tex, Cal, Mex, and Monty — it always surprised people that they were brothers; they looked and spoke and behaved so differently.

In 1962, Charles met a moody French American model named Suzanne de Bidart. He was being drunk and noisy on the streets of San Juan, and she told him what a jerk he was. Even in disarray he had a wounded charisma. They were married in New York in 1964, and they traveled and photographed well together, sharing a self-mocking chic. But when Suzanne gave birth to my cousin Andrea, known as Daisy, in 1966, the circumstances were squalid. Charles, who had moved to Mexico City to work for General Foods, had wanted Suzanne to abort the baby, and when Suzanne was nearly eight months pregnant, she caught him having an affair. In a state, she boarded a plane to fly off to Zihuatanejo — but the cabin was unpressurized, and her water broke as the plane made an intermediate stop in the jungle. A local doctor listened for a fetal heartbeat by pressing his ear to a metal egg cup on Suzanne's stomach and said, "I don't hear the baby." Yet that evening Daisy slipped into the world, weighing less than three pounds. When Suzanne's next pregnancy miscarried, in 1968, she was relieved: Charles was in New York, conducting another affair. Two years later, Suzanne and Daisy abruptly moved to Ghana — "You can't love for two," Suzanne says — and Charles stayed in Milan.

As he took increasingly prominent jobs in advertising with Norman, Craig & Kummel and J. Walter Thompson, he picked up local ways wherever he went. In Mexico City, he sang along with the mariachi bands; in Milan, he pinched his fingers to make a point. When his daughter Lili was married, he flew in from London and gave a toast at the rehearsal dinner, and friends asked her afterward, "Who was that Englishman?"

Because Charles would lose interest in his wives, we didn't really get to know his children—and they didn't really get to know Charles, either. Lili recalls, "I didn't see him at all from when I was eight to fourteen or fifteen, when my mother had to suggest to him that my brother and I visit him in Milan." Charles was so nervous when he met the children that his hands were shaking; he wanted to do this right, to make amends. He took them to a bullfight and later introduced Lili to steak tartare, Mongolian hot pot, and dim sum. He made life seem so cosmopolitan and amusing that Lili tried to work out a plan to leave her dreary mother and stepfather and live with glamorous Charles. However, she says, "I don't know if he ever thought of me if I wasn't in his plain sight."

"I was always sending him soppy cards and saying, 'I love you, I love you,'" Daisy says. "He saved all the letters and drawings I ever sent him in a file—I found it after he died—and on the phone he'd say, 'I love you, too, Daisy.' He wouldn't ever say it first, though. And he had the best for himself—Turnbull & Asser, cashmere—but he was frugal with us. He always thought we were all after his money."

I WORRY a lot about money, in a defensive sort of way, but I have nothing of James Wood Friend's Midas touch. In 1980, Day gave the three of us a Christmas gift of $200 each to invest in stocks, as a way of encouraging an interest in fiscal management. Timmie sold her Eli Lilly position twelve years later for $735. Pier sold his Citibank stock after five years for more than $650, which he used to buy his first car. And I took a plunge on National Mobile Concrete—an oxymoron only Grandpa Ted could have loved.

In 1986, my parents gave us $60,000 apiece to cover three years of graduate school or to help with the struggles of early adulthood. My father was understandably proud of being able to stake us, proud that he had begun to repair the family fortunes, taking salary put by during the years at Swarthmore and investing it diversely, as he'd learned to do by sitting on the college's investment committee. He had broken with the Wasp habit of letting children fend for themselves until it no longer matters. (Uncle Wassa, after reneging on his promise to pay for his daughter Anne's college education, told her, "I'd rather stand on my head and spit wooden nickels than give you a dime.") Day's note said that the money had been placed with his adviser at Smith Barney, in our names, and that "even as we try to arrange your further independence, we will be eager to hear your thoughts, and glad to advise you whenever you ask. Love, Day."

I remember brooding about the idea of arranged independence, and being pleased that after borrowing $2,000 from Mom and Day, to help me survive in Manhattan on my reporter's salary at a magazine called *The American Lawyer*—$15,500—I had paid the loan off before this gift arrived. While I was grateful for my parents' offers to "pave the way" with their friends in publishing, to help me "get a foot in the door," I was also glad that I had gotten this first job on my own. One of the reasons I loved New York was that unlike Boston or Philadelphia, the city was run less by the old-boy network than by the noisy claims of talent. Still, when I heard of a new satirical monthly, *Spy*, I introduced myself by letter to one of its founders and mentioned that I'd been on the *Harvard Lampoon*, as he had (no reason to renounce the old-boy network *entirely*).

I was crazy about working at *Spy* as a writer and then a senior editor; it was thrilling being part of a young, underpaid underclass and blowing spitballs at the city's old, overpaid overclass. We spent our days together in laughter, competing to think of more shivlike headlines, and our nights discussing stories and headlines we could never do—"The Yellow Peril," say, about moguls and their Asian wives—over rounds of stingers ordered up by the coeditors, Graydon Carter and Kurt Andersen, old friends from *Time*. "More hooker drinks!" Kurt would call, and Graydon would cry, "Drink up, Taderino!" One evening, a few stingers in, Graydon challenged me to arm wrestle, beat me soundly, and gave me a sweet, confiding little speech about how I needed to make a six-year plan to rise to the top, needed to understand how the city truly ran, the false heat—the relentless, unembarrassed self-promotion—that fueled it. He ordered another round and pinned my arm again. Then he told me how to prevent hangovers: first, coat your stomach before going out with four aspirins dissolved in milk; second, upon awakening in the morning, drink a raw egg in whipped Worcestershire sauce. Third, squeeze a little Visine into your eyes, shave twice, and wear a bow tie, because you feel better when you look natty, and people will notice your tie instead of your wan expression.

I soaked it all in: the hurly-burly of adult life was not nearly as bad as I'd feared. I even copied the bookish way Kurt nudged the bridge of his glasses up with his forefinger as he cracked wise. My mother was pleased that I was enjoying myself at a publication that swiftly became remarkably popular and influential (and, nearly as swiftly, fell apart). But she suggested, a few months in, that constant attack would ruin me: "Walter Kerr was a famous theater critic for the *New York Times*, and one reason everyone read him and loved him was that he always looked for something to praise." I didn't agree—it hadn't occurred to me yet that my ambivalence about money informed my appreciation for this line of work, where we reflexively attacked the visibly rich, people like the Viscontis.

But I was beginning to wonder about our targets. The first three people I profiled at the editors' suggestion, an intellectual, a judge, and a tycoon, were all Jewish. We weren't pillorying them for their religion, but for their hypocrisy, megalomania, stupidity, cupidity, vulgarity, pretension, sexual peccadilloes, and self-glorifying excess: all satire's usual piñatas. But we didn't know what we didn't know. Thirty years earlier, Edmund Wilson had made a criticism of *Time*, then run by upper-crust Wasps, that also applied to *Spy*'s middle-crust Wasps:

> Time's *picture of the world gives us sometimes simply the effect of schoolboy mentalities in a position to avail themselves of a gigantic research equipment; but it is almost always tinged with a peculiar kind of jeering rancor . . . a general impression that the pursuits, past and present, of the human race are rather an absurd little scandal about which you might find out some even nastier details if you met the editors of* Time *over cocktails.*

At one of *Spy*'s many parties, a friend who wrote for the magazine, Melik Kaylan, issued a challenge: "Tad, for God's

sake say something controversial about someone powerful."
"Graydon Carter can blow me," I replied. Melik laughed,
then said, "That's the best you can do?"

I sometimes felt that I was cheating at *Spy*, using humor
not as an expression of feeling but as a crafty shortcut, a way
of winning the writing game by lowering the stakes. Yet I
felt no urge to ennoble the magazine's mission—which, occasional excesses of meanness aside, I approved of—or to
right larger wrongs. I had become a writer because the life
came fairly easily to me, because everyone in the family from
Grandpa John on down was overly encouraging about my
early work, and, mainly, to seem mysterious and desirable. I
hoped my byline would attract women for me, serving as a
highway teaser like the Wall Drug billboards: ONLY TWO
THOUSAND MILES TO TAD FRIEND. FREE ICE WATER.

Well into my thirties, though, I dreaded the actual process of writing. It felt like a chore. My work bore the traces
of having been labored over like a dry garden in Japan, the
sand raked into formal patterns by workmen in conical
hats. When I met with editors from *Esquire* to discuss a
potential freelance profile and they began anatomizing my
prose—"He's got the perfect style for it, that dry, acerbic
thing"—I tried, while looking attentive, to stop my ears. I
didn't want to have a defining style, even a situationally perfect one. A defining style would express a personality, and a
personality would have to be expressed by a person, and then
I would be stuck, accountable.

I also felt uncomfortable thinking of myself as a writer or
an artist, rather than a journalist; serious art, rife with feeling and conflict, is not encouraged among Wasps. *Christina's*

World is as near as we care to get to the abyss. When Mary Cassatt returned home for a visit, the *Philadelphia Public Ledger* revealed the culture's hierarchy of values by reporting the arrival of "Miss Mary Cassatt, the daughter of Mr. Alexander Cassatt, president of the Pennsylvania Railroad, who has been studying art in Paris, and who owns one of the smallest Pekinese dogs in the world." After the documentarian Dickie Rogers learned that a growth on his foot was a melanoma, he told me, "I was relieved. My first thought was, *I'm going to die — I don't have to make a great film*." Part of his relief, I think, came from the knowledge that his people never wanted him to make a great film, and now he wouldn't have to vex them by doing it. Two years later, he was dead, the documentary about Georgica he'd been working on for a quarter century still unfinished.

Because *Spy* was such a success, I realized I might soon be offered jobs at other magazines and find myself on track to become an editor in chief somewhere by age thirty-five. I didn't want to be an editor in chief somewhere by age thirty-five; I wasn't yet ready, even in anticipation, to be another attendant lord. So I quit to travel and regroup.

A few years later, in the early nineties, my literary agent called me to give me a pep talk, afterward referred to between us as "the contender speech." Her point was that I was treading water with the array of pieces I was writing for *Esquire* and *Vogue:* "The reputation you have, among your friends and enemies, is that no one knows what you care about, d'you know what I mean? You have to decide if you're going to be a contender, channeling your talent in a straitjacket, or just do your pieces one by one on the sidelines. I keep wanting to bump you up to the A level, but honest to God, Tad, if you don't want to be focused, if not committing to any one thing makes you happy, then I'd be the last person in the world to not keep a happy client." *Enemies?* But she was right. I did want to dumbfound the world with my abilities yet leave no trace. I'd thought of myself as the consummate freelancer, beholden to no one, but ambition expressed in the serial execution of others' ideas is the hallmark of a corporate man.

AFTER CHARLES Friend's first wife remarried and became Joan Turnure, she moved with her children and her husband and his children to Caracas. When Joan and Charles's son, by then known as Juan, was in first grade there, he began throwing up during roll call. The school psychologist suggested he might be expressing his desire to be part of the same family as his stepsiblings. "So we changed his name from Friend to Turnure, but not legally," Joan says, "and I wrote to Charles to explain the circumstances, that he was getting ill in class. But Charles was very bitter about it. At Lili's wedding he told me, 'He's not my son—he changed his name.'"

"I remember mostly negatives," says Juan, who a few years ago legally changed his name to John Christopher Friend Turnure, completing his trek of identity. "When I was twenty, Charles visited me at Columbia Presbyterian Hospital, where I'd just had spinal fusion surgery for a crushed lumbar disk. I'm lying there on morphine in a room without air-conditioning, and he comes in and says, 'I don't know why you had this surgery—it's a big mistake. I wouldn't have done it.' We had a whole blowup over it. Then, at Lili's wedding, when I hadn't seen him in years, he said, 'Boy, you got fat!' "

Juan observes that among the values he learned from his father's side of the family, and has tried not to pass on to his daughters, are the following:

> *--Kick your kids out of the nest early.* . . . *It's good for them.*
> *--Drinking at a young age is acceptable.*
> *--You're marrying a girl from where? But your backgrounds are so different (read: not our class, dear).*
> *--You should uphold the family name, despite all the deadbeats who preceded you.*
> *--Family conflict should be avoided, not confronted.*
> *--When the going gets tough in a marriage, the Wasps get out.*

In the early 1970s, Charles met Karin Kretschmer, a generous, smiling German who worked in advertising in Milan and had come to see him about a job; he drew her in by talking enthusiastically about his travels to Yemen and Iran, and by admitting—his brow drolly furrowed—that he was lonely. When he introduced her to us later, she proved candid and inquisitive, curious about our interests in a way that seemed to puzzle Charles *(They're just my brother's children.* . . . *)*. Karin teased him, calling him Carletto and refusing to countenance his sulks, and he began to open up at last. But only after Karin stopped seeing him, early on, when she learned that he was not yet divorced from Suzanne, as he'd let her believe. It was Grandpa Ted who reunited them, by dying. Charles called Karin in tears to say that he was leaving for the funeral in Pittsburgh the following day, and asking her to meet with him and to forgive him. When they married, he neglected to tell his children; Daisy, seeing the photos in Charles's Milan apartment, was shocked not to have been invited.

At fifty-five, Charles discovered that he had cancer of the thymus, news he would relay offhandedly: "It's such a bore." When he returned to America after this blow, he and Karin settled in Sarasota—Charles having dismissed her suggestion of Delray Beach as "Too close to Mother"—where he began to employ a pain-reduction technique called Dynamic Meditation. After "constructing" an imaginary room inside himself where he could invite people in to advise him, he invited in Ronald Reagan. Always a conservative Republican, he now began listening to Rush Limbaugh, which can't have helped much.

After decades of infrequent contact, my father sent Charles a $12,000 check for six months' worth of cancer treatments with Taxol, together with an apology for having borrowed his comic books a half century earlier. "My additional and deeper purpose," Day later wrote, "was to enjoin correspondence on our brotherhood and its meaning—a difficult project, given the intense aversion of the Friend family compound to talk realistically of human emotions and relationships." He added that Charles "thanked me warmly for the gift . . . and returned the check, saying I should use it as a down payment toward the renovation of our garage workshop into my study." My father believed that the gift, although returned, had achieved its purpose, but Karin suggests that it left Charles nonplussed.

He could be hard to read. When Karin broached the topic of cancer or mortality, he would say, "There's nothing to talk about." Nothing to report. When Karin and Charles went to Jess's for the holidays, Karin got mad at them both: "I said, 'Do we have to talk about the stock market on Christmas Day?'" My father flew to Sarasota in late February of 1994, when Charles was in extremis, and found his brother still very much in character. When the nurse said, "You just lay there quietly," he replied, "No, I'll just lie here." When she looked at him, he said, "I'm still the house grammatician." (My father later told the nurse, "That's okay; the word is 'grammarian.'") Day sat by his brother's bed and read him the Twenty-third Psalm from a Bible Mom had sent him at Christmas; he had been asking for a Bible, but everyone else had resisted such a fateful gift. When Charles said that the Twenty-third was the only psalm worth reading, Day told the story of declaiming the First Psalm in the woods after he'd failed his orals. "Did you tame Bambi?" Charles inquired bitingly.

The final night, Karin woke my father to listen to Charles's increasingly ragged breathing. He took his brother's pulse and whispered, "It's over 130!" and Karin whispered, "It's been high ever since his thymectomy"—the removal of his thymus gland two years earlier. Day had the disturbing sense that Charles had spent the last years of his life sprinting. As the dying man's breathing slowed to three gasps a minute, Day and Karin began to sob. Finally, at 7:30 a.m., a becoming flush spread across Charles's face.

My father wrote up an obituary, listing, at his brother's

insistence, Lili and Daisy as his only children. Juan was not only stricken from the record, but advised not to come to the funeral. Nonetheless, he wrote a generous condolence letter to Grandma Jess, who was in the hospital recovering from her fourth heart attack when Day called to tell her that her younger son was dead.

> *It makes me sad that he never knew his granddaughter, Jessica, or knew me as a father and successful businessman. . . .*
> *Since we always lived so far apart, he never visited and neither did I. Time just slipped away and now it is too late. I can't say anything more except I regret it all very much.*

Though Joan Anderson Turnure and her second husband had been careful to keep Lili in Charles's good graces—even suggesting that she ask Charles to give her away when she married—Charles's will disinherited Lili, too. Joan finds this poignant, seeing how much of him is in them: "I call Lili and Juan real Friends," their mother says. "Lili because she never discloses her feelings beneath her sweet exterior, and Juan because he keeps you at a distance by being blunt and prickly." The influence was instinctive and reactive, as Charles told his children almost nothing of their ancestors. He never spoke of his childhood except in bleak vignettes, recalling the icy flowers formed by the frost on his window at St. Paul's. Coming from an unhappy family, he left two more unhappy families behind, and all unhappy families are alike in their silences.

Karin wasn't sure what to do with Charles's cremated remains. "I had told Charles, 'Why don't we have you here, in

Florida, where I can visit you?' Because I come from a tradition where you visit. He came from the American tradition, so he said, 'Just throw me on the heap. When it's over, it's over.' " Despite his family antipathy, however, he'd always worn a gold ring with the Friend crest, and there were still spots available in James Wood Friend's Pittsburgh mausoleum. So Karin parked Charles's urn there and asked my father if she could have her name cut into the final tomb beside him. She had promised Charles she wouldn't leave him there alone.

Yet Karin now says that when she dies, she wants her ashes mingled with Charles's and scattered in the Atlantic. They were always happiest just the two of them, without family to muddle things. "I went back to the cemetery two years after he died," she says, "and there was a violet growing by the front door. I was so excited, because I'd put cut violets with Charles's urn when I'd brought him there. It was fall, and the grass was cut low, and there was no way a violet should be there, but there it was. It was like Charles was saying 'Hello!' I do wonder, though, if Charles really wants to be in that place, where it's so cold and dark. I think he wants to get out of there and travel freely."

GRANDMA JESS not only never got over her father's death, she never got over what happened after his horseshoe company was sold in the 1920s. Mrs. Holton gave the lion's share of the proceeds to Jess's older brother, Oliver, and her older sister, Kay. Forever after, Jess was watchful about money. She taught her sons how to balance a checkbook and track their investments, and when she gave the three of us a hundred shares each of General Motors, in 1993, she appended a lengthy explanation of the company's vicissitudes and dividend history—lengthy because she had held the stock for sixty years.

In 1995, she wrote a memo to her heirs laying out her preferred disposition of her jewelry, clock, wineglasses, and silver; it began, sniffily, "First of all I would like to say that I am pretty sure that Eliz."—my mother—"will not want anything I have, as she showed no interest in any of Kay's things except linen napkins. However, I would like my grandchildren to have anything they need, or want." She then phoned my father to say that as Charles had mistreated Juan and Lili in his will, she wanted to leave them an extra portion in hers. Day said, "It's your money to do with as you like."

"Yes, but is that all right with *you?*" she kept asking.

"Whatever you want to do is fine with me."

"Don't you want my money?" she finally asked, plaintively. Jess seemed to understand that expectations of inheritance ratchet impossibly high because Wasps tend to express love not as a flow of feeling but as a trickle of side tables—leading their children to look to recoup in dead money what they lost in live affection. As Muriel Rogers once told her son Dickie, "I give you money because I love you at that particular time."

The day after the phone call, Day wrote Jess a letter that turned up in her desk with a small cache of treasures when she died. After beginning "Dearest Ma," he reiterated that he'd be happy to receive whatever money she wanted to pass on.

Now I want to talk about your greatest gifts to me:

Your beauty. . . . I had the most beautiful mother of anybody.

Your passionate feeling. . . .

Your prudence.

I've commented on this often and recently. Let me say it again and differently. What kept me from becoming a gambler (and a loser) like my father? Surely your example.

Your independence.

Yes, as you put it on the phone last night, I "got a good start" in life. I not only got schooled, I got educated. I learned to love learning. Then, when you and Pop divorced, I made myself as financially independent as possible. I got small scholarships my first two years in graduate school. I earned money teaching the next two years. And I have never asked anyone for money since then. . . . My independence consists partly in choosing work and a way of life that none of my family have followed. In the course of that I've developed some values that Friends, and perhaps Holtons, don't readily share. For instance, I cannot bear the phrase "time is money." I know what that means in business terms, and I've proved I know it as an executive. But the phrase itself is philosophically atrocious. Time is much more important than money. Time is life itself. . . .

What I am writing to thank you for, in the first place, and always, is for gifts of life — your beauty, passion, prudence, and independence. These, far more than any other influence, have formed my character. The flaws in that character are my own. Thank you for my strengths.

The following year, I asked my father if there was any

money salted away that would enable me to join some friends in buying a building in Soho—a loan of $100,000 would secure me a large apartment. He said there wasn't, and gave me a talk about stocks providing the foundation that eventually led to the "oasis" of real estate. Three days later, Grandma Jess died, leaving us each more than $100,000 in stocks. I felt guilty and spooked, brushed by the monkey's paw. But by the time the will had been probated, the apartment was gone. I decided to spend the money on psychotherapy, having already put the $60,000 from my parents to that use. My birthright in wherewithal seemed to me almost perfectly balanced by my birthright in repression.

So the money Amanda and I have now is almost all money we have made. Still, she suggests that my real issue with ambition and money is my residual belief that I don't have to do anything I don't feel like doing in order to establish our family's financial security, because there will eventually be some sort of inheritance to tide us along. This charge is one of the things we sometimes fight about, all the more bitterly because I worry that she might have a point.

TWELVE

Guilt

L ATE IN MY sophomore year, I went to my first tea at
the Signet Society. Having just been elected, I made a
slow victory lap of the library, examining the framed
letters of admission of such former members as T. S. Eliot
and John P. Marquand; the tradition was to send your first
book to the Signet along with your letter of election and
the red rose you got at initiation. I was puzzling over the
society's motto, a Virgil tag that translates as "So do you
bees make honey, not for yourselves," when Paul Sax tapped
my elbow. I followed his nod and saw a slight, dark-haired
beauty in a black cardigan. Melanie Grayboden was smoking and bestowing upon her companion an extraordinarily
wide-mouthed smile that seemed, apprehensively, to promise everything.

Paul was the Signet's president. I'd gotten to know him on
the *Lampoon*, and had the feeling that he'd supported my
Signet candidacy at least in part to recruit a witness to his
feelings for Melanie, the Signet's secretary, who'd written

my letter of election in back-slanting blue script. "She writes poetry," he said now. "*Good* poetry. And she looks like that. And that's her boyfriend, who's this . . . *great guy*." Her boyfriend was a quizzical Wasp, a promising writer who wound up in trusts and estates. Paul laughed, stewing: "Goddammit!"

She was one of those women—there are a few in every class—whose choices reverberate. Though I felt she was out of my league, I flirted with her at parties for years, sometimes eliciting that lingering smile. Afterward, I would find myself musing about her pretty feet, and her scent of jasmine and fresh-cut flowers—Beautiful, from Estée Lauder, a patient of Melanie's doctor father who gave him gift packs. Melanie had a snobby, what-can-you-do-for-me air: pure Manhattan. She also surrendered to laughter and stood extra close, radiating warmth. And there was that amazingly hopeful smile. And I still believed that elusive women had a soft, secret, yielding side locked away just for me.

By the summer of 1990, there was a slow build and then a lovely dinner on Long Island at an inn near her family's summerhouse on Shelter Island, so lovely I missed the last ferry home. After all the circling, there was an instant connection: the "It," we called it. Waking in her West Side apartment, we'd call Elite Café and have them bring over bagels with lox and lattes and a *Times*. Sometimes I'd bring Melanie her latte in the shower, where she liked to muse in a cloud of steam. Following my family's tannic ways, I'd never really drunk coffee before, but I took to it now as if it were LSD or Karl Marx.

Not that she wanted me to change, yet: she liked my time-worn clothes—that oatmeal-colored Shetland sweater—and the sense of tradition I gave off, which she felt meant I'd know how to raise children. She said she saw me as a lion, lazy but innately strong. That fall she was in Mississippi a lot, working on a documentary, but she wrote regularly, at one point recalling the final time we met as friends and wound up, in irony, at Tavern on the Green:

> *So foreign for New Yorkers because it is a destination for foreigners. . . . But there was something very powerful in feeling foreign with you. It's an image I've retained strongly from* The Great Gatsby — *you can be far more intimate with another person at a big party than you can at a small one.*
> *The world to me today seems like an enormous party.*

I liked how she found people and paradoxical ideas "delicious" or "scrumptious." She seemed to swallow life, savoring it all. But it was my first real relationship, and I was faking my way along. Relationships were a net of restrictions and obligations, and, finding myself caught much faster than I expected, I thrashed about resentfully. So I'd greet her with a "What should we do for dinner?" not, as she kept hoping, "I was thinking of you at lunch because . . ." She'd never met anyone with as many barriers, which worried her, but also intrigued her, which further worried her.

I recoiled from her lack of self-control, the thing I'd been drawn to: if she was feeling neglected at a party, she'd have an extra glass of wine and swing from cool to mushy, noisily confiding the problems with shooting a documentary in "Bumfuck, Nowhere." I'd tighten up—and she'd notice and frown and have another glass. And I was troubled by the tenderness I felt, dimly aware that tenderness was a precautious feeling I had toward someone I was going to hurt. In the time we saw each other—four years all told, with some time off for bad behavior—I would sleep with four other women. Each time it seemed like the answer, until it obviously wasn't.

On her birthday, six months in, she said, "Can I ask you something? Do you want to break up with me about half the time?"

"No," I said. "About a third. What's your fraction?"

"About a quarter."

Two weeks later, after we'd been together three nights in a row, I told her I needed a night off. We were due at her parents' for Passover, and Melanie's face took on the wounded look I'd begun to dread. I knew I'd be in trouble with her mother: Laurie liked her parties to go just so, and already seemed to doubt my intentions. And her husband, Eric, reminded me of a nineteenth-century policeman, down to the disapproving mustache.

I really liked Melanie's younger brothers, the family's joyful way with barbecuing and visitors, and how her great-aunt Esther and grandmother Sharon jumped to instant, full-throated dispute: "If your stomach hurts, take Alka-Seltzer!" "Mylanta!" "Alka-Seltzer!" I had expected more of that from Laurie and Eric, the clamorous unconditional Jewish love my friends were always feeling smothered by. But Melanie's parents were surprisingly Waspy. Finally, to have something we could all do together, I took up golf. Melanie and I had a wonderful time fooling around at her parents' club on Shelter Island until the four of us played a round. On the first hole, Eric, a low-handicapper with a flowing swing, hit a 250-yard bomb that kicked behind a tree. I hit a low quacker that fluttered mournfully left and then zipped forty yards right, into the middle of the fairway. "Oh, sweet pea," Melanie said, "that's beautiful!"

"That's a banana ball," her father muttered from the cart. "A slice."

"Give him some advice, Eric," Laurie said.

"Don't slice," he said, tromping the gas.

A few months later, Melanie told me that her father had taken her aside to say, "It's time you got married. To someone wealthy enough to support you. And to a Jew." The religious qualification was a surprise to both of us. Yet if we'd paid attention, we'd have noticed that her mother kept setting her up on dates with Jewish men. Years later, when I called their house in Shelter Island to wish Melanie a happy wedding that weekend, Laurie picked up and said Melanie was out. "Could you give her a message?" I asked. "Depends what it is," she replied.

No ONE in my family or its circle ever spoke to me about Jews as a topic, except Uncle Wilson. But Jews were always there in counterpoint. Grandpa Ted was hardly alone, among the Wasps on Squirrel Hill, in fretting that it was turning into "Kike's Peak."

The length and breadth of Wasp anti-Semitism remains astonishing. When the *Social Register* began, in 1887, it numbered no Jews among its nearly two thousand families; noting the volume's success, Ward McAllister—the arbiter who had established the "four hundred" people who constituted New York Society—suggested that "our good Jews might wish to put out a little book of their own, called something else of course." A few years later, Dr. Melvil Dewey, inventor of the Dewey Decimal Classification system and the hanging vertical file, founded the Lake Placid Club with the goal of a membership that would be "the country's best." Toward that end, signs on the club lawn warned: "No Dogs. No Tuberculars. No Hebrews."

In the 1920s, the elite eastern universities instituted an unpublicized quota system, capping Jews at 10 to 15 percent of each class. At Harvard, admissions officers would look at an applicant's birthplace, family names, and parental occupations to determine whether he could be classified J1, conclusively Jewish, or J2, preponderantly likely to be so. These maneuverings were ostensibly intended to manage what the Yale admissions chair, in a 1922 document entitled "The Jewish Problem," referred to as "the alien and unwashed element." The real Wasp fear, which also inspired the reactionary Immigration Act of 1924, was that the two million Jews who had arrived from Eastern Europe since 1870 were beginning to surpass them. The Wasps' underhanded response made clear that they'd lost confidence in being the chosen people.

In his incisive book *Old Money: The Mythology of Wealth in America*, Nelson W. Aldrich Jr. suggests that Wasp anti-Semitism

> *is qualitatively different from their anti-Catholicism or anti-black racism. It is more like a deadly rivalry — not over which set of values captures the soul of America, but over which ethnic group wins custody of Old Money values. If Jews are an obsession with the Wasp Old Rich, and they are, it is not because they spell the destruction of the things Old Money holds*

dear but because the Wasp Old Rich half-suspect that Jews take better care, can afford to take better care, of the patrimony than they can.

THAT FIRST Christmas, Melanie came to Villanova and was bowled over by my mother's standard greeting: Mom raced to the door, crying, "Darling!" and "Melanie!" After a hug that left an imprint of Chanel No. 5, and a bit of hostessing—"Would you like some milk? Tea? Some lovely, cool grapes?"—Mom displayed her latest coup: the hand-painted three-quarter-scale powder room sink she'd carried on her lap on the plane from Albuquerque! Ta-da! She did a Charleston step or two in triumph, and led Melanie to the crèche, to which she'd just added a tiny sheep on wheels. Mom had grown a little weary of the Christmas production, but visitors always brought out her razzle-dazzle, as if she were auditioning the house for the pageant at Radio City.

Melanie joined right in with odd family rituals like decorating the tree to the tune of the New Christy Minstrels' "Sing Along with Santa," reading *The Tailor of Gloucester*, and marching downstairs to "Hayfoot, Strawfoot." The number of gifts in her pile by the fireplace moved her to tears. Mom, who liked advising Melanie about her career and about home decoration, had gone all out. This was us at our best: bountiful, traditional, swishing the wadded-up wrapping into the garbage bin. Melanie loved it all. "In my family," she told me, "there is no yesterday, there is only today."

That summer, she and I went in on a summerhouse in Sagaponack, ten minutes from Georgica, a charming saltbox that sparrows circled at sunset. But soon enough I spoiled it. First Alessandra Visconti came for a weekend, and on Sunday night Melanie cried into the bedspread: Alessandra had only talked to me, and therefore didn't take our relationship seriously, and therefore must know I still cared for Giovanna.

"That is an amazing series of inferential leaps," I said.

"I feel lonesome," she said. "More when I'm with you."

In August, I fooled around at the saltbox with Francesca. Bookish and wry, she was me in a frock. Her father had waltzed with my mother in dancing school, a fact I stupidly mentioned to Francesca, who, in a flourish of independence, promptly canceled our next date. I left messages on her machine every day for a week, certain that she would reschedule once she realized how rude she was being. (A few years later, she sent me a postcard suggesting we get together. Then she didn't return my phone calls. Yes, I made more than one.)

After my first—and, as it turned out, only—night with Francesca, I called Melanie in Mississippi to break up. It was a painfully murky conversation, particularly as I omitted the Francesca part to spare myself. The next day she called back, sounding bravely optimistic, to remind me that I always overreacted when she went away. I should just tell her the real trouble. "Don't spare me," she said.

Finally, stumblingly, I said that I was very happy with her at home but always anxious about how she was going to behave in public.

"You're not proud of me?" Melanie said in a small voice.

———

THE SUMMER before college, when I worked at the Jersey Shore, I was seventeen and the drinking age was eighteen. A friend gave me an old fake ID that set me up as "Mike Epstein," a nineteen year old whose photo looked vaguely like a brown-eyed, curly-haired, chubbier me. I memorized his address and date of birth for the bouncers, then realized the new identity gave me running room. In a crowd of strangers, that summer and in summers following, I sometimes introduced myself as Mike. Mike went to the University of Pennsylvania, wasn't as worried about what people thought of him, and cared deeply about your orgasm. It felt great to be Mike to the extent that it was a trying on of the person I might have been, or might possibly still become. It felt shaming and miserable to the extent that I was lying to every Sharon I met, and I finally gave Mike up.

By the time I graduated from college, I realized that almost everyone I'd hung out with was Jewish: Rich Appel, Dave Stein, Paul Sax, Julie Glucksman, Deb Copaken, Jonathan Sapers, Jean Castelli. Bruce Monrad had known precisely where he and I would end up: as vice presidents somewhere. Rich and Dave seemed to think any of us could be almost anything. They seemed not to see me as a Wasp, and thereby to open up possibilities my background had threatened to foreclose.

Largely similar but just different enough, upper-middle-class Jews and Wasps are magnets with flickering polarities: attraction, retraction, compulsion, repulsion. When my colleagues at *The American Lawyer* gathered to watch the Mets in the playoffs, I cringed when a Jewish coworker I was quietly sleeping with announced, "Gary Carter has the nicest tush in the National League!" *Why "tush"? Why compare them? Why say anything whatsoever on the topic aloud?* Later, I had a running Scrabble game with, and crush on, a Jewish friend named Lisa. She said she had her heart set on a $20,000 platinum engagement ring with an emerald and a two-carat sapphire, surrounded by diamond stars. *That sounds kind of busy—and expensive.* Crush over.

MELANIE AND I got back together two or three months later, depending on how you count. The interim was messy: Melanie found out about Francesca because she started dating Francesca's boyfriend. And there was a Giovanna night in there, too. My mother gave me a little talk about the difference between love and infatuation, and I could see that she might have a point. But I hadn't gotten over my infatuation with infatuation.

That Christmas, Melanie stayed in New York, saying she wasn't ready to see my family yet. At home, I began to view my parents through Melanie's newly skeptical eyes, noticing how Mom sought praise for every meal, and how Day, annoyed with her, downed three rum-based Red Lions before dinner. Mom drew me aside one morning to say, "Don't you think Day is drinking too much?"

"Yes," I said, bracing myself. She often asked one of us to carry her water.

"I don't know how he can do it, after Grandpa Ted," she said worriedly. Then, switching tacks, she asked, "Where does male rage come from?"

"Women, probably," I said.

She thought about it and shook her head, "No. No, I don't think so."

She later brought up the drinking with Day. He went to the family doctor and asked how much alcohol would be too much, then told Mom he was only two-thirds of the way to the red zone. She felt he was making the problem mathematical and abstract—but, having made his point, Day cut back, and the threat receded.

By the following summer, trust had provisionally reestablished itself, and Melanie and I were living together on the top floor of an old tenement above the Holland Tunnel, a railroad apartment with two fireplaces and a surprising amount of light. I liked her constant nearby bustlings, just as I liked folding laundry for two. When Melanie visited William Faulkner's home, Rowan Oak, she remembered that he and I shared a birthday and picked a gardenia blossom to press into her note to me: "I love sharing my treasures, my collections, small as they may be, with you. And it fills me with such joy to be around yours. I look forward to going home as I never have before."

Georgica celebrated its one hundredth anniversary that July Fourth weekend. The night before the party, Day had a dream in which Melanie told him, "Slovenly hats are best for heads with many memories." I wanted to tell her this—she believed in dreams and psychics, in the I Ching—but it would have meant calling her in New York, and the medium would have been the message: I'm here, and you're not. Melanie loved Georgica. She loved sitting in the kitchen with Norah and getting the skinny on the rest of us, or trying to anticipate the silent summons that told us all when to go to the beach. But she wasn't there, because the celebration was for families only.

I had been fighting with my parents about whether

Melanie and I could sleep in the same bed in Villanova and Wainscott—a battle I eventually won by declaring, "Okay, we just won't visit." I didn't have the stomach for another dispute, especially when I was uncertain: was she family? So Melanie and I fought instead, because she sensed that if I wouldn't fight for her now, I wouldn't fight for her later. As I was heading out the door, she ran up in a puff of jasmine and said, "I hate feeling like this shrew who drives you away—but you drive me to it!"

"You think it's all because I don't love you enough," I said. "But it's a full-time job staving off your insecurities."

"So get a Wasp girlfriend who doesn't have any emotions!"

That was the weekend that Mom told us about Grandpa John's vanishing act.

As the celebration began, in a white tent on the softball field, I wandered to the windmill, where lovely old photos revealed the continuity of ritual across the generations: softball, tennis, beach picnics, children doing headstands by the lifeguard chair. My heart misgave me to see a young, blazingly pretty Muriel Rogers, Dickie's mother, arrested in impatient motion by the bathhouse as she hurried toward her throat cancer, her larynx surgery, her ravaged old face. No one could infer such youth from such age.

Back at the tent, Elliot Ogden made a speech of welcome, and then Wilson stood, a little unsteadily, to address us. Prostate cancer now riddled his bones, though he never spoke of the pain. "One of the reasons for the success of Georgica has been the absence of speeches," he began, drawing a laugh. He fiddled with his bow tie, waiting for quiet, then went on to make a plea for preserving those properties that did open up for "desirable candidates" who would perpetuate the Association's "character and congeniality," for keeping up a certain standard that could be met by the money of the old and the energy of the young. Though lightly delivered, his remarks seemed like a coded plea for informal restrictions. (In the surrounding Hamptons, a number of properties still carried covenants prohibiting their sale to "Jews, Negroes, and entertainers.")

Georgica's founding documents contain no racial or ethnic qualifications, but its members maintained themselves as an all-Wasp group until the 1950s, self-selecting for "our kind of person." The first Jews got in, as one longtime Georgica resident puts it, "because one was so Waspy he's not really Jewish, and one was Yale and played beautiful tennis." But there was still anxiety a few years later when Estée Lauder's son Ron became an associate member (a membership status accorded renters and those whose houses lie outside the Association). A resident says, "What you heard was 'The Lauders are lovely people, but we're afraid of their friends.' That was the way it was couched—that their friends would come and see the place and buy in, and we'll turn around and it'll be all Jews."

In the 1980s, Conrad and Peggy Cooper Cafritz were admitted as associate members: Peggy is black, and Conrad is Jewish. (Conrad's real-estate-development business ran up more than a billion dollars in debts in the early nineties, which is something of an accomplishment.) My parents liked them, and I got on well with Conrad, enjoying the way he'd purse his wine-taster's lips and twirl his reading glasses like a lariat as he tartly recounted the local gossip. But we were in the minority. The feeling against them and their splashy parties wasn't bruited about so much as passed invisibly, the way the signal to break into a trot flashes through a herd of caribou at the sight of a wolf. After a few years, the Cafritzes' membership was not renewed.

The following summer I invited Conrad over for tennis. Later that week, I was approached by an affable older member, who said, "I understand that you had Conrad Cafritz playing with you the other day."

"Yes."

"Ah."

I felt my neck begin to tighten. "I wasn't aware that that was against the rules."

"Oh, it's not," he said. "You can bring any guest you like. It's simply that he was a divisive figure, and his reappearance was felt not to be . . . auspicious." I invited Conrad back the following week, but he suggested we play at his place.

Wilson's centennial speech made me glad Melanie wasn't there, after all. She was always particularly demure around him, fearing to put a foot wrong, even as I was particularly voluble, trying to forefend the kind of remarks he'd occasionally made to me about how "Jews are spoiling the character at Yale, sophisticating the collegial atmosphere." He was a textbook anti-Semite of his era: opposed to Jews as a group but willing to make exceptions for outstanding individuals of his acquaintance. Maybe he liked Melanie, or maybe he didn't know she was Jewish—he was often surprised that people he liked were. I never knew if his silence on the topic around her was owing to courtesy, or conscience, or simple luck.

MELANIE AND I had lived together for a year when she quit producing documentaries to focus on her poetry. Soon she was down to her last two thousand dollars, and I was grumpily paying the rent for both of us—grumpily because it put the question of joint property in sharp relief. When we went away together for my travel stories, to Egypt, Morocco, and Greece, the holiday mood would darken as Melanie realized that I wasn't, just yet, going to propose. When I traveled alone, I'd come home to find her at the top of the stairs, studying my face as I mounted. Her questions grew more pressing: would we raise the kids Christian or Jewish? Have a bris or a christening? My suggestion of a "brisening" bought me a little more time. I had no desire to raise our potential children as Christians—I didn't believe in God—but I didn't particularly want them raised as Jews, either. I had in mind some kind of traditional yet nonreligious household that treasured Christmas. She began talking about having a baby without me, if necessary. "Are you still taking the pill?" I asked. There was a mutinous silence.

Walking near Macy's, I saw a small woman in her seventies eagerly selling blue and pink baby bonnets from a grocery bag at her feet. "I knit them myself," she kept saying to the indifferent throngs: "I made them all myself!" The caps weren't particularly attractive, but I was moved to buy one to ease her increasingly crestfallen look and reward her for hoping. I began to pull out my wallet, then put it away—what would I do with a baby bonnet? I didn't tell Melanie about the incident, because it had brought her so to mind.

Late that summer, while tidying up for a poker game, I was carrying one of Melanie's notebooks back to her office when a poem fell out. "Maplewood Farm, 1993 (for Tad)" was about sifting through Grandma Tim's paintings after her death, the year before, about memory and loss. It ended:

> *In the hayloft's yeasty nave*
> *We lay listening to pigeons*
> *In the rafters, pigs mucking below, alive*
> *In all that dark.*

Replacing it, smiling, I saw my name in the notebook in a journal entry, and the words "he has many problems, very deep." Startled, I read on, my face growing hot. Then I settled in to proceed chronologically from our breakup in 1991 — when there was a lot of abuse of me, most of it deserved — and learned that I was self-centered, cold, uncaring, and emotionally immature. I had developed my defiant solitude to cope with my mother, while modeling my inexpressiveness on my father. She'd canvassed some of my close friends, and they agreed with her.

I felt a little better about reading her journal when one entry revealed that she'd begun reading my journals a few months earlier, but also much worse, because my journals were the repository of all my doubts about our relationship. Privy to them now, she had written: "DO NOT HAVE CHILDREN WITH THIS MAN." And yet here she still was. During our next fight, when she kept asking about Giovanna — actually not a threat, just then — I shouted, "Goddammit, I do love you," and hurled my glass of iced tea onto the kitchen floor. After I sheepishly mopped the linoleum and swept up the broken glass, I found her sitting pensively on the edge of the bathtub. "So there's my lack of self-worth and my fear of abandonment," she said. "I'm more frightened than you are, as you once told me," I said. We rested our foreheads together.

She was seeing a psychotherapist, and at her increasingly determined suggestion, I began therapy myself that September. I acquiesced in part to buy more time. But I'd been thinking about talking to someone for two years, ever since Grandpa John's wife, Sherleigh, tumbled down the stairs and sustained a skull fracture that would, within weeks, carry her off. After her fall, I called Grandpa John but couldn't get him to understand who I was. I repeatedly identified myself—- "It's your grandson Tad!"—but he said, "I think you have the wrong number," in polite, going-away tones.

After hanging up in bewilderment, I waited ten minutes and called back. "It's Tad!" I yelled, and he said, "Oh, hello."

After saying how sorry I was about Sherleigh, I asked how he was.

"Bearing up," he said briskly. "Still traveling?" With a sense of unreality, I mentioned that Melanie and I were about to go to Egypt, where I'd be writing a travel piece. "When I had the bad taste to climb on the dome of the Taj Mahal seventy years ago, the novelty of foreign places had not yet worn off," he observed. "Now it has, and travel per se is no longer enough to write about." Yes, I said, that's right. Dismayed by the thickness of his shield, yet unable to think of a single consoling thing to say to pierce it, I worried, after we concluded the call, that I'd end up just like him.

Still, I went into therapy with the idea that my shrink should be able, within six weeks or so, to tell me whether the problem in my relationship with Melanie was me, or her, or us. I ended up on the couch for thirteen years.

Just before Christmas, Melanie and I saw *A Perfect World*, in which Kevin Costner plays Butch, a convict in Texas in 1963 who escapes and, more or less by accident, kidnaps an eight-year-old boy named Phillip. I had just begun, haltingly, to talk about my childhood with my therapist, Sylvia, after she'd observed, "I'm beginning to wonder why you feel it's so important to seem chipper, in here. I mean, you came to me for a reason, no?" Now, as I watched the growing bond between Kevin Costner and an uncertain boy, the exchange of confidences and physical affection, I felt my chest tighten. Butch carries a postcard his father sent from Alaska after he took off when Butch was young, and near the end of the film, as the Texas Rangers are closing in for a showdown we sense won't end well, he reads it to Phillip:

> *Just wanted to tell you that me leaving has nothing to do with you. Alaska is a very beautiful place, colder than hell most all the time. Someday you can come and visit and we'll maybe get to know each other better.*

By the time the lights went up, I was sobbing. Melanie put her hand on mine. I flung it off, then reached for it again. "Just—I love you, but just don't," I said. "I can't talk about it right now."

That last spring, Melanie kept calling from a puppy store, saying she'd fallen for a Cavalier King Charles spaniel that wriggled with joy whenever she tapped on the window. "She won't bark, I promise," Melanie said. "She never barks." Our landlord, who worked downstairs, had a phobia about dogs and our lease forbade them. But after a week of Melanie sobbing herself to sleep, we brought Lulu home. Cavaliers are a quirky, overbred group—former hunting dogs with a lousy sense of direction—but they are wonderfully affectionate. Lulu was fond of scooting toward us on her butt (which turned out to mean she had worms) and prodigal with face licks. Soon Melanie was paying more attention to Lulu than to me, and relishing the instant reciprocation. It both vexed and surprised me that though I was doing a considerable share of the kibble pouring and let's-go-for-a-walk-now-ing, Lulu responded more to Melanie's rapturous embraces.

In May, after a happy ten days in Ireland, Melanie and I fought on our last night. It was a strange fight, a fight in reverse. She said she'd be willing to postpone having kids. Feeling stricken by this desperate sacrifice—feeling unworthy of it—I told her she should find someone better than me to have children with. I suppressed the gamy knowledge that I was relieved, as I could now leave seeming noble, rather than just slinking off. As we were falling asleep, exhausted, in our small white room near Shannon Airport, she whispered, "Stay with me." I began crying, and it took me a while to say, "I just don't feel your love the way I should." "I'm sorry you don't feel you were loved enough," she said, still very quietly. "I had high hopes for you."

When our landlord told us we had to go, it forced the final reckoning. I went to Georgica that August, and Melanie went to Shelter Island, and we made slow-motion plans for movers to divide our furniture. She kept Lulu, naturally, but for years afterward when I saw them, Lulu would still give me a face lick, a touching washcloth swipe of remembrance.

For the first time, the house and the beach and the lawn

in Georgica didn't restore me. Mom came into my room one
night and said, "I just realized that if you're breaking up with
Melanie, that means I have to break up with her, too."

"That's how it usually works," I said wearily.

"But I don't want to break up with Melanie," she said.

You HEAR a lot about Catholic guilt and Jewish guilt,
but very little on the topic among Wasps. In *Exit Ghost*,
Philip Roth's alter ego, Nathan Zuckerman, ponders the
late George Plimpton, the founding editor of *The Paris
Review*—an exuberant Wasp apparently unconstrained by
second thoughts as he flung himself into participatory
journalism, designing fireworks displays, birding, and party-
going.

> *George afforded my first glimpse of privilege and its vast re-
> wards — he seemingly had nothing to escape, no flaw to hide or
> injustice to defy or defect to compensate for or weakness to
> overcome or obstacle to circumvent, appearing instead to have
> learned everything and to be open to everything altogether
> effortlessly. . . . When people say to themselves "I want to be
> happy," they could as well be saying "I want to be George
> Plimpton."*

Yet I felt nothing but guilt about Melanie. If Catholic
guilt is "I've been bad" and Jewish guilt is "You've been bad,"
then Wasp guilt is "You probably think I've been bad." Wasp
guilt derives from knowing your ancestors would say you'd
let down the side. I felt that in shying from Melanie's
full-hearted if messy love I had not lived up to my inherited

expectations of candor and decency and, well, menschiness. Later, I would begin to think that the guilt long pre-existed Melanie, and was not the result but the motive of the crime.

Wilson seemed to feel intermittent guilt toward our family; in the 1970s, he'd asked my parents if they wanted to buy his back three acres, and my father had offered him our entire savings, $55,000. Wilson instead took $75,000 from Donald Petrie, and then we all watched as the property's value began doubling every three or four years. "I thought, *Twenty thousand dollars, in family — Wilson, you should have sold to us,*" Day says. "Petrie and I used to rag each other. He knew he'd gotten a good deal."

In April of 1993, Wilson sent off a letter to Mom and Paddy and Norah that Mom passed on to us. It was a pained statement of reckoning; he announced that he'd been dipping into capital just to meet expenses, and that after he died, he feared it would be "imperative that my heirs or my estate sell Wainscott or rent it for some profitable part of each summer." Melanie and I wrote him to ask if we might rent Century House for two weeks that August for $2,000, much less than market rates but a lot for us. He replied, "I feel greatly restored and cheered and strengthened! Wainscott has been a joint venture from which we have each of us drawn great pleasures but to which we have each also made sacrifices and personal contributions. May it long so continue."

When we saw Wilson in Wainscott, he could only walk halfway across the living room behind his walker. He would be dead by October. One afternoon in the kitchen, Norah told Melanie and me that her father had confided that he kept seeing an entity: the head of a woman with cornrows, an alien countenance who hovered peacefully near the floor, smiling at him. "It's like he's open to a whole other set of possibilities, now, at the very end," Norah said.

"It's amazing!" Melanie agreed.

My father had come in for a cup of tea and heard the end of this, and he remarked, "He's on a lot of medications, is he not, which could explain such an apparition?" I was irritated by this characteristic response, and irritated with Norah and Melanie for the credence that provoked this characteristic response—one I recognized, from seeing Melanie's face close down, as my own.

Late that summer, Grandpa John and his third wife, Hanny Duell, visited Wilson for what everyone knew would be the final time. Without Hanny's happy return to his life, I doubt Grandpa John would have returned to Wainscott then, the site of his ignominy in 1938 and of the consequent shift in authority to Wilson, who would essentially become our substitute grandfather. He'd only been back once since Tisha Pierson was married on the lawn in 1962.

John had escorted Hanny to her debut in 1928, and she'd saved his letter to her afterward; when he came to Villanova for Christmas in 1990, she sent the letter back to him, care of my parents, in a gift stocking. Embarrassed by our curiosity, he slid the letter into his jacket and muttered, "No comment." Hanny, on the other hand, was a marvel of forthrightness. She wrote to her grandchildren to say: "I have known John Pierson ever since my brother Charles brought him home from Yale over sixty years ago. He has always been my friend. It seems it was ordained for us to live our lives separately and fully, albeit along converging lines, until our turn came. That is now." It was clear that she and

Grandpa John should have been married all along—though then none of us would be here.

Melanie and I joined the three of them in the dining room for their last meal; John and Hanny were catching the ferry very early in the morning. I mentioned the trip Melanie and I had taken to Greece that summer, and how after we arrived on Syros we took a caique around the limestone cliffs to Grandpa John's land and spent an evening in the cottage there. Melanie spoke feelingly of the walk up from the dock through the reforested tamarisks and Aleppo pines.

Grandpa John asked whether we'd heard or seen any goats.

"We did, I'm afraid," I said. Hanny put her hand on John's. "They had amazing food at the market," I continued, with determined cheer. "We packed it in with us and ate on the porch, by candlelight, listening to the crickets. We had Kavarnis wine, *tzatziki*, Kefalotiri cheese, and about six amazingly sweet tomatoes."

From the head of the mahogany table, a vast wooden raft carrying him out, Wilson roused himself: "Tomaytoes!"

After dinner, he went straight to bed. But he summoned the strength, when he'd arrived at the stairs in three slow tacks of his walker, to conclude his hostly duties. Turning to Hanny, he inclined his head and said, "Very nice getting to know you better."

"Good night, then," John said.

"Good night."

THIRTEEN

Reconstruction

T HE FIRST FEW times I edged into Dr. Sylvia Welsh's office, a formidable room saved from austerity by a wooden dollhouse, I thought her censorious. In our second psychotherapy session I tried to recall how we'd ended the first time, and she said, "With the girl who was too young for you," dispatching Giovanna in a phrase. So I decided that Sylvia lived alone with a Manx cat—even as I couldn't help noticing that she was sexy, animated, and nearly fearless. In fact, she was married—her husband's office was next door, which I somehow *could* help noticing—and had a daughter. I was gazing at the world through X-ray glasses that revealed every woman as an enchantress.

Sylvia was a slight woman in her early forties who looked great in Lanvin suits and Louboutin shoes whose brazen red soles reminded me where my money was going, a subject I kept bringing up. I knew I was being stingy and overparticular—a real Wasp—but I couldn't help myself: the only way out was through. She'd observe that she was charging me half her usual rate and that I could see the transaction as a gift, not a theft. Finally, she'd say, "*Oy vey*, shut up, already." She brought out the Wasp in me and I the Jew in her. Eventually, that would change.

Early on, I mentioned that I was a good dancer. "What?" Sylvia said, cackling. "*I'm* a good dancer — I'm a great dancer, in fact. You, not so much, I'm guessing." The subject was fraught: an ability to waltz and foxtrot is the Wasp's traditional ticket to inclusion. In 1888, Ward McAllister explained why he'd set the limits of society at four hundred people: "If you go outside four hundred," he said, "you strike people who are either not at ease in a ballroom or else make other people not at ease." Yet tutored ease was the opposite of what Sylvia and I were talking about: rhythm, attunement, a bluesy willingness to sweat and shake and throb. Namely, sex. That her barb stung only proved her point that, off the dance floor, at least, I seemed about as funkadelic as Richard Nixon.

After eighteen months she encouraged me to try psychoanalysis. I stopped sitting up and talking to her once a week and started lying down and talking to her bookshelf four times a week. I knew I must be making progress, because I felt so much worse. Across the months and years my anxieties came to seem intensely repetitive yet implacable. Why didn't she call back? Why hasn't my editor responded yet? Why am I so ashamed of anger, or any strong emotion? Why has this couch become the most important place in my life? I could buy an apartment, load up on Berkshire Hathaway stock, and travel the world *if I weren't bankrupting myself here.* Sylvia finally brought me up short: "Do you really have a better use for the money?"

My PARENTS' Villanova house was in some ways a compromise. Mom had wanted a sun-filled modern home, but Day urged heritage, which was cheaper. They wound up, in 1989, with a two-hundred-year-old gardener's cottage on the corner of an old estate. The two-acre plot came with a brook and a pond and more than a hundred trees, including, looming over the roof, a sugar maple that Mom gazed at fearfully in high winds. As for the house itself, with its hulking front-door hood and its ragbag of additions . . . her kinder friends merely murmured, "Oh, Libby!" If it had been up to Day, the decor might have remained as it was, the drab walls and defiant shabbiness of reflexive Wasp style. But over the next decade Mom corralled all the talents and energies that she had poured into painting and needlepoint and being a college president's wife, and hitched them to the house, dragging it where she foresaw.

Three sets of architects were called in to realize her ideas, eleven major projects in all, each of which she had drawn up without allowing for such blemishing inconveniences as ventilation equipment or smoke alarms. When she was reminded of these necessities, her lips would set, and then, switching on her twin high beams—one of charm, one of acute distress—she would bulldoze the architects into making it all work. Three small bedrooms became the master suite, the old kitchen became a mudroom, a passageway became a bar. Above the bar she carved a pass-through so you could relay glasses to the new kitchen, a festive command center with ribbons of shelves and a blue-and-white Portuguese-tile backsplash. Between the kitchen and the dining room she hung sliding barn doors on iron braces, so that you could close off the kitchen when you had catered dinners and no one would be the wiser. There weren't any catered dinners, of course, and the sliding doors slid only for illustration; the whole idea was a revenant wish from a bygone way of life.

Day, aside from frowningly monitoring the cost and halting construction when the bills grew too preposterous — delays she chafed at, hating parsimony — ended up leaving most of the details to her. His taste was earthier; by surrendering on any number of other points, he was finally able to persuade her to preserve the rough stone of two internal walls that she had intended to plaster over. One of my mother's friends, observing her tenacity in these struggles and seeing her as a chatelaine on a par with E. M. Forster's Mrs. Wilcox, took to calling the house "Doric's End."

Day liked to walk the grounds, to supervise the koi in the pond and return with an armload of wood, but Mom preferred her nature domesticated. When she created a garden behind her bedroom, she bounded it with locust posts topped by copper caps like upside-down pie tins and filled it with dwarf cherry and tiny cypress and a miniature pine that popped out of a blue-and-white pot. The centerpiece was a stone bull that she hoped future grandchildren would ride. This secret garden turned the out-of-doors into a drawing room. At the same time, by some alchemy, the house was opened up to the out-of-doors, made into the sunny villa she had always wanted. She detested darkness and confining spaces — the womb, Buick 8s in a storm, the grave.

———

WHENEVER ANYONE rang the bell, Mom would shanghai him or her, be it beloved son or bewildered Girl Scout, into a house tour. These lasted almost forever: like Russian dolls, her rooms held stories nested within larger stories. En route to her handmade sink from Albuquerque, for instance, she'd see the ironwood chest she'd found in Seoul and be reminded that when she'd received her MasterCard bill for it she'd become convinced that she had made a killing on the exchange rate at the dealer's expense. Later, when she couldn't make the dealer see how he'd shortchanged himself—"I placed an *international* call, but, nonetheless . . ."—she had made a compensatory donation to a Korean eye hospital. The logic was characteristic, as was the punctilio, as was the guilt, as was the belief that she could have taken advantage of an antiques dealer.

In the living room, she placed her mother's silver gravy boat and travel alarm clock on a table alongside a maple burl and a bowl of marble eggs and shells. She was ravenous for choice objects, telling more than one friend that she wanted their embroidered sofa pillows after they died. Looking down on the table were an oil painting by Guy Pène du Bois that showed Grandma Tim in her glamorous twenties and, on an adjoining wall, ten of Grandma Tim's own ink drawings. Each room was intended as a Joseph Cornell box, and the living room was a wonder cabinet dedicated to the Hartford Butterfly.

The house began to resemble one of the virtual-memory palaces imagined by the Greeks as an aid to recollection. Mom was now terrified of Alzheimer's, so memory-laden talismans were a source of tremendous comfort. Her idea was to both acknowledge and subdue the past—her past, particularly—by giving it a cameo role among her present pleasures. Goggy Coxe's desk was gathered along with Goggy Pierson's desk and Goggy Robinson's *poudreuse;* all the Goggies were given one chance to shine.

If you lingered by the silver menagerie, she would hand you the small elephant that she had acquired in 1968 through her acquaintance with Connie Mangskau, a Bangkok antiques dealer. Connie Mangskau had asked Mom to carry a letter to a dealer across the border in Siem Reap: "Just an innocent little old letter, she said." When my mother handed the Cambodian dealer the padded envelope, he sliced it open and tipped out a pile of diamonds. In appreciation, he invited her to take a memento from his shop, and, while she was *furious* at Connie Mangskau, she had finally picked out this elephant, but later she was *furious* at herself for not picking out the much larger one nearby, an elephant the size of a basketball! She would mention, in passing, that she had first met Connie Mangskau in 1955, when she was in Bangkok teaching English. She would not mention that she'd gone there for Grandpa John.

Driven to whisk everything unsightly away, she also sought to coax applause by demonstrating how the trick was done. A rolltop panel in the kitchen, an "appliance garage," would be raised to display the huddled coffeemaker, Cuisinart, and blender. And Day grumbled about how she herded visitors into his bathroom to show off the louvered cabinet that hid—ta-da!—his drying jockstraps.

Timmie suggested that Mom start a business designing tiny spaces and call it Martha Store-It. But Mom couldn't have endured anyone else's inexactitude. Before laying out her kitchen drawers, she took a tape measure to a variety of bread loaves and determined that three of them would fit snugly in a drawer that was five inches high, seventeen inches wide, and eighteen inches deep. And she had a group of architects sit in a circle while she measured the mean length of their shins to determine the proper depth of a Japanese tea well for Day's study (sixteen and a half inches). She designed as if she were on a ship, where space is scant and items may have to be battened down in a storm. Some of her nooks and cubbies were so small—*so* small—they looked as if they had been made by little mice.

Sylvia pointed out how strong my incest taboo was, and as we discussed my "type"—Mediterranean-Jewish, short, mysterious, built—she suggested that I might eventually see my mother, who was none of those things, as attractive. "Maybe someday you won't even have a type," she said.

"Of course you'd say that, because you're just my type."

"But you don't have sexual feelings for me, either," she pointed out.

"Not that I want to talk about with *you*."

In the first month after I broke up with Melanie, I slept with two women. "You feel guilty about sleeping with women you don't have feelings for," Sylvia observed.

"Yes, but maybe it would be better if I could just sleep with people and not feel guilty."

"Maybe it would be better if you could just *murder* people and not feel guilty. Trust your guilt."

"*Veh is mir*," I said—"I am pain itself"—and she laughed.

We got into my dreams, naturally. So many came clamoring then: an occasional flight over a crescent beach, or a bike ride on Highland Avenue in Buffalo under a canopy long since felled by Dutch elm disease, sunlight powdering through phantom limbs. But more usually slogs along wintry roads where I couldn't see my own reflection in the black ice, dreams almost too schematic to repeat that afternoon and often erased on waking anyway, leaving only a seam of unease. Recurrently, I was playing soccer on my usual left wing and ran down my line to find myself thwarted by a stand of mangroves. Or, on the squash court, a thicket in midcourt hid both the ball and my opponent. "It's interesting to me," Sylvia said one day, "as we've been talking about how you equate intimacy with submission, a loss of self rather than an increase, that your sports in these dreams are soccer—'sock her'—and squash, a verb of violent suppression."

"Oh, come on!" I said. "I didn't *name* the sports; I just played them."

"But you had the dreams."

The intimacy of analysis is uneven: Sylvia came to know nearly everything about me, but while I came to know aspects of her very well—the tenderness, the feistiness, the disdain for hypocrites and Republicans—her biography was a near-blank. I knew only that she'd been married before, that she'd once had a job driving a Thomas's bread truck, and that she was a blocked novelist (which we both knew informed her eagerness to help me find myself as a writer). One gray day she seemed low—much later, I would learn that her father had just died—and I remarked on her mood, and we got to talking in a quieter vein than usual, and suddenly she told me how her parents had come to Cleveland from Poland after the Nazis wiped out most of her family, including her grandmother and her mother's five siblings. The Holocaust was still alive for her, having loomed over her childhood as a recurrent summons to despair. I felt an awed pride that she was confiding these details to me, that being attentive really did elicit confession. And I felt guilt at having been so comparatively favored: fortune's child.

Recognizing this—recognizing she'd made a textbook error—Sylvia began our next session by apologizing. "I feel much closer to you because you trusted me," I said. "How can that be bad?"

"Trust me," she said. "It can." And then she told me that even when I was just lying there, listening, my vigilance was seductive. I took this as a great compliment. Later, I began to see it as a warning.

FOLLOWING MOM everywhere as she renovated was Sam, her Tibetan spaniel. When she shopped for pile rugs or a bellows, he perched in the passenger seat of her Honda with an expectant look whose acuity was not increased by one of his eyes being brown and the other blue. I was jealous of Sam, of their mutual adoration: he barked rapturously whenever she returned. After he was hit by a car and clumped timidly around the house with a splint on his left hind leg, a one-dog conga line, Mom dropped everything to ply him with treats. Nothing knits a fracture like crème brûlée. In a profile of her in Swarthmore College's magazine, in the late seventies, Mom had said, of our Newfoundland, "I always wanted to have a lion, and Molly is what I have instead. She has a small brain but a large heart, and gives us lots of love. She seems to be more expensive, more time-consuming, and to require more medical attention than any of the children, but I adore her because she is totally uncritical." After Molly died, Day said, "I want to be your dog for a while." "Oh, Dorie," she said lightly. "Who would train you?"

Molly would search your face with myopic benevolence, then lick it as much as she felt you needed. *The Official Preppy Handbook* observed that "massive size and saliva output make this breed almost uncontrollable and nearly impossible to keep indoors—no one outside the serious Prep Family even considers this dog for a pet." Wasps prefer outdoor dogs, both as an emblem of our pastoral and sporting roots, and because they help us get muddy. They are transitional objects, allowing the otherwise unseemly romp and snuggle. Another, darker view of the preference for such dogs was expressed by Jean-Jacques Rousseau, in conversation with James Boswell:

> ROUSSEAU: *Do you like cats?*
> BOSWELL: *No.*
> ROUSSEAU: *I was sure of that. It is my test of character. There you have the despotic instinct of men. They do not like cats because the cat is free, and will never consent to become a slave. He will do nothing to your order, as the other animals do.*

Like Mom herself, Sam was a cat in dog's clothing. His wicker basket in the Villanova mudroom was a perfect replica of her Christmas bassinet for the Christ child, only at 100x. When Mom first showed Sam the new basket, thoughtfully positioned near his water and food bowls, he made two anxious circles inside it and then threw up. He preferred to sleep in my parents' bedroom, because the eccentric heating system blew gusts of hot air toward their bed while leaving the upstairs rooms, where we slept, meat-locker cold. Sam would lie by the vent with his front paws formally arrayed, like the stone lions guarding the New York Public Library, the mistral fanning his fur. In the middle of the night he would bound onto my parents' bed, wriggle over Mom's back, and sleep cradled between them.

Sam's waywardness echoed Mom's inability to follow her own dispositions. Though she had designed a phone-booth-size study for herself off the master bedroom, she preferred to answer mail and tackle problems from one of at least six other places in the house. Each of these areas overflowed with catalogues and *Architectural Digest*s, from which she'd grab ideas for cabinets and cubbies, which were no sooner built than they, too, overflowed with catalogues and *Architectural Digest*s. After she died, Timmie and Pier and I went through the epic scatter of her files, trying to decipher her system. Her system turned out to be stacking or bundling all the stray paper within reach on a given day. In her computer, I found a poem that she'd written recently on the sly, her first real poem in nearly fifty years, a time she described to friends as a prolonged writer's block. It began, "My husband is watching me iron. / Steam reassures him. The hiss of starch / The probing slide around each button of his shirt / Speaks to him of Solway Street in Pittsburgh." And among its lines were the following:

> *My house specializes in these challenges.*
> *Bags of mail I did not ask to receive*
> *Choke the floor of the linen closet.*

A photograph of me, holding a baby on a beach.
But which beach and, for that matter, which baby?
A Japanese chest whose bottom drawer has
*   irresponsibly locked itself,*
And who can remember where I put the key?

WASPS SHOULD love therapy, as it stops you behaving in uncontrolled ways, and makes you responsible for your actions—that stock phrase of parental admonition. Yet many Wasps, my family being a partial exception, distrust the talking cure because it also reorients you from collective adherence to individual need, from loyalty to inquiry. Two months after beginning analysis, I had lunch with Day at a pasta place near my apartment. After we'd eaten our salads, I nervously launched into what had long been troubling me, saying that I thought our relationship could be more emotionally candid. I said that while love was all around in our family, he and I talked only about sports and books and money. I faltered and trailed off, having hoped to say something more, something like "The fact that love wasn't voiced much was supposed to illustrate the richness of our attachments, but it seemed to just save everyone the risk of expression." But first I needed to feel that he was with me so far.

"I'm glad you're getting a chance to work on some of these difficult matters with your doctor," Day said. After he delivered a few observations on the benefits of self-examination, bright spots flushed his cheeks, and he said, "But I do love you." He told me how when I was eighteen months old, he was babysitting me in my stroller outside—*Babysitting? You can't babysit your own child*—and dribbling a stone between his feet, soccer player that he was, and he gave it a kick, and it skimmed off at an unexpected angle and just missed my head. "I was almost knocked down by the force of my love and mortification—what had I done?"

You kicked a stone at my head? But I was touched that he was trying. A few days later, he wrote me:

> *I hope the conversation was as useful to you as it was illuminating to me. I do not imagine you found much wisdom (unlike those coffeehouse conversationalists who enjoyed "dipping in the honey pot of Oliver Goldsmith's mind"). Or that you uncovered illuminating secrets (as did the FBI, rummaging in Aldrich Ames's trash bin to discover his true mentality). But I am ready for any such exercise any time that may serve your need, and the joy of family discourse.*

It was hard to tell whether he wanted to open up the discussion or close it down. Both, maybe.

IN THE summer of 1995, my mother finally asked her father, then nearly ninety and suffering from Parkinson's disease, why he'd kept leaving. She placed Grandpa John on her built-in sofa at the center of a house designed, in a sense, to facilitate his return: here was lovingly gathered all the best that she and Grandma Tim had had to offer. She spoke in her determined way, with a premonitory toss of her head that indicated both her wish not to offend and her intention to carry on regardless. She began with the hurricane and worked up to the airport in Bangkok, the years of feeling that she was a disappointment. "Oh, Weenie," he said at last. "I'm sorry I was such a skunk."

Two days later, still elated by the exchange, she discovered a lump in her left breast. On the operating table, she felt an entity beside her, a big dog she decided must be Molly. The mastectomy revealed that the cancer had metastasized into thirteen of her lymph nodes. She underwent radiation and chemotherapy and weathered it all very well, palliating her claustrophobia during her CAT scan by clutching Malta in her right hand. Then her oncologist recommended an experimental regimen of stem cell replacement and high-dose chemotherapy as a further firewall.

When she checked into the hospital for it, I sent her a Care Bear with a gauze bandage attached to its paw and a card that said, "It's going to be all right." She sobbed when she opened it, and kept the bear with her in the hospital, and later on her desk at home. I liked being reassuring; it reassured me. But the high-dose chemo almost killed her. After years of freezing out her body's needs, she suddenly found her body responding in kind. Three years later she recalled the experience to her fellow parishioners at the Bryn Mawr Presbyterian Church:

> *You stop eating, you are nauseated, your bladder is unreliable, you have uncontrollable diarrhea, you develop terrific diaper rash, you vomit, you're dizzy, you bleed from the sores in your mouth, which, for one week, are so bad you can't speak — just make gurgling sounds — you have terrifying Dante-esque nightmares — and all of this goes on relentlessly, spiraling down for days and days and days. . . . Suddenly death, which had always been fearsome, seemed like a wonderful resource.*

When she came home, wretched and weak, my father unexpectedly arose from his books. He had been thriving as president of the Eisenhower Exchange Fellowships Foundation, in Philadelphia, expanding its programs and increasing its endowment from zero to $24 million in just a dozen years, but now, at sixty-five, he stepped down to be with her.

As they were brushing their teeth one night, Mom studied her bald head in the mirror and said, "I look like a Martian."

"A dramatically intelligent-looking Martian," Day said. "Really you look more like an actor made up for Noh drama."

Mom gave a soft scream and shook her head in the Japanese tremolo. "Do you love me?" she asked.

"Yes, I love you."

"Why?"

"Only three reasons. Because you are courageous, tender, and amusing."

She thought it over. "That's enough, I guess."

Later, she would paint a self-portrait of this new way of being, *My Beasts and I: In Memory of My Father.* Robed in red, she surrounded herself with Grandpa John's tiger and other animals, like a priest in some ancient ceremony. Wiped clean of gaiety, her face looked scourged, gaunt, and wise. "It's quite something," I said when she showed it to me. "Very powerful." I knew I sounded mealymouthed—she was obviously proud of the work—but the painting frightened me. I had longed for greater candor between us, but not this candor, not death as the mother of beauty.

Later that spring, Grandpa John called to see how Mom was doing; they had grown much closer since she challenged him in Grandma Tim's old manner. He asked Day, "How's my bride doing?"—then caught himself, with a chuckle, and said, "I mean, How's *your* bride doing?"

Mom was doing increasingly well. For months there was napping, and constant nausea, and an auburn wig. And then, after a year, she was back. As a consequence of gazing into the abyss, perhaps, she had stopped feeling unappreciated, mostly, and she and Day had never been closer. Her hair came in short and sleek and gray, and she looked like a wise elf. Now that she'd ripened into a true grande dame, her crotchets were a vital constituent of her character. Proud of her hard-won victories, Mom would correct anyone who congratulated her on being in remission—a word that, to her, suggested that the cancer was merely in abeyance, tucked away. She was *cured*, and just the person she had hoped to be when, in 1955, she wrote a "Memo to Myself" on a sheet of blue stationery:

> *Today, when I am twenty-one, just fresh from what will probably be the last of my formal education and full of misgivings about my future, wondering especially if I will ever fall in love with someone and marry him — today John Bishop [her boyfriend] said to me one of the nicest things that I have ever heard. In answer to my suggestion that I might, you know, be an old maid after all, he told me: "No, that couldn't be, for I know that the older you become the more beautiful and the more charming you will be." How good if that were true.*

IN 1997, I fell in love with Christine Wells, a book editor. Smart and precise and sensitive as a seismograph, she had a laugh that was all the more eruptive for being reluctant. She also had a fiancé, and I spent a long time lining up saucers of milk beneath her tree as she stared down at me, her eyes shining through the darkness. We had a wonderful five months, and I particularly remember how happily intent she was one afternoon when we went for a long bike ride on Long Island and stopped to pick blackberries, her face crimson with juice and exertion. Then, after we'd traveled in southern Portugal, she said she needed to be alone for a while. Well, it hadn't always been wonderful: I had gone that summer to Mongolia and Los Angeles and Vermont in part to weather her storms of sorrow, hoping they'd blow over while I was gone, as if depression were a nor'easter. But it had always been promising, and breaking up didn't seem to make either of us feel any better. I missed her smell, a distinctive combination of laundry bluing and anxiety.

My father faxed me from Jakarta to say, "I think you are wise to use time as a resource for whatever it offers that you may wish to choose, including (1) repair toward commitment or (2) easing off to affectionate detachment; or (2) enabling (1) but not, obviously, (1) entropic to (2)." Then Christine wrote that she had "a few lovely pictures" from a weekend we'd spent with her parents, including "one where you're poised on the cliff above the beach, looking out to a misty sea, Cortez-wise, and I'm laboring up the slope. Isn't that funny." We got back together, on and mostly off, for five more months. So (1) entropic to (2), if I understand what that means. She was different now, wary of me not on principle but from experience—a verdict that only made me redouble my foredoomed efforts to retrieve her. I seemed to have perfected, with Christine, my ability to inspire women to progress from writing long e-mails burgeoning with declarations to short e-mails as clenched as a thistle. Later, she wrote:

You seemed quite sure (as I probably was as well; we were two prickly people cautiously attempting to disarm ourselves) that there was no such thing as a surfeit of affection and regard, that the supply was always going to be finite, and that any giving of it had to be counterbalanced quickly by a getting of it. This didn't seem ungenerous to me, just exacting. But I noticed a real shift from when we went from being friends — and you were a kind and very generous friend — to being in love. Then things that might not seem to be about love and attachment itself — who paid what part of the check, who performed which errand, who went uptown and who went down — all began to symbolize who had been loved more, and this, for you, in a very concrete way. And I began to get the sense that an imbalance in these things would be killing.

When I told Sylvia of Christine's views, she said, "Yes, you seem all needy and sensitive and then, once you've lured them in, you get mean." I scowled at her textbooks. "You've kept this analysis very clean, you know—you don't talk dirty," she continued, gathering speed as she ran for one of her trains of thought. "It's why you were relieved to break up—you basically told her, 'Go off and work on your mess.' It's all connected, don't you see? —your fear of intimacy, of your own imagination, of mess, and of expressing emotion. This is very exciting!"

"*You're* excited," I said. "But you're not the one who has to work on all these problems."

"But I am working on them," she said gently. "I'm working on them with you." I lay quiet, trembling. "Why is it so hard for you to acknowledge that you want me to love you?" Her perceptiveness, just then, made me hate her.

When I came home that Thanksgiving, Mom asked me whether I had any romantic prospects. I said, "No," in a leave-me-alone tone.

"It's possible," she said carefully, "to look at my interest as an acknowledgment of having done damage in the intimacy area, and a wish to help."

"Well, I appreciate that, but I'm not sure you can at this point."

"It seems easier now to raise children, because they have those carriers where you go into a museum and the child goes with you," she said, referring to BabyBjörns. "I can imagine, as a grandmother, wanting to take a child to a museum. But when I was a child that never happened, so I basically liked to spend time alone. At camp, when I was nine, I would go into the woods, scrape leaves from a rock, and commune with it—my only friend." She pouted, jokingly.

"I'm sorry for that, but didn't that teach you what loneliness is like?"

"Day and I tried very hard to pass on less loneliness than we got."

I could see that that was true, but said only, "That's a worthy goal."

She frowned at the slight stress on *goal* but continued, "You were a very nice baby. Mrs. Krushke said you were one of the sweetest babies she'd ever seen." Mrs. Krushke was my baby nurse. "But I wasn't really sure I wanted this baby, and you were always spitting up and going through your whole wardrobe." She sighed. "Well, it was my loss."

No. Mine.

Then she touched on another mutual sore point. "I think it might just be too much therapy," she said. "You can think about these things too much and be paralyzed." This was an idée fixe of hers: everything would improve if I just stopped analysis. It was striking how much, in this, she resembled my insurance company. A few years later, she would meet Sylvia at a party in Georgica and, flustered, introduce herself by asking, "When will this *wretched ordeal* be over?" I stood between them, feeling a confused wish to let the moment play out but also to rescue Mom with a joke or two. She was at her worst with Sylvia, awkwardly changing the topic from analysis to real estate — Where is *your* house, exactly? — because she feared that she was being supplanted.

"Do I seem happier to you than when I started?" I said to Mom now.

"Oh, yes, much."

"So why would you want me to stop before I'm done?" I was trying to take charge of the discussion, but we were in her living room, and I was slumped in her custom-designed armchair, upholstered in blue-and-white batik, with my feet on her ottoman. It's hard to hold court when you can't plant your feet on the floor.

"You know, I was in analysis for two years, a long time ago, and it was what made me feel I could be married," she said.

"I didn't know that."

"But you do have to get on with your life at a certain point."

I frowned but stopped myself from saying, "Two more years and you might even have felt you could have children." She continued, "I like about ninety-five percent of your character very much. There's five percent I don't like, and I know that five percent is important to you, and I know you blame me for it, but I don't understand it."

"That's a terrible thing to say," I said, not wanting to know what, exactly, that five percent was. I suspect it was the part that had not forgiven her.

She went on to lament that Timmie and Pier were elsewhere that weekend, and that I came down so infrequently from New York. "We have this beautiful lawn here, perfect for two soccer teams of grandchildren," she said. "And there aren't any grandchildren. I'd always thought my children would live nearby, just down the road, and would be over all the time. But everyone lives so far away."

"And why do you think that is?" I said.

She began to cry. I felt sorry, and guilty, and started crying, too. Sam trotted into the room and looked worriedly back and forth. She gathered him up and wept into his fur.

FOURTEEN

Lawns

B Y MY MIDTHIRTIES my career, at least, was angling
toward contenderdom. In 1998, I became a staff
writer at *The New Yorker*, adapting easily to its under-
stated tone and with more difficulty to writing long pieces
that fit together like jigsaw puzzles. But the late nineties had
been a turnstiling period of married women and bored
women in skimpy sweaters, and, dismayingly, I was now on
my agent's "extra man" list for dinners. A few months into
2000, my friend Jennifer Steinhauer called me in my Los
Angeles hotel room at five a.m. local time to say that her *New
York Times* colleague and good friend Amanda Hesser, a
graceful food writer with a darting sense of humor, had just
broken up with someone and I should call her. Right this
minute, in fact. When I groggily said, "Okay, but what time
is it, right this minute?" Jenn scoffed, "Oh, wake up! It's your
lucky day."

When Amanda walked into the bar where I'd suggested
we meet, I thought, *Yes, yes, exactly!* I loved her face—a mix

of Audrey Hepburn and Modigliani—and her warm brown eyes, her shy yet purposeful walk, her demure yellow shoes. I loved how she weighed any number of factors with a tiny frown before deciding what to order as an appetizer. She was, in her deliberation and determination, not my traditional type. Nor was I hers. Gun-shy, we both took our time doing due diligence. During that period, she didn't call me by name, or by a nickname, leaving a telltale gap in "Hey . . . want to get something to eat?" It was the way I'd behave with a Wasp friend's father before he invited me to call him Wink. Sometimes, she would pat my head with a meditative look, and I'd say, "Old Pokey, he was a good horse."

Two little moments began to convince me. The first was when Amanda dropped by my apartment one night with a bright-eyed look, carrying an apple tart that tasted like apple nectar. She was putting it out there, leading with her strength, making me raise my own game. "Come right in," I said. "May I offer you, um, a vodka? Some scallions?"

The second was when we were sitting on my bed a good half hour after we'd agreed to go out for dinner and a movie, and Amanda was still running her fine-point marker through items on her pages-long to-do list and writing little reminders to herself, making the list longer than when she began. "Oh, come *on!*" I said.

"I just need a *minute.*"

"Nobody, on her deathbed, wishes she'd spent more time on her to-do list," I said.

She sprang onto her haunches and declared, "I'll take you down!" then tried to wrestle me to the quilt. I started laughing, which increased her advantage of surprise, and she almost had me pinned before it occurred to both of us that I outweigh her by seventy-five pounds. From then on, whenever I was being too much me, she would cry, "I'll take you down!" and launch a sneak attack, like Cato bushwhacking Inspector Clouseau.

After four months, she began to write about our relationship for a column called "Food Diary" for the *New York Times Magazine*. I scowled when she told me her plan, hating the prospect of being publicly embarrassed. Whenever I said something unorthodox about food—how a roast chicken tasted like "pork chop seasoning," say—I could see her making a gleeful mental note, which further reduced my already-thin stream of culinary opinions. Then, at Christmas, Amanda showed me her first few planned columns, and I relaxed. While there were sly riffs on my dining foibles, she not only addressed what I thought of as my good qualities—capturing what I cared about and how it felt to be me—but she also exaggerated my virtues, describing me as "witty, impossibly smart, and very, very funny," as well as "thoughtful and generous." Plus, the watercolor illustrations made me look like a Gallic Gregory Peck. Nobody had overvalued me so since Melanie, but with Amanda I wanted to live up to her idea of me. And I felt ready to try.

We didn't fight much, at first, arguing mostly about temperature: she likes to shower and sleep in equatorial warmth, and I dislike sweating while doing either. As we relaxed into our natural selves, issues came up. I left my office messy; she was always late. I withdrew and she nagged—who started it? I was behaving like my father, she like her mother. (Being in therapy, as we both were, is like taking a commando course: you learn where the pressure points are, and how to kill with a single blow.) But when she wasn't driving me berserk, I found her fierceness on these fronts endearing; our disagreements usually felt not dire but merely puzzling or hilarious. One night after we'd sparred about how I wash dishes—I had not soaked them for forty-eight hours in a sinkful of caustic potash—I thought, *I could fight with Amanda for the rest of my life.*

There were so many moments, really, a continual gathering of texture and ease, and of the fizzy feeling that I wanted my friends and family to meet Amanda so they could begin thinking better of me. It turned out that she cackled when amused. And that, unlike anyone else I'd been interested in, she couldn't tell a lie without blushing. I came to delight in how her slow, curtain-raising smile disclosed the stage of her inmost self. For the first time, I felt little of that frustration and blowing up the air mattress that I'd assumed relationships required. When I worried, in Sylvia's office, that it seemed too easy, she cocked her head and said, "Why be loyal to all that?" Perversely, still, I sometimes felt the sadness of happiness, of no longer having to fight to prove I was worthwhile.

A year in, as I was beginning to think of proposing, in a middle-distance sort of way, Amanda and I went to a wedding on the South Fork. When we arrived at the reception at a restaurant called East Hampton Point, surrounded by a dozen close friends, milling in our finery on a soggy fall afternoon, I knew, suddenly, that it was time. I led Amanda down an empty hallway behind the bar. The passage was damp and chilly, her two least favorite qualities, but she followed calmly, thinking I was positioning us by the kitchen for hot hors d'oeuvres (one of my moves). She looked astonished when I swung her around with my hand on the small of her back, as if to music, and said, "I've been thinking. . . ."—which wasn't true. My thinking cap was off. When she said, "Yes!" the future compacted to her ear, pink with excitement, and her sheltering lock of hair.

IN 2000, Mom launched her culminating campaign. She had always wanted Day to have a proper study, but she also needed to remove his desk and filing cabinets from the front hall, where they gave visitors a hodgepodgy first impression rather than the desired Japanesey effect. With him gone, that space would become a new entrance hall, a tiny powder room, and a playroom for the future grandchildren. Having redesigned the garage as his office, she attached it to the house with a passageway she called "the Link." Day didn't think the Link necessary, in part because of the expense—which she ended up paying for out of the money from Maplewood, house begetting house—and in part because he declared himself happy to walk outside to get to his study. "Oh, now, Dorie," she said. "You won't be happy trudging through snow up to your knees." She understood that his stoicism was reflexive, a fear of self-indulgence. But it was also vital to her that the new wing be connected, that the house encompass us all.

Wild with excitement about "the playhouse," as she called it, for two years she talked of little else. She filled its shelves with books from Grandma Tim's childhood (Howard Pyle) and hers (Beatrix Potter) and ours (Maurice Sendak). There was a sunlit reading nook by a bay window, a little drawing table that slid out from beneath it, a corkboard, and a peeka-boo TV. Yet the room seemed intended not only for toddlers but also for Mom herself. Its furnishings included one of her mother's Sheraton love seats that she had upholstered in easy-to-ruin gray trapunto, two large bolsters in even-easier-to-ruin blue-and-white Marimekko, and two enormous ginger jars steadied on wooden disks. The sliding door that would keep the children in had a porthole to allow for adult observation (there they are, still not playing with the enormous ginger jars). The ceiling was a Prussian blue, covered with stenciled stars and comets and a single crescent moon.

The first potential playhouse user, Pier's son Wilson, came along at last in late 2000. The following February, Mom sent around an e-mail asking us to help her decide her grandmother name. Such nicknames usually emerge from the grandchildren, but she wasn't taking any chances:

> *Every time I come up with a name for Wil to call me, Pier has a (no doubt sensible) reason why it wouldn't work. For example, I thought "Puff" sounded nice, but he pointed out that that has connections to marijuana. . . . "Grandma Elizabeth" is too much of a mouthful, "Grandma E." becomes Grammy. Here are some other thoughts: "Pom" (after Babar's third child, who, I know, was a boy) or "Pom Pom." "Mouse" (from Day's new name for me, "Mousehead") — actually, Goggy Robinson had a cook called Mouse, which is fine by me. Tad and Tim, you will someday presumably have little ones who will have to latch onto whatever name we choose now, so please,* GIVE IT SOME SERIOUS THOUGHT.

She eventually settled on "Foffia" — as a young girl, that was how she had pronounced "flower" — and put it on her license plate to cement the granny-branding. "Foffia," impossible for any small child to say, or at least for any small child except my mother, inevitably became "Foffie," a tweak she tolerated with a slight frown.

That April, Grandpa John celebrated his ninety-fifth birthday by holding Wilson in his arms. Trembling in his wheelchair, he murmured to his great-grandson, "Be the best at what you do, and be kind to those who are not." He died that fall, three days after 9/11 — for a UN stalwart, a killing blow.

I thought of Grandpa John one warm evening last spring, as Amanda and I came home by taxi with Walker and Addie, then twenty months old and utterly adorable in their blue pajamas with fleecy clouds. We'd spent the afternoon with Adam Platt and his family in their Manhattan apartment, where Addie, mistaking a sculptural assemblage of clay spheres for the foam balls we played with at home, grabbed one and flung me a no-look pass. When the ball exploded just short of my lunge, Addie was outraged, and her storm of accusatory tears nearly drowned out my offers of restitution and Adam's affable refusals. Addie takes misadventure personally: when she runs laps around our dinner table with her right arm pumping, her tenacity, her merry refusal to be diverted from these vital private errands, reminds me extraordinarily of Mom.

Tuckered now, Addie was asleep in Amanda's arms. The sudden, mortal fatigue of small children. When we check on the twins before we go to bed, tiptoeing into the hay smell of their night sweat, she often half-wakes to laugh at us — *Of course you want to see me!* — before diving back to sleep, squatting with her head just touching the pillow, as if at prayer. Walker, for his part, clicks and wheezes, sprawled on his back with a strip of belly gleaming like a wino's. This 11:30 p.m. visit, night watchmen keying our clocks, has become Amanda's and my new favorite ritual, replacing the seigneurial morning life of coffee and the *Times*.

Walker was in my lap. Fighting sleep, his blond hair wet with sweat, he reveled in lower Broadway's rain of light, pointing and insisting, "Thass! Thass!" I returned his sweet, beseeching smile without having any idea what he was talking about, as his roaming finger targeted stoplights, lampposts, and sky. The few words he possessed were necessarily protean because they stood in for so many others—for everything, really. When I bent over his crib to tuck his blanket or ease *Goodnight Moon* from under his cheek, he sometimes cried out in his sleep, "Milk!" or "Shoes!" or "Daddy!" which moved me enormously. Now he placed his hands atop my forearms, drowsily settled into me, and murmured, "Bish!" There was indeed a large Atlantic City–bound bish beside us. "Our son is a genius," I told Amanda. *Not that that always turned out well. . . .*

"He takes after me."

Six months after her father died, Mom sent me a photo of a baby polar bear curled up on its mother's back on an ice floe. Both bears were asleep and seemed contented in their landscape of blue and white. "Dearest Taddio," she wrote. "Since I was a tiny child, Daddy and I sent pictures of animals to each other. When I saw the enclosed I wanted to send it to him. But since that is no longer possible I'm sending it to you instead. With much love, Mom."

AFTER INITIALLY seeing my family as hothouse flowers, Amanda came to appreciate our courtesy and humor. Or so she says now, when it's too late. She enjoyed baking a peach-and-almond tart with Mom and getting tips from her, requested or not, on how to paint with watercolors. She also took to Century House, and we had the world's shortest wedding venue conversation, agreeing to get married there in mid-September 2002, and to have a clambake rehearsal dinner on the beach.

Almost everyone was there for the wedding except Baba, who was far into the mists, and Mom's spaniel, Sam, who was lame, deaf, and almost blind. His existence had been reduced to indiscriminate licking, hopeful expressions of love for whatever open palm or chair leg came near. He always loved to sprint down the lawn in Georgica, his belly whistling through the grass like a hydrofoil, but he was now too infirm to travel.

The evening of the rehearsal dinner proved cool and quite breezy, so after scarfing lobster rolls, we all huddled around a bonfire as my best man, Rich Appel, introduced Mom's toast. I could feel Amanda's heart rabbiting as she shivered through three sweaters; she really does hate the cold. Looking stylish in a puffy red coat, Mom unfolded her reading glasses and her typed-out remarks, and began. But she had trouble holding everything steady in the wind, which gusted through the microphone in stormy shrieks. Rich trained a flashlight on her notes and Timmie held the mike, and Mom began again: "Wainscott has been a charmed part of our family since 1914, and has been cherished by five generations: starting with my grandparents, Charles and Elizabeth

Pierson. Our house, which you will see tomorrow, is over a century old. In the hurricane of September 1938, ocean waves crossed the bar and Georgica Pond, and broke on our front porch."

Just when I was wondering if she had mixed up her notes, and we were getting "Tribulations of Ye Pierson Clan," she pivoted: "Tad was my firstborn. He showed early promise of a literary imagination. Not long after learning speech, he invented a companion to play with called Foogin. Foogin became a part of our family life, referred to whenever anything interesting was happening, and especially present at bedtime." She went on to discuss my other imaginary friends, and then to observe that once I was grown, she wondered if I'd ever find the right flesh-and-blood companion. "And then one day, miraculously, there was Amanda. When I first asked Tad to tell me about her, he gave me only one adjective: shy. *Well*, I thought, *that sounds like his old friend Lelvin*. And when I actually got to meet Amanda—right here, in Wainscott, getting off the jitney in the middle of the night—and found how easily and generously she laughs, I was reminded of no one so much as Geeshee. As our friendship—hers and mine—deepened, I discovered her quick mind, a mind as bright and clever and full of color as Dato's. Mrs. Bawsbaw had been a competent but ordinary cook; Amanda's crème fraîche, on the other hand, is sublime. To top it off, Amanda is beautiful, as Lunar had been. And finally, like Foogin, Tad's first, best beloved friend, she is brave."

There were many other toasts, including affecting remarks from Timmie and Pier. It was our family at our best. Several friends told me that seeing that current of private feeling undammed in public, that mix of love and wit, filled them with envy. Then Jenn Steinhauer stood to mention her role in bringing us together and to recount our first date. After I had walked Amanda to her building—or near it, anyway; she gave me the Heisman fifty yards from the door—I'd asked to see her again, but she just stared at me until I said, "Or, not . . ." and turned away. She maintains that she was nervous and thought she'd said yes. Only when Jenn phoned each of us the next morning did she sort it out and demand that I call Amanda again. Recounting this circumspect confusion, Jenn said, "I would like someone to explain to me: how do Wasps mate, unaided?"

NEITHER AMANDA nor I is a churchgoer, so, at Day's suggestion, we had asked Barrie Shepherd to perform the service; he had been the minister at the Presbyterian church in Swarthmore. When Amanda and I met with Barrie to discuss the ceremony, he was as thoughtful and bracing as I remembered, and he said that as he'd wed Catholics and Buddhists, agnostics wouldn't be a problem. Then he asked us to pray with him. As we sent drafts of the service to and fro, and Barrie disclosed that he always presented the newlyweds with Bibles, we began to realize that he wished God to not only preside over but ordain our marriage. And while we didn't mind having God as a witness, we didn't want it to be His day. So we regretfully told Barrie we needed to look elsewhere.

Most of my early ancestors would have taken Barrie's part. Jacob Hemingway, Yale's first student, became a Congregationalist pastor who characterized households with unbaptized children as "the nurseries of Hell"; when his daughter married an Episcopalian, he turned her portrait to the wall. In the past century, though, many of my forebears began to lose faith in Christianity, without necessarily gaining a corresponding sense of freedom. Grandma Tim, for instance, left the Congregationalists for the Unitarian Universalist church, which has no official creed. My parents accompanied her and Tom to a Unitarian Christmas service in the early eighties, and Mom observed that there weren't any familiar carols. "Why are Unitarians embarrassed by the baby Jesus?" she asked.

"We aren't embarrassed," Timmy said. "We just don't believe in Christ as a deity, that's all."

"Well, that's pretty much the end for Christianity, isn't it?"

Day remains a devout Presbyterian with an amplifying belief in Buddhism and Sufism; Mom seemed to me less a Christian than a Christmasian who believed in talismans and fate. She would walk the aisles of airplanes after boarding, looking for babies, guarantors of safety. And she often told the story of how a man she knew had once boarded an elevator and seen that everyone on it had just lost his aura. "Excuse me," he said, "I have to get out," and he thrust his way into the corridor, then watched the elevator plunge through the basement. Once, irked by her definition of an aura as something distinguishable only by its absence, I asked why her friend didn't tell the others in the car about their auras, why he didn't save them, too. "If they all left the elevator without their auras, the entire *building* would have collapsed," she replied. "He had to allow some to die so that others might live."

To trust entirely in feeling, one must believe that this life is all there is: that no moral duties are owed. But the modern Wasp like me is uncertain, and tries to straddle both paths as they diverge: attending church occasionally for the hymns, trying to earn enough for a summerhouse without becoming a philistine. So Amanda and I weren't confident that we could cherry-pick our traditions, that the Wasp menu is à la carte as well as prix fixe. But we decided to risk it, and wrote our own service to include bits from William Carlos Williams and Rainer Maria Rilke and Raymond Carver's "Late Fragment," which we asked Pier to read:

> *And did you get what*
> *you wanted from this life, even so?*
> *I did.*
> *And what did you want?*
> *To call myself beloved, to feel myself*
> *beloved on the earth.*

It's the "even so" that always lays me out.

Before the ceremony, Amanda and I stood in the master bedroom holding hands. I was wearing a new gray suit, and she was in a knee-length pink Prada dress with cap sleeves. Her hair was blown out, and she stood two inches taller than usual on gold sandals, but she had none of the bride's freeze-dried look; she was blushing, quivering, alive. From the window, we spied on our friends and families on the lawn. There was Amanda's brother Dean and his wife talking with Day, and George and Pablo with our two mothers, and Norah prowling the perimeter, and Alessandra Visconti, and Sylvia

Welsh, and Paddy and Karen and my cousin Eliza, who'd done the centerpieces—blue and white hydrangeas in bowls filled with sea stones and sand. My life, our life, telescoped.

In the previous months, Mom had kept e-mailing us reports from the *Farmer's Almanac* and "hurricane forecast experts" that predicted a devastating blow for September 14. She bought a hundred and fifty ponchos for the guests and put them aside—in a huge, attention-getting box near the front door—just in case. That the wedding day had dawned sunny and mild was due, she felt, to this precaution. The late-afternoon sun lit up the lawn amid the lengthening shadows. Wilson had reclaimed that lawn from the poison ivy and crabgrass and the tunneling moles, widening it by degrees across his lifetime, and now it glowed as a living promise. I wished, then, that I had said something to him before he died, something appreciative. But that's not how we roll.

Our guests were migrating toward the pond, so Amanda and I slipped downstairs to the path that would bring us through the shoulder-high goldenrod and out by the altar, usually known as the birdbath. As we waited in the rushes, I had a sudden vision of a cocktail hour on the porch twenty-five years earlier. Uncle Wilson was in a poplin suit and Aunt Letty in a blue dress with her hair pulled back and Mom in an even bluer dress and Day in his red-checked blazer, each sipping from the contents of Wilson's frosted cocktail shaker. It was just a flash—all of them young and smiling and lacquered by light.

The cello and flute struck up our processional music, "Simple Gifts," a Shaker dance tune I'd always loved, and we started down the path. I was clamping down on my fluttering spirits, trying not to start tearing up then, knowing I was going to later—as I did when I said, "I am marrying you, Amanda, among many other reasons, because my heart jumps up with gladness whenever I see you."

"Hey, slow up!" Amanda said now. "I want to take it all in."

"I'm excited," I said, taking her hand again. "Here we go!"

AT DINNER, Day stood beneath one of the Japanese lanterns bobbing from the tent poles and welcomed everyone. "Elizabeth says that I'm really much better at responding to queries than giving speeches," he began. "So—are there any questions?" Then, taking up Jenn Steinhauer's rhetorical question from the night before, he explained that the first step for Wasps seeking to mate was to "cloak in obscurity a mutual self-deference," which everyone thought was very funny, perhaps because it proved her point.

"I think your father's a little squiffy," an older Wasp remarked, smiling. Day wasn't the only one—I was having a wonderful time. After scuttling Presbyterianism, we'd decided it was all up for grabs, and so we had the band play "Hava Nagila," and did a twenty-minute hora. Our groomsmen twirled Amanda and me around on our chairs, and once Mom was aloft, she waved her green scarf like Isadora Duncan. Just before eleven p.m., she took me aside to say that Don Petrie had told her the day before that Georgica had a no-amplified-music-after-eleven rule. "First of all, the band quits in fifteen minutes," I said. "Second, we haven't had a wedding here in forty years, so let's enjoy this one. And third, if Don Petrie comes over, I will be happy to personally tell him to fuck off."

Mom smiled, unexpectedly: "Okay, darling." She danced on the lawn until the last song, a twangy, foot-stomping version of the gospel standard "Jesus on the Main Line," adoring it all. The next morning, recalling the highlights over bagels on the porch, she exclaimed, "And then there was that part of the evening where we all became Jews!"

On their way home, my parents picked Sam up from a kennel. They took him back to the house, fed and walked him, and stroked his thinning corona of fur. At dawn, they found his body stretched out in the Link, still warm.

THE FOLLOWING summer, in June of 2003, I took Mom to the hospital at the University of Pennsylvania for an outpatient procedure on her bladder. In the car afterward, still dreamy from the anesthesia, she told me about her first period. It had arrived when she was fifteen and riding the Long Island Rail Road. In every way unprepared for this calamity, she had locked herself in the bathroom and sobbed. It was an odd conversation for us to be having, and yet I remember thinking, *This is how we should be talking, calmly and intimately, just two adults discussing their periods.* Laughing and chatting, we bowled off to Rite Aid. When I came out with her prescriptions, I tapped the window and she awoke from a catnap, smiling.

She began to recover from the operation—and then to fail, rapidly. One morning she just fell down. My father called and said that she wanted to speak with me but had wanted him to prepare me for how she sounded. She got on and said, "He . . . llo, Tad-di-o . . ." Her clarion voice was slurred and quavery. I tried to make a casual reply, but we each heard the other's alarm—the fear of impairment, of dwindling.

She checked back into the hospital, where tests determined that the mitral valve of her heart had become clogged with a strange puttylike material, flecks of which had passed into her brain. The root problem remained mysterious. As the doctors ran more tests, we tried to brighten Mom's surroundings, to distract her from the applesauce, the beige walls whose color she termed "baby couldn't help it." Timmie rubbed her feet with citrus lotions, and I brought in Malta. Antibiotics began to alleviate her symptoms, and in a few days she was sitting up and making plans to attend Timmie's wedding in Georgica, two months off, declaring, "I'll be borne in on a palanquin!" She began hostessing the nurses—"Have you met my daughter-in-law, who writes for the *New York Times?*"—and apologizing to everyone for her unwashed hair. As Amanda and I left for the train, she was trying to find *Sex and the City* on television, and I told her that the hospital didn't have HBO. "Well, how do they expect anyone to get better in here if they can't watch *Sex and the City?*" she said.

The doctors decided that her mitral valve ought to be replaced. When I called the night before the operation, Timmie picked up and said that a rehabilitation therapist had taken Mom for a short walk down the hall. When she got back, I told her, "I hear you were running up and down the stairs like a mountain goat."

"Oh, yes," she said instantly. "Leaping from crag to crag."

The next morning, as they were rolling her in, Malta somehow vanished from her pajama pocket. And that afternoon, after they stitched her up, her heart just stopped.

As we signed paperwork at the hospital, I kept seeing Mom as she was afterward, bundled in a sheet, her hands folded on her chest and her mouth parted slightly, a small scab on her lower lip. Her skin had felt cool, like home. Day had broken down over her, his tears falling onto her closed eyes. When the doctors asked permission to do an autopsy, Timmie suggested that we allow them to examine everything but those eyes, her last blue-and-white element: "She's an artist; she may need them." The autopsy later revealed that the cancer had returned, everywhere and all at once.

We drove back to Villanova in silence. Paddy and Karen were there with us, comfortingly; and Pier's wife, Sara, came down from Montclair; and Pier flew in from a trip out West, and soon the house was full. Amanda and I ended up sleeping in my parents' room, because Day said that he couldn't stand to be there just yet. He took the futon in his study, and I thought of him lying alone beneath his porthole, looking west. Her porthole. The house was a minefield of memory—every painting, well-scrubbed pot on her pegboard, phone message in her hand. Upstairs was a trove of presents she had wrapped but not yet addressed, awaiting Christmas, five months away.

Amanda and I stayed awake for hours. I wished I smoked, because it would have killed some time—time, then, the coward enemy. After she dozed off, I found myself thinking about *The Tailor of Gloucester*. I was almost able to soothe myself by thinking of Grandpa John as the tailor, absent from his shop only because he was sick and frail, and Mom as a faithful brown mouse, sewing busily in the dark.

At dawn, I was awoken by a soft rap on the door between the bedroom and the Link. Thinking it must be Day, I mumbled, "Yes, come in." When there was no reply, I decided I must have dreamed it. Then came another rap. Thoroughly awake now, I got out of bed and walked to the door and said, "Hello?" A series of raps, two feet away and distinct, answered back. It wasn't *tip tap, tip tap, tip tap tip*, quite, but nearly.

I opened the door and peered into the Link. The passage was empty. It was empty, that is, if you didn't count the pewter mirror where Mom liked to primp in passing, or the door to the garden with its nested dog door (six inches wide, with an inch of leeway), or the tidy bureau and rack for Day's suits and overcoats, or the cunning shelf for his hats she'd asked the carpenters to notch out above the lintel—he disliked hats, but you never know—or the closet that she had said would be perfect for him and later appropriated for herself. She kept her suitcases on top of it, ready to go.

FIFTEEN

Home

THE DAY OF hard feelings occurred on the winter solstice, a black day just before Christmas of 2006 that began with us firing our babysitter, who was brusque with Walker, and continued with Addie bellowing at our creeping progress down the New Jersey Turnpike and Walker foghorning periodic agreement. When we got to Villanova, it took a while to unload the car and feed the twins and address their complaints about sleeping in Pack 'n Plays—"Look, here's your dog, Foo! Oh, now, Foo doesn't like being thrown into the fireplace!"—before we could finally make it downstairs for dinner.

The New Yorker had published my piece on Mom ten days earlier, and Day had asked me to bring home the alternative layouts: a variety of early photos of Mom and me together. As I was scooping out a carton of ice cream for dessert—Pier and Sara and Timmie and Scott had all just arrived, too—Day leafed through the layouts, frowning. He hadn't shaved in five weeks because of a skin rash, and his Unabomberish scruff made him look older; at dinner he mentioned that, according to the IRS's actuarial tables, he had nine years left. He suddenly held up the sheaf of paper and asked, "How can you look at these photos and not know that your mother loved you?"

I was taken aback by his tone, particularly as I'd shown him the article months earlier, and he'd responded warmly. "I do know that she loved me, just as I loved her, and I think the article reflects that," I said.

"Judging by many of the eighteen responses I have received, that was *not* apparent to many people," he said. Glances flashed around the table, and I saw Pier's face assume a careful neutrality. Knowing I'd regret whatever came out of my mouth, I willed myself to count down from ten, and fortunately Timmie jumped in to defend the piece, and to say, "It was Tad's story of Mom, and it would have been different if you wrote it, or I did." The fragile peace held.

After dinner I started to change for bed, still stewing even after bending over Addie and Walker, who were curled up like pole beans, and listening to them breathe. I told Amanda I had to go talk it through. Yes, she said, I think so. So I put my pants back on and went downstairs, past Mom's dressing room with its faint smell of old wood and Chanel No. 5, to rap on Day's bedroom door. He was in his armchair, taking off his cordovan boots. I sat on an ottoman facing him and said, "So what was all that about at dinner?"

He cleared his throat and said, "I'm just trying to give you the range of responses your piece has provoked."

"I'd rather hear what you think, directly, rather than try to guess where you are behind the screen of eighteen strangers."

"Since you ask, and in the spirit of candor," he began slowly, "I feel that the piece didn't capture Mom's love for you, or suggest that you loved her. It failed in those respects, and it also failed to capture my relationship with Elizabeth, as well as our family dynamic. To speak in metaphor, it was well written, a shrewdly chosen series of snapshots, but it was an X-ray rather than an MRI. It failed to illuminate the soft tissue. And that failing suggests an emotional aridity that I fear pervades your work."

"I can't believe you would say that," I said. "No one would read *Family Laundry* and think you didn't love Grandma Jess or Grandpa Ted. But they were complicated people, and so was Mom."

"She was complicated, but—"

"Yes, she was wonderful, but she did dominate things," I said. "Maybe you want to forget that now, forget that there was a reason you spent all your time in your study, because it seems disloyal or petty to bring it up when she's gone. And maybe that's understandable—probably, it is. But pretending there weren't problems means denying what it was like to grow up in this family."

"It's *your* article and *your* career, and you will do with them what you like. You will do well—you have done well—and you will continue to do well. But this is my view," he said, frowning. "The emotional sterility is what troubles me."

"I feel extremely misunderstood," I said, starting to choke up, and hating that. "And it makes me want to leave this house." He looked at me levelly, listening. "How can you say that about aridity, when your son is sitting across from you, obviously upset, and you're sitting there dry-eyed? *You're* the arid one, you've always been that way, and I wish you weren't.

I so wish you weren't." He still didn't say anything. "I know you have feelings. But why, why do you have to present everything as a syllogism?"

He sighed and shot his cuff, deciding which of several avenues to take. "I have told others, and I don't know if I have told you, that you're my favorite living writer."

"You had mentioned that to me, and I appreciate it," I said, feeling oddly formal, as if I were accepting a prize that had been announced years before.

"I look forward to everything you write, and read it with great pleasure, as Mom did. But I would remark that I worry about you being a prisoner of Freudianism, which is a thread that wends through the article. Life is about saying yes to the mystery of the future, not about endless refinements of the past."

"I stopped my analysis last month, actually," I said. He brightened, so I hastened to add, "But just because I had reached a natural stopping place. I'm not trying to push you away by clarifying that, just trying to tell you what's on my mind." He nodded and clasped his hands around one knee. So I went on, jumping some barrier at last. "Okay, it's not about therapy, and whether I shouldn't be in it or you should. You should do whatever makes you happy, and there's no reason it has to be what makes me happy. And it's not about the article. I guess we'll agree to disagree about that. But what it *is* about is our relationship. Why won't you talk about that, and about your feelings?"

"I will try harder," he said. He took a deep breath and sat for a while, thinking. "I suppose that in response to watching my father suffer so many defeats and humiliations, I overcompensated and became very well defended."

My mouth seemed to know what to say: "I'm sure that had a purpose, and has served you well in the past, but it doesn't serve you now with your children. You've always been very articulate—"

"Not always," he said softly.

"Well, since I've known you, which is a long time. And I'm pretty articulate myself; I learned that from you. But I can imagine a whole different sort of conversation, where I came in here and we talked honestly, without being so carefully fluent, and you told me that you were angry with me—"

"It's hard to imagine being angry with you—"

"Well, you are now. This is what it feels like. And I have been angry, at times, with you. And it would be better if we could just say so, instead of having it all leak out in disguise, which just leaves both of us grumpy, and distant, and exactly where we started."

He seemed to shrink into his chair. And then, with a visible effort, he shook himself forward again. "I appreciate your attacking me in such a sportsmanlike manner," he said. "And I do love you."

"And I love you, too," I said, feeling both the truth of it and my reluctance to say it, just then, the words feeling rote and niggardly.

"Yes," he said. He stood heavily, in one boot, and we hugged. His beard rasped my cheek, and he didn't seem to want to let go. At last he stepped back and gripped my upper arms. "I tried to get her out of that hurricane," he said. "But I never could."

———

IN THE new year, Day had Mom's contractor begin building two bedrooms over the garage, to accommodate the late boom in grandchildren—Timmie was pregnant, a year and a half after her liver transplant—and solidify Villanova as the family's winter gathering place. He pulled the Rouault mother and child out of storage and hung it above the spiral staircase to the new bedrooms. And he and I talked often about the family, relaxed chats at the butcher-block dining table.

The seams were being sewed together again, and last Christmas, when Walker and Addie were finally old enough to run around the house on their own, they loved the place. Walker was particularly drawn to the playhouse, and would squirm backward into the hidey-hole beneath the drawing table, pull a pillow half over his head, and announce, "I playing hide-in-seeks!" Amanda had told Addie who Foffie was, and now Addie would occasionally say, "I see Foffie," in a different tone than the one she used when pointing to a newspaper mug shot and saying, "That's Uncle Pier!"—one of her favorite jokes. She was fascinated by Mom's last painting, *My Beasts and I*, and would scramble up the stairs to study the work, in the hall outside our bedroom, in silence.

The morning of our Christmas celebration, I woke Addie to get her dressed for "Hayfoot, Strawfoot." She rose anxiously from sleep. "Where's Foffie?" she asked. "Foffie's not here?"

Tears sprang to my eyes, and I had to collect myself before I could say, "She's outside," meaning in the hall.

"Foffie's taking a nap outside?" Addie and Walker saw life as binary: you were awake, and then someone made you take a nap.

"Sure," I said.

"Foffie's saying bye-bye?" she asked.

"In a way."

"Foffie's in the painting," she cried. "Foffie's *home*."

IN LATE summer, Day suggested we plan a visit to Pittsburgh, an idea I loved. It would be my first visit since the Ice Cream Spoon controversy, and our first trip together since we visited the Hall of Fame in Cooperstown when I was ten. One Friday in December, I took the train down from New York and Day came aboard in Philadelphia for the haul to Pittsburgh. When we arrived, we checked into the Duquesne Club, which Big Jim Friend and Dorie Friend Sr. once frequented. It's now a stately pile where gilt-framed portraits of Andrew Carnegie and Henry Frick overlook acres of empty function rooms. We were the guests of Henry Phipps Hoffstot Jr., a lawyer at the city's renowned Reed Smith firm and the grandson of Frank Hoffstot, Big Jim's partner. Henry and Day had become friends at Eugenia's parties after Grandpa Ted died — Henry a rare kindly face in her aspic milieu.

In the morning, my father called Allegheny Cemetery and arranged for them to open James Wood Friend's mausoleum so we could visit the following morning. And then Henry picked us up for a day's sightseeing. "This is our new car," he said, as we settled into the red-plaid interior of his 1979 Jeep Cherokee. He also had a 1952 Bentley and a 1931 Pierce-Arrow, his father's car, which he kept tuned by driving it five hundred miles a year. Henry himself, at ninety, was like his cars: so well maintained he appeared no more than seventy. Soft-voiced, anticipating and accommodating our every wish, he appeared supremely comfortable in a tattersall shirt, a green crewneck sweater with brown elbow patches, and a herringbone jacket from London that must have been forty years old.

I had on a wool hat and gloves and a heavy overcoat, but I was still shivering as we stood with Henry on a promontory above the city; it was one of those brilliant winter days when the cold bores into your bones. Henry, wearing no hat, gloves, or overcoat, pointed out landmarks with custodial pride, including the former riverside locale of our ancestors' foundry, Clinton Iron and Steel. "The steel flowed through a channel in the floor of the Clinton furnace like a river of milk," he said, "and the sky was always black with smoke and soot." "Hell with the lid taken off" is how journalist James Parton described the city in 1868; a half century later, H. L. Mencken wrote, "Here was the very heart of industrial America, the boast and pride of the richest and grandest nation ever seen on earth—and here was a scene so dreadfully hideous, so intolerably bleak and forlorn that it reduced the whole aspiration of man to a macabre and depressing joke."

Henry took us next to the Phipps Conservatory, a vast greenhouse and gardens built in 1893. His great-aunt had been married to Henry Phipps, the steel and real-estate tycoon who endowed the place, and Henry himself had served as the conservatory's president. All that airy transparency enclosing orchids and fan palms must have seemed miraculously weird as it rose from the ambient grime. Henry observed, "The mayor of Pittsburgh said, 'We need a hospital more.' And Phipps told him, 'No, the city needs a conservatory.' " *Jews build hospitals*, I thought, *and Wasps conserve*. The word "conservatory" chimes in our guilty souls.

On the long drive to Frank Lloyd Wright's Fallingwater, Day asked about the 1909 McKees Rocks strike, and our ancestors' method of squashing it. "I never heard my grandfather mention it," Henry said. "He was rarely chatty. And, of course," he added with a small smile, "it was not reported in the main Pittsburgh papers of the time."

After a tour of Wright's masterpiece, we drove to Pike Run Country Club, in rural Jones Mills. Day hadn't been back since he proposed to Mom here in 1959. "Our family would stay at Pike Run every weekend from May to August," he said, as we walked onto the nine-hole golf course, deserted now, in the off-season. Henry had his hands clasped behind his back, the image of perambulation. We stood near the tee box of the fifth hole, a short downhill par-four whose green was surrounded by oaks. There was a snap in the air from distant leaf fires, and the flat cast of the setting sun lit up the oak tops like torches. "I scored the only eagle of my life here," Day said. "Two miracle shots, driving the green and sinking a thirty-foot putt."

"And isn't this where you proposed?" I asked.

"Yes," he said, "here"—he turned to the green just behind us. "We stayed in Wood's End"—he pointed to a squat cottage nearby—"an ugly clunk of a house then and it still is. Elizabeth and I went for a walk in the fading sunlight, and I just blurted it out." After Grandma Tim's funeral, Mom had told us all about it: how, just when her mother was beginning to say, "I'm not sure I want that young man in my house anymore," Day brought her onto the golf course and said, "After you're finished with Dr. Higgins"—her analyst—"will you marry me?"

We walked inside the low fieldstone clubhouse: hunting prints, chintz, floral wallpaper, and a card table. "Essential to the culture," my father said, scrutinizing the table as if it were an arquebus in a museum. Above the bar was a caricature from 1949 of Ellis Burrows, the African American bartender, dispensing fifths of gin and scotch to sozzled-looking members. "Ellis used to rescue those who had been a little too free with the bottle," Henry said. "He carried certain members to bed night after night."

Day responded with one of his most characteristic expressions—a complexly humorous shrug. Then he drew my attention to a photograph of the interior of the old clubhouse, which had burned down in 1947. It showed a spacious great room bordered by a second-floor balcony. "Joan Fisher, who was always doing things like that, was challenged to jump off the balcony," he said. "Everyone laid pillows on the floor to cushion her landing, but, unsurprisingly, she—"

"Broke her back," Henry said mournfully.

"No, only sprained an ankle," Day said, smiling at Henry.

We visited Henry's son, Henry Phipps Hoffstot III, known as Phipps, and his wife, Darlyn, on their nearby estate, which featured horses, cattle, and a squash court. The Hoffstots had evidently managed their finances well, while we had spent our capital, one way and another. As soon as I stepped inside the house, I knew what it would be like, because the smell—dogs and fires and soup—was exactly Maplewood's. It was just as I'd imagined, only better maintained: a hard-used mudroom, a crooked stairwell, sloping floors beneath low ceilings, a fire blazing out of a stone hearth. Soon we were sipping Earl Grey on a chintz sofa with Phipps, who was looking gray after recent knee surgery for a squash injury, and Darlyn, in a down vest and a blue turtleneck, who was eager for news of New York. They could have been Grandma Tim and John McDill a half century ago.

"Poor Phipps is not flourishing," Henry said after we were back in the car and heading, in twilight, through meadows owned by the Mellon family. Soon we were on Route 30, drawing nearer to Pittsburgh amid shopping malls studded with Arby's and Steak 'n Shakes. "I wonder who goes to those things," Henry said. "They're always full."

"Americans are buying things all the time," Day said.

They shared an elegiac silence as we drove through Squirrel Hill to the block the Friend compound once occupied. "Now, slow down, please, Henry!" my father said, once we came to the Tree of Life, the synagogue that now bestrode much of the property. My father began describing everything as it was — the three houses, the lawns and the boundary of poplars and the large garage where chauffeurs buffed the family's Pierce-Arrows; and how Didi's ear trumpet never worked, so everyone used signals to bid at bridge: spades was a shoveling gesture, and hearts was touching your heart. "It was wonderful territory for a little boy," he said. "My great-grandfather thought dynastically, God bless him, imagining his family living there forever. It lasted fifty years."

We cruised down Solway Street, where a dozen small houses now sat near the former main entrance. "Here's the driveway gate!" Day cried. Two mighty brick pillars stood by the curb, bracketing an asphalt drive that now ran only twenty yards before it dived into a sunken garage. Rearing from the frozen ground, the pillars were like the femurs of a brontosaurus. We looked at them in silence awhile, and at last drove on.

Henry had organized a dinner for us at his house on Fifth Avenue, and as a treat for my father had asked the daughter of the Pike Run bartender Ellis Burrows to cook. Day recalled her helping out at parties, long ago. When we arrived at Henry's house, a neoclassical beauty, Day went to the bathroom and I wandered about admiring the parquet floors. When I came into the kitchen, Gretchen Burrows, a slight woman in a white work shirt, started up from the stove with a smile. "I remember you, Mr. Friend!" she said. "You haven't changed a bit!"

SUNDAY MORNING, we put on suits and check out of the Duquesne Club, then wait for Henry in the club's front room, where a small toy train circles a plastic Christmas tree on a platform covered with green felt. Someone, feeling that the tableau was too schematic, has surrounded it with an abundance of red poinsettias. "It's exactly the way it was at our Christmas Eve party in my youth," Day says. "Except that we had steel tracks instead of plastic, and my parents and their friends would build a whole village, with trucks and houses and villagers, after Charlie and I had gone to bed."

As a cold rain falls, we walk with Henry to his church. Shadyside Presbyterian, a massive granite muffin around the corner from Henry's house, was Grandpa Ted's church, too, if you believe his obituary. Henry says proudly that Shadyside features perhaps the best singing and preaching in the country. The pews are two-thirds full, a mix of well-dressed older Wasps and younger people like the mother and daughter in front of me, who wear stretch pants and have matching tattoos. Bemused to find myself in church for the first time in years, I listen carefully to the fine sermon about why we, all of us, find ourselves here, on this first Sunday of Advent. The explanation, the minister suggests, is that none of us have life figured out yet, nor can we, because God's purposes are beyond our anticipation. God is not finished with us yet.

Afterward, I hasten back to Henry's house to meet the cab we called earlier; the driver, a bear of a man in a Pittsburgh Steelers fleece, smokes a cigarette as I sit in the back watching the windows bead up with rain, heavier now and turning to sleet. Day and Henry come along a few minutes later, sharing Henry's tartan golf umbrella. Something about the two men picking their way together through the puddles in Henry's gravel drive, each with a hand on the umbrella handle, touches me. They seem still to be observing the proprieties of their departure from Shadyside, the long recessional. There is a round of handshakes and warm well wishes, and as we pull away for Allegheny Cemetery, I turn and give Henry a final wave, and he smiles.

The cemetery, rolling lawns outlined by spreading maples, would be beautiful much of the year. But the trees are gaunt and wet now, and the weather and absence of visitors give the old Wasp graveyard the aspect of a potter's field. Shoulders hunched against the sleet, Day and I stork-walk from the cab across the grass to James Wood Friend's granite Greek temple, a crust of ice crunching underfoot. Despite the cemetery's promises, the tarnished brass doors are shut tight. We peer through the tiny window into the nearly black interior, making out a damp floor of polished granite and the dim outlines of sarcophagi: James and his wife, Martha; his four children and their three spouses; Eugenia and Ted (and my stowaway Roberto Clemente and Danny Murtaugh); and Uncle Charles. The number of us eager to lie among that company has tapered, and the one empty crypt may never be filled.

Our cabbie tools us around in search of an attendant, and finally, in a small office just inside the Temple of Memories, we find a friendly woman named Sandy. She has twin pearl earrings stapled into the helix of her left ear and sits huddled between twin space heaters. Day settles into the chair opposite her desk and explains the situation, beginning with his phone call the day before, as she takes notes. "My son would like to see his ancestors," he concludes gently, "so we certainly hope you can help us, Sandy."

She calls the main office and makes a sympathetic moue when she gets the answering machine. "This is Sandy," she begins. "I have James Wood Friend here, and he needs to get into his mausoleum." Day and I exchange an amused look. Hanging up, she says, "Of course, no one's ever there on Sunday. But you can always open a family mausoleum with your family key; did you try that?"

"What key?" Day says.

"You have a key and we have a key. That way it's fail-safe."

"I've never had a key," he says in consternation. "No one, to my knowledge, has that key."

It suddenly seems fitting that the key has been lost. It is

like the task set in a childhood fable: he that opens the tomb shall have all the treasure that waits within. Only I have no magic staff or singing bird to show me where the key lies. "That's okay," I say. "We'll see it another time." Day will be flying back later, but my train for New York—the only train of the day—leaves in twenty-two minutes. Our cabbie lead-foots it to Union Station, and I jump out and grab my suit-case. Day opens his arms, and we hug. And then I run for my train, turning at the door for one last sweeping wave.

As the locomotive labors to take me from the city, snow begins whirling down, beating at the bleared windows of the old steel carriage. I find myself thinking about those brick pillars on Solway Street, and how, soon, no one alive will know why they're there. Events escape us at light speed.

Eleven hours later, I am back in Brooklyn, turning my key in the lock. Stepping into a pitch-black apartment, I slip off my muddy shoes and stand a moment in the hall. No one stirs. There is only the tick of the radiators, marking time. But I am comforted knowing that, all around me in the darkness, my family sleeps.

ACKNOWLEDGMENTS

I AM OBLIGED TO the many friends, family friends, and relations who spoke with me for this book, entrusting me with their thoughts and memories. I am especially indebted to those who tolerated questions on delicate topics or extensive follow-up inquiries, including Brett Bourne, Nicki Bourne, Tom Bourne Jr., Karin Friend Dempsey, Liz Gray, Lizz Greene, Anne Robinson Murphy, Eliza Pierson, Kate Pierson, Donny Robinson, Anne Santos, Jane Smith, Ted Terry, and Gillian Walker.

In thinking about this subject, I found several books particularly provocative, useful, or inspiring: Nelson Aldrich Jr.'s *Old Money: The Mythology of America's Upper Class*; David Hackett Fischer's *Albion's Seed: Four British Folkways in America*; Walter Russell Mead's *God and Gold: Britain, America, and the Making of the Modern World*; Peter S. Jennison's *The History of Woodstock, Vermont 1890–1983*; and George Howe Colt's *The Big House: A Century in the Life of an American Summer Home*.

I am beholden to Robert Bryan for his guidance in sartorial history; to Nicholas Prychodko and Lila Byock for thoughtful research into tiny points on my behalf; to Chrissie Crawford for sharing her letters; to Henry Hoffstot for his unparalleled generosity; and to my agent and friend, Amanda Urban, who has not only represented me for twenty years in the faith that I would someday write a book, but who urged that it be this one. David Remnick at *The New Yorker* ran the piece on my mother that inspired the book, and then was an early and encouraging reader of the book itself. Graydon Carter and Kurt Andersen were generous boosters of the book—as well as inspiring bosses when I was starting out as a writer—and Susan Morrison was a wonderfully helpful friend and counselor.

Judy Clain at Little, Brown sat with me in her office late on a winter's afternoon as I described the prospective work and said, "Oh, I can see it all!" Which, at that point, made one of us. Her unswerving enthusiasm for the project, and amazingly swift response to the completed manuscript, was immensely comforting. Judy's assistant, the omnicompetent Nathan Rostron, kept the book bounding toward publication with a blizzard of farsighted, task-assigning e-mails that often arrived before I'd had my morning coffee; nonetheless, working with him was a pleasure. And Betsy Uhrig seemed able to keep the whole manuscript in her head as she copyedited it, thereby saving me from a raft of infelicities. Those that remain are my fault, not hers.

I am blessed to have so many friends who volunteered, or agreed to be volunteered, to read the manuscript. The book is much the better for the suggestions of Dan Algrant, Jeff Frank, Wade Graham, David Grann, Deborah Copaken Kogan, John Burnham Schwartz, Mona Simpson, Jennifer

Steinhauer, John Tayman, and Edward Wyatt. After sitting with me for two chats about Wasps, Franny Taliaferro later read the first draft and offered numerous helpful thoughts. Nora Ephron not only gave me the hilarious benefit of her view of Wasps, but then, after reading a draft, her incisive take on where the narrative was too reticent (that is, Waspy).

My good friend Rich Appel does not appear in the book as much as he would like—I have agreed to put his entire wedding toast on my Web site, when I get a Web site—but he read two drafts and significantly improved each one. I came to rely on his judgment entirely. Sylvia Welsh not only offered editorial suggestions aimed at clarifying just how terrific an analyst she was but, through her aid in time of need, made it possible for me to write the book at all.

I would like to thank Jason Brown, who suggested, at a *Lampoon* party in 1982, that I start keeping a journal. And I would also like to thank myself for remembering, the following morning, what he'd said.

My brother, Pier, and sister, Timmie, have my deep gratitude, both for their careful readings of the work in progress and for their willingness to help me recall long-ago events and to forgive me for the worst of them. Yes, I socked Timmie in the stomach and hurled a baseball bat at Pier—sorry! Most of all, though, I appreciate their indulgence: it can't be easy to have your brother publish his take on events that happened to all of us yet resonated differently with each of us.

This book would simply not have come together without my father's help. He was invaluable as a collector of photographs and letters, an interpreter of family dynamics, and as a close yet forbearing reader of the manuscript. Despite his concerns about what I was doing and about how he and others might appear in print as a result, he spent many, many hours helping me do it. This is love, surely.

My children, Walker and Addie, often scrambled onto my lap to type into the manuscript. Usually this produced epiphanies such as woldt344~1,,,&yyv, but one night before bedtime they stayed with it and wrote all of Chapter Nine. So to them I say: tqqy6BVOOO$e! When they weren't on my lap, I kept them in my head, trying to make the book one they might enjoy, someday.

Amanda's support for the idea of the book, her patience as it was being written, her impatience to read it when it was nearly finished—her eagerness to live through every wrinkle of the process with me as confidante, coach, commiserator, editor, long-sufferer, and, of course, nutritionist—epitomizes what marriage vows mean by "For better or for worse." Throughout our marriage, Amanda has been entirely for my better. I am truly grateful.

TAD FRIEND is a staff writer at *The New Yorker*, where he writes the magazine's "Letter from California." Prior to that, he wrote regularly for *Outside*, *New York*, and *Esquire*, reporting from all seven continents. He lives in Brooklyn with his wife, Amanda Hesser, and their children, Walker and Addie.

BACK BAY · READERS' PICK

Reading group guide

CHEERFUL MONEY

*Me, My Family, and
the Last Days of Wasp Splendor*

TAD FRIEND

Start a Wasp Book Club!
Tad Friend's Tips for Cheerful Reading

*Creating your own Wasp book club is easy
and surprisingly inexpensive.*

Overview
First, assemble a group of people who are *just like you* and whose book choices will not inadvertently provoke some sort of "new perspective" or "opportunity for empathy."

Next, pick someone who's almost like you, but not quite, and blackball him or her from the club. Fun!

When your club first meets, spend the session murmuring about how book clubs have fallen on hard times since the war, and how it's a real shame. Just a darn shame, is what it is.

Weekly Necessities
Drink
Astringent, gin-based
concoctions in endless
quantities
A reserve flask, just in case

Clothing
You should wear clothing.
This isn't one of those
seventies key-party-
in-Darien deals.

Extra Credit
Food (at the Club or prepared at home)
Hors d'oeuvres
Deviled eggs

Ritz crackers topped with
peanut butter and bacon

Watercress sandwiches
  (crusts removed)
Pigs in a blanket
Oysters Rockefeller
Triscuits with cheddar
  cheese
Dip

Entrees
Salisbury steak
Fish option (species to be
  determined, once unfrozen)

Sides
Green beans (blanch until
  soggy)
Creamed spinach
Creamed onions

Beach option
Lobster rolls
Steamers
Corn on the cob
Pony bottles of Rolling Rock
Season all liberally with sand

Diversions
Conversation starters (the slow build to discussing the book itself)
Summering
Wintering
Exact date your trust fund
  matures
General decline of everything

(Each subject should be
considered wrapped up
whenever someone utters a
cheery "Oh, well!")

TV shows (a further light diversion)
The Dick Van Dyke Show
Lost in Space (in which the
  Robinson family tries
  to avoid becoming
  entangled with strange
  life forms)

Gilligan's Island (spotlight
  on Lovey and Thurston
  Howell III)
The Mary Tyler Moore Show
Gilmore Girls
Mad Men

**Movies (an even more time-killing way to postpone
discussing the book)**
The Philadelphia Story
Holiday

Love Story
Gentleman's Agreement

Evening
Meet the Parents
Annie Hall
Ordinary People

The Good Shepherd
Caddyshack
Trading Places
Dead Poets Society

Oh, all right, then: Books

The Big House: A Century in the Life of an American Summer Home by George Howe Colt
Prep by Curtis Sittenfeld
The Catcher in the Rye by J. D. Salinger
The Late George Apley by John P. Marquand
The Stories of John Cheever
The Rector of Justin by Louis Auchincloss

The Great Gatsby by F. Scott Fitzgerald
Monkeys by Susan Minot
Oh the Glory of It All by Sean Wilsey
Revolutionary Road by Richard Yates
A Separate Peace by John Knowles
The Wind in the Willows by Kenneth Grahame
Cheerful Money by Tad Friend

(Spend a few months discussing this last one: Is the book not profound? Is it not like an onion? Or perhaps an onion wrapped in a mystery, inside an enigma? Doesn't it feel just like the author is talking to *you*? Just like he's beaming his mind-control rays right through your tinfoil hat? That's because he is. And he's telling you to go out right now and *buy additional copies*. One for Grams! One for the housekeeper! One for those lovely people at the Salvation Army!)

A Conversation with Tad Friend

When did you first decide you would write about your family?

In 2005, not long after my mother died. I sat down to write a shortish piece instantly about how if you walked into my parents' house you would know what kind of person my mother had been. The way she arranged her objects and paintings and furniture, the emphasis she put on both clarity and coziness, was as distinctive as a fingerprint. I made several attempts at the piece, but it languished until I saw my father standing on the lawn in the snow, which somehow brought the whole thing together in my head. And as I was finally writing the piece, I discovered that I had the urge to write about my whole family, and at greater length. It seemed like a good way of trying to explain how I became me.

What are the Wasp virtues? What are Wasps good at?

At their best, Wasps seem to me very good at serving some larger ideal; at carrying out a mission. Though perhaps that sense of mission has waned over the years. The historian John Lukacs has written about a photograph on the wall of the Yale Club that shows Yale men at the Plattsburg officers' camp in 1916, training to go fight in World War I. Lukacs suggests that their smiles embodied the zenith of

Wasp confidence, in being "characteristic of American optimism, meaning that it is vague but strong. The strength matters more than the vagueness, in the short run at least. It reflects the belief of this company of men that their duty to their country and their duty to their class and their duty to themselves are completely and unquestionably in accord....Plattsburg embodies the ideals and standards of Athletic Christianity, American Patriotism, and such Teddy Rooseveltian nouns as *Zip* and *Pep*."

As I discovered in my research for the book, a collateral ancestor, Harold Ludington Hemingway, was a shining example of that kind of unironic decency. After graduating from Yale, in 1914, he volunteered the moment the United States entered the Great War, and headed off to Plattsburg. Harold had always been modest and polite: when Santa Claus visited his first grade class, he stood apart from the turmoil. The teacher asked, "Have you spoken to Santa Claus?" "No," he said quietly, "I haven't been introduced." When the teacher gravely performed the introduction, Harold shook hands and said, "How do you do, Mr. Santa Claus. I am very glad to meet you. Will you bring me a pair of skates?"

His roommate at Yale, where Harold played varsity football and rowed crew, later observed: "If you were losing at golf, or tennis, or cribbage, he could prove that you had the winning advantage, and strengthened by his faith, it often turned out so. He seemed to be a living spring of optimism. He could cheer others because he was inherently cheerful himself. I have seen him burning with malarial fever, suffering with neuralgia, with sprains and dislocations, but I never heard him complain once of the pain of it."

As a lieutenant and, later, captain in the infantry, Harold

wrote letters to his family in which he said he would miss his chocolate boxes from home "like the deuce" and that the Boche 88 shells "make the darndest whir you ever heard," but that "it seems to me the darned old fools will come to pretty soon and see they're licked and call it off." Though he corresponded faithfully with his parents, he tried not to worry them. So it was left to other soldiers to write and tell them that Harold's zeal under fire had earned him the nickname "Fearless Hemingway," and that he'd been recommended for a Distinguished Service Cross for exceptional bravery in the fighting at St. Mihiel, and had volunteered, in the repulse of a German offensive at Château-Thierry, "to crawl through a field raked by machine guns" to reconnoiter, and then led his men to safety "with Boches on four sides of them."

In early October 1918, Harold wrote, "We are having a rather hot time here. Last night we pulled off a raid in which three of my men were killed. It has broken me up a good deal. I feel as though they were my children and I ought to have taken better care of them." When his men came under artillery fire on October 20, he shouted at them to take cover. Hearing no reply, he said, "I'll have to go and get them." As he was shepherding them home, a shell burst blew shrapnel into his abdomen. In the hospital at Glorieux, Harold asked if he was going to die and the doctor, unable to bear his glittering look, said that he had an even chance for recovery. "Well, then," Harold declared, "I will beat it." His men sat down and cried when they learned of his wounds, knowing the course of intestinal perforations all too well. When Harold died the following day, three weeks before the armistice, his men decorated his grave with asters, like those blooming then in his native Connecticut. Then they laid down a single red poppy.

Conversely, what are Wasps hopeless at doing?

They're not good at fixing that funny sound the washing machine makes. Or at noticing it.

What has surprised you about the reaction to the book?

I've been struck by the number of people who find it useful because they are married to Wasps, or engaged to Wasps. I hadn't intended this, but for some people the book serves as a kind of field guide, or handbook. It's comforting to know that if your husband is behaving like a block of wood, it's not because of anything you did, it's because of something his great-great grandfather was taught at Exeter in 1886.

What Wasp rituals do you look forward to participating in with your children as they grow older? Which will you avoid?

We will continue the family membership in the Trilateral Commission and the secret baptisms in the meltwater at the North Pole. We will discontinue our subscription to *Consumer Reports.*

Will you encourage them to read Cheerful Money?

Yes, by forbidding it entirely.

Questions and Topics for Discussion

1. Tad Friend opens his memoir with a scene in which his father, Dorie, is documenting the family house, which the author's late mother, Elizabeth, had perfected in her own way. Why do you think Friend chose to open his memoir with this scene? How does this scene resonate through the rest of the book?
2. Friend notes on page 9 that his four grandparents constitute a Wasp compass: loquacious and madcap; brainy; haughty; moneyed and timid. Which of these four sets of characteristics seems most universal among Wasps? Which compass point does Friend himself seem to pursue?
3. Friend suggests that Wasps are defined less by skin tone and religion than by a certain cast of mind (page 12). How would you define that cast of mind?
4. In what ways does Tad Friend himself seem like a true Wasp? In what ways not?
5. What do you make of the Wasp affinity for mud that Friend details in chapter 2?
6. Friend's relationship with his parents is sometimes problematic. How has their family dynamic been shaped by

their broader heritage? What part of the Friend family dynamic seems to you typical of all families? What part seems peculiar to Wasps?

7. The book's title is taken from a ritual from Friend's childhood, in which good humor under duress or spontaneous helpfulness among the children was rewarded with a quarter. How might you relate this practice with other themes of the book?

8. When Tad Friend was in his twenties, he lived a fast-paced life in New York and fell in love with Giovanna Visconti—a period he calls "the most hopeful chapter of my life" (page 116). Why do you suppose Friend considers this chapter his most hopeful?

9. Which Wasp characteristics do you most admire? Which would you rather not experience firsthand?

10. Near the end of the book, Tad Friend's father takes issue with Tad's portrayal of his mother. Do any other issues seem to underlie their confrontation?

11. By Friend's own admission, he spent most of his inheritance on two decades of therapy. How might "the talking cure" have worked to alleviate some of the personal and cultural attributes that Tad was trying to leave behind?

12. In some ways, *Cheerful Money* is a record of the decline and fall of the Wasps. Given the course of American history, do you think this decline was inevitable? How would you compare the Wasps to other American tribes?

13. In what sense is it significant that the key to the Friend family mausoleum has been lost (page 343)?

14. Which Wasp traits and traditions do you think are here to stay?